Ecclesiological Investigations

Series Editor

Gerard Mannion

Volume 11

Denomination

Other titles in the series:

Denomination:
Assessing an Ecclesiological Category

Edited by

Paul M. Collins
and
Barry Ensign-George

B L O O M S B U R Y

LONDON · NEW DELHI · NEW YORK · SYDNEY

Bloomsbury T&T Clark
An imprint of Bloomsbury Publishing Plc

50 Bedford Square	175 Fifth Avenue
London	New York
WC1B 3DP	NY 10010
UK	USA

www.bloomsbury.com

First published by T&T Clark International 2011
Paperback edition first published 2013

British Library Cataloguing-in-Publication Data
A catalogue record for this book is available from the British Library.

ISBN: HB: 978-0-567-13131-7
PB: 978-0-567-26352-0

Library of Congress Cataloging-in-Publication Data
A catalog record for this book is available from the Library of Congress.

Typeset by Newgen Imaging Systems Pvt Ltd, Chennai, India
Printed and bound in Great Britain

CONTENTS

Contents

List of Contributors

Paul Avis, General Secretary of the Council for Christian Unity of the Church of England, Canon Theologian of Exeter, honorary professor of theology in the University of Exeter and editor of *Ecclesiology*

Paul M. Collins, Parish Priest of Holy Island, Berwick-upon-Tweed, Northumberland UK

Barry Ensign-George, Associate for Theology, Presbyterian Church (U.S.A.)

Steven R. Harmon, Adjunct Professor of Christian Theology, Gardner-Webb University, School of Divinity

Kirsteen Kim, Associate Principal Lecturer and Director of Programmes in Theology and Religious Studies, Leeds Trinity University College; Research Coordinator, Edinburgh 2010 project

Peter De Mey, Professor of Systematic Theology, Chair of the Centre for Ecumenical Research, Catholic University of Leuven (Belgium)

Amy Plantinga Pauw, Henry P. Mobley Professor of Doctrinal Theology, Louisville Presbyterian Theological Seminary

Russell E. Richey, William R. Cannon Distinguished Professor of Church History, Candler School of Theology, Emory University

Ann K. Riggs, Principal and Academic Dean, Friends Theological College, Kaimosi, Kenya

Gesa Elsbeth Thiessen, Milltown Institute of Theology and Philosophy, Dublin

Elena Vishnevskaya, Assistant Professor of Religion, Central College

Wolfgang Vondey, Associate Professor of Systematic Theology, Director of the Center for Renewal Studies, Regent University

INTRODUCTION

PAUL M. COLLINS

The concept of "denomination" and "denominationalism" was the focus of several seminal studies during the twentieth century. Perhaps the most notable are those written by H. Richard Niebuhr and Russell E. Richey.[1] More recently scholars have returned to this focus to raise the question of the place of denomination in the twenty-first century.[2] This volume of essays has been written in response to the paper offered by Barry Ensign-George at a session of the Ecclesiological Investigations Group at the meeting of the American Academy of Religion held in Chicago in 2008. In his essay Ensign-George puts forward a simple and (it seems to me) inescapable argument about the conceptualization and practice of being "Church", which takes place between the local congregation and the "global Church". He designates this conceptualization and practice with the term "denomination", which arises from his experience of his own tradition (Presbyterianism). Having identified and designated this manifestation of the Church, Ensign-George goes on to ask how such manifestations relate to the quest for Christian unity today. He describes the concept he wishes to identify using five characteristics: *contingent, intermediary, interdependent, partial* and *permeable*. It is in response to this construal of the manifestation of the Church between the local and the universal that the authors of the other essays have written.

The main purpose of this volume is to encourage a conversation about the reality of the Church in its concrete manifestations, particularly in this instance, between the congregational and the global. In a variety of Christian traditions the language of "denomination" is eschewed as irrelevant or abhorrent. However, Ensign-George has produced a compelling argument for revisiting the understanding of what the churches of the Reformation have often called "denomination". Whether "denomination" is a preferred or an abhorred term, Ensign-George has raised important ecclesiological questions about the theorization and practice of the reality of the Church between its micro and macro manifestations. It seems to me that it is only through engagement with the understandings and questions which Ensign-George's conceptualization raises that the quest for Church unity can be taken forward today. This volume stands as a testimony to the need to be clear about what binds Christians together in their particular allegiances as well as about the disputes the Faith and Order agenda has sought to resolve. So while this volume is an invitation to conversation, it does not seek to prescribe how such conversation will take place. But it seeks to open up a set of ideas and questions concerning the reality of the Church, as manifested in terms of denomination. The editors hope that others will seek to respond to Barry Ensign-George's essay from their own perspectives and that there may be other opportunities in conferences and in print to take this discourse forward.

As you engage with the essays in this volume, you will find that the responses to the concept of denomination elicit strong feelings and ideas and a great deal of diversity. In the first essay, "Denomination: An Anglican Appraisal", Paul Avis raises the bar with a fierce critique of the use of the language and the conceptuality of denomination. The questioning of the use of the term "denomination" continues in Steven R. Harmon's essay, "The Ecumenical Dimensions of Baptist Denominational Identity", but he concludes more positively that denomination has a place in facilitating the journey towards Christian unity. The theme of critique is also pursued by Gesa Thiessen in her placement of the language of denomination in the context of Luther's thought, as well as in the context of the quest for unity. In his essay "United Methodism: Its Identity as Denomination", Russell Richey explores the more positive understandings of denomination and denominationalism. But he also grapples with the question of how a tradition such as Methodism is to understand itself both as a "denomination" between the local and the universal, and yet also as a global phenomenon. In the essay "The Orthodox Church on Denomination", Elena Vishnevskaya confronts the abhorrence for denomination found among the Orthodox churches, and she questions the formulation of the quest for Christian unity around Western preoccupations and terminology. Offering a Pentecostal perspective, Wolfgang Vondey also explores the implications of a tradition which eschews the language of denomination and provides an ecclesiological understanding of the term "movement". He articulates a classic Pentecostal understanding of movement as a concept which challenges a typical view of denomination, and yet sees both movement- and denomination-based ecclesiologies as capable of contributing to the transformation the quest for Christian unity necessarily requires. In her essay based on her experience of the Society of Friends in Africa, Ann Riggs explores the different ways in which Quakerism responds to the concept of "denomination", sometimes rejecting the term and at other times seeking to embrace it. In particular, she explores an ecclesiological understanding of the concept of "agency" which might at times be seen as parallel to the concept of denomination. In her essay "Presbyterianism and Denomination" Amy Plantinga Pauw identifies the tradition which is perhaps most at home with the language of denomination. She does this based on the fact that the Reformed tradition readily accepts the legitimacy of other Christian traditions, and also that denomination is a category which speaks of the precarious and provisional status of the Church. The perception of and problems for the Roman Catholic Church, particularly in the United States, are analysed in Peter de Mey's essay. He also evaluates the possible different outcomes of the ecumenical project and how they might relate to the concept and reality of denomination today. In the final essay Kirsteen Kim draws out key themes of this collection and sets them in a global context, from which perspective she also reflects on the possibilities for the ecumenical project.

So, this collection of essays clearly demonstrates that the question of the concept of "denomination" *per se* and in relation to the quest for Christian unity remains as lively and controversial as ever. The diversity of the responses suggests that the reality of the Church, as Barry Ensign-George describes, between the local and the global is a topic which continues to need clarification and honesty

Notes

1 H. Richard Niebuhr, *The Social Sources of Denominationalism* (New York: Henry Holt and Company Inc., 1929); Russell E. Richey (ed.), *Denominationalism* (Nashville, TN: Abingdon, 1977; reprint ed. Eugene, OR: Wipf & Stock, 2010); Robert Bruce Mullin, and Russell E. Richey (eds), *Reimagining Denominationalism: Interpretive Essays* (New York: Oxford University Press, 1994).
2 Russell E. Richey, "Denominations and Denominationalism: Past, Present, and Future", *Word & World*, 25, 1, 2005: 15–22; David S. Dockery, Ray Van Neste, Jerry Tidwell (eds), *Southern Baptists, Evangelicals, and the Future of Denominationalism* (Nashville, TN: B&H Academic, 2011).

Chapter 1

DENOMINATION AS ECCLESIOLOGICAL CATEGORY: SKETCHING AN ASSESSMENT

BARRY ENSIGN-GEORGE

Denomination: Need and Possibility

One of the most significant theological problems confronting American Protestantism today is its failure to develop a theological account of denomination. Is there a legitimate place for denomination as an ecclesial structure? If so, what is denomination, such that it could have a place in the church that the triune God brings into being?

Denominations are a primary mode of trans-congregational structure and life within the church today, particularly in America, but also around the globe. For American Christians, denominations have been a (and arguably *the*) primary mode of trans-congregational structure and life since the early days of the nation's life. Yet little beyond the bare rudiments of a broadly shared theological assessment of denomination exists in the theological literature today.

Systematic theology offers at present no meaningful help in understanding denomination theologically. While denomination has been a standard concept in the fields of Sociology and Church History for decades, systematic theologians have, over the last 75 to 80 years, largely ignored the concept of denomination.[1] Indeed, when systematic theologians speak of denomination they most often reduce it to denomination*alism*, and denominations are widely, vociferously denounced.[2] Denounced, in fact, with great regularity by theologians who are themselves generally members of, and frequently ordained ministers in, well . . . particular denominations. Veli-Matti Kärkäinnen's survey of ecclesiology, for example, a recent survey of the topic, has no index entry for denomination.[3] Other standard introductions to and compendia of theology also fail to offer a theological account of denomination.[4] These examples are representative: we have no significant theological analysis and discussion of the major structure in which large numbers of Christians have lived and do live out their faith. This is a significant lacuna in the scholarly literature.

As for the denominations themselves, they have been unable (or unconcerned) to provide a theological understanding of themselves.

My own denomination, the Presbyterian Church (USA) PC(USA), offers abundant examples. Not least among them is the basic polity document of the PC(USA), the *Book of Order*. The failure to provide a theological understanding of denomination is evident in the way in which the *Book of Order* uses the word "church" with sliding referents. Thus, its first chapter ("Preliminary Principles") begins with a general statement about the church, which states in its second paragraph: "Christ calls the Church into being, giving it all that is necessary for its mission to the world, for its building up, and for its service to God."[5] At this point, "church" clearly means the church across denominations—including but not limited to the PC(USA).

A few pages later, however, in the fourth section of the first chapter, there is a statement on "The Historic Principles of Church Government." That section reads in its entirety as follows:

> The radical principles of Presbyterian church government and discipline are: That the several different congregations of believers, taken collectively, constitute one Church of Christ, called emphatically the Church; that a larger part of the Church, or a representation of it, should govern a smaller, or determine matters of controversy which arise therein; that, in like manner, a representation of the whole should govern and determine in regard to every part, and to all the parts united: that is, that a majority shall govern; and consequently that appeals may be carried from lower to higher governing bodies, till they be finally decided by the collected wisdom and united voice of the whole Church. For these principles and this procedure, the example of the apostles and the practice of the primitive Church are considered as authority.[6]

The passage that follows the initial colon is taken from a statement worked out by American Presbyterians in 1797. While Presbyterians in 1797 might have been ready to declare that the boundaries of "emphatically the Church" were coterminous with the boundaries of their denomination, the PC(USA) today rejects such a claim. Hence the referent of the word "church" in the quoted paragraph is elusive. Does the first statement, regarding congregations and the definition of "church", mean to prescribe for those beyond the PC(USA)? Perhaps. Is the indicated pattern of authorities (representative government, larger ruling the smaller, and so forth) a prescriptive statement of what should be the case even beyond the PC(USA)? Perhaps, but probably not. And the final clause, "till they be finally decided by the collected wisdom and united voice of the whole Church". Does this prescribe the PC(USA)'s submission to the authority of a "whole Church" that stretches beyond the PC(USA)? Certainly not. Such submission is not, at present, even a remote possibility. Again, we see that the notion of denomination is a theological aporia. Not only have theologians failed to offer close analysis of this notion—the denominations themselves have failed to do so. I believe that efforts to fill in this lacuna are a high desideratum.

This theological gap has practical consequences. Absent a strong, coherent self-understanding, denominations will be unable to provide compelling accounts of their own continued existence to their own members, to other denominations and ecclesial bodies, or to a watching world. Unable to provide a compelling account of their own existence to their members, denominations find they have no meaningful internal coherence, and they are unable to resist centrifugal forces appearing within. Unable to provide a compelling account of their existence to other denominations and ecclesial bodies, the ecumenical movement has reached what many experienced ecumenists tell us is an ecumenical impasse (the so-called ecumenical winter). Unable to provide a compelling account of their own existence to a watching world, denominations find they have no way to explain why newcomers might want to join their particular embodiment of the Christian faith.

Yet, though much maligned, denomination is potentially one of God's good gifts to the church. Denomination is a form in which Christians can live out varying understandings of faith in Jesus Christ and of what that faith requires in terms of right belief and right practice. Denomination provides a form in which new insights into the faith, or new applications of old insights to changing contexts and circumstances, can be tested by being lived out. Denomination provides a form in which human creatures, finite and creaturely, can live in the freedom to pursue the multiplicity of patterns of life and belief that are generated by the richness of the Gospel, and to do so in a way that is partial and fragmentary, and thus dependent on and essentially connected to the wholeness of the Gospel.

Providentially, the present moment is a particularly opportune time for careful assessment of denomination. Formal ecumenical dialogue has raised the level of understanding across denominational lines, undercutting both explicit and implicit claims that the boundaries of one's own denomination are identical to the known boundaries of the church. A host of institutional structures and agreements embody this acknowledgment of one another.[7] There is also a vernacular ecumenism at work at the ground level among individual Christians and congregations, a relativizing of denominational claims for reasons both good and bad.[8] In this situation, it is easier than it may once have been to see and claim the distinctions between church, denomination and congregation.

In this paper I will sketch some features of an understanding of denomination that characterizes denomination as having a legitimate place in ecclesiology.

This understanding of denomination is not simply descriptive. It is prescriptive, and as such is an attempt to counter false understandings of denomination. It is merely a sketch, and grows out of a larger project of theological assessment of denomination as an ecclesiological category. Furthermore, this sketch is drawn from within a Protestant—indeed, specifically Reformed—theological, and therefore ecclesiological, outlook. Nevertheless, because denomination is a reality across Protestantism, and because denomination is so strikingly under-analysed, providing an account of denomination from within one strand of Protestantism will have ecumenical value.

Two brief notes; First, I draw heavily on the reality of my own denomination, the Presbyterian Church (U.S.A.), not simply because it is the denomination I know best, but also because I believe it embodies conceptual issues common to denomination in general. Second, for the purposes of this paper, I am bracketing the question of whether the Roman Catholic Church and the Orthodox Churches can correctly be identified as denominations on the basis of the defining marks I offer here. I do so in part because the matter is strongly disputed, but primarily because one cannot rule on this question until one has a fairly clear idea of what denomination is and a fairly clear judgement about its legitimacy. At present we have no such thing—hence, this paper and the larger project of which it is a part.

Intermediary Structures in the Church: Denomination

Denomination is a middle term between "congregation" and "church". Denomination brings together a number (often a very large number) of congregations in a pattern of life that is thick and concrete, and in doing so, enables congregations to begin to live out their affirmation of the existence of "one holy catholic and apostolic" church in thick and concrete ways.

As such, denomination is one form of intermediary structure in the life of the church.[9] The need for, and legitimacy of, intermediary bodies is generally recognized. Within the Roman Catholic Church there are conferences of bishops who gather with one another on a national or regional basis. There are religious orders that live a distinctive life together built around the gift of a particular way of understanding and ordering elements of a common faith. And there are the uniate churches, which are even more clearly intermediary structures within the whole, gathered around distinctive and particular patterns of rite, language and culture. Among the Orthodox, there is the reality of autocephaly, the various Orthodox churches being, each one, an intermediary structure within Orthodoxy, again allowing particular patterns of language and culture to find standing and embodiment within the unity of the church. The worldwide church communions also, from a different angle, indicate the necessity and legitimacy of intermediary structures. In the Roman Catholic and Orthodox churches the whole is assumed to be primary, and the finer conceptual work is done in specifying the legitimate grounds for and limits of the intermediary structures named above.[10] In the world communions the logic flows in a reverse direction. The communions start with intermediary structures (various denominations that understand themselves to be within a particular Christian tradition), and these intermediary bodies find themselves drawn to one another, fashioning together a global body to provide a structure in which those intermediary structures may embody something of the whole of which they are fragmentary parts.

The key question for denomination, then, is not, "do diverse intermediary structures have a legitimate place in the church?" The key question is, "is denomination one of the legitimate forms of intermediary structure in the church"? The central task of this essay is to sketch an affirmation that denomination can be a legitimate intermediary structure in the church.

Denomination

Denomination as intermediary structure

As noted above, denomination binds congregations together in formal patterns of mutual life. These patterns of mutual life are built upon shared theological commitments (commitments about both belief and practice) that are broad and deep enough to hold the congregations and their members together in mutual commitment to a particular form of life together. This requires, necessarily, agreement about a number of disputed theological matters.

Denomination plays a role in such disagreements in two ways. First, it provides a space in which to discern. As the history of Christianity amply demonstrates, some theological disagreements cannot be settled immediately or in a brief period of time. The nature of many theological disagreements has a complexity that defies quick analysis: matters of disagreement sometimes reach into the life of the church and its members with a level of seriousness that requires responses of enormous care and sensitivity. In such cases the authoritative sources fail to provide immediate clarification, and their relation to a matter of disagreement requires careful sifting of the authorities themselves. Often the relative authority of allegedly authoritative sources is itself a matter of disagreement. Yet life must be lived now. Lived in response to and on the basis of decisions one way or the other about these very disputed matters. Life cannot be put on hold while we resolve our differing insights and understandings. Denomination provides a structure in which to live out differing beliefs in these situations—provided that denominations are understood to be a form within the church, not the whole of the church.

Denomination does more than create space in which to discern, however. It also provides a means for living out differing forms of a faithful Christian life. Must the functions of a bishop be exercised by an individual, or may they be exercised by a collective body such as a presbytery? Must ordinations include a laying-on of hands that runs in succession from the Apostles? Must commitment to Jesus Christ as Lord and Saviour be manifest in particular evidences of the presence of the Holy Spirit in a believer's life? Such questions must be answered by every congregation for it to function as a distinct body, and such questions must also be answered when multiple congregations come to live in a common denomination. Denomination rests on the affirmation that there is more than one faithful response to questions of this sort. Denomination provides a form in which multiple faithful possibilities for Christian life can be lived.[11] Denomination is a structure for a living disagreement in matters about which faithful Christians may disagree.

Denomination: Contingent, intermediary, interdependent, partial, and permeable

How, then, shall we understand denomination? I offer five characteristics of denomination, understood as a structured entity between congregation and church. Denomination is a contingent, intermediary, interdependent, partial and permeable embodiment of the church.

Contingent. Denomination is "contingent" in that denomination is not a necessary pattern of Christian life together. There was a time when there were no denominations. Denomination arose in a particular time and place because it served the purpose of faithful Christian living in a particular moment. Denomination has continued because it continues to serve that purpose.

Intermediary. Denomination is "intermediary" in the sense that denominations exist to mediate between two realities: the church universal and the local congregation. Denominations exist rightly only when they serve as a means for something else—a means by which congregations live into the affirmation that the church is one. It is idolatry for denominations to proclaim themselves to be ends, whether the proclamation is made in word or deed.

Interdependent. Denomination is inherently "interdependent" in that any given denomination depends on the existence of other denominations for the fullness of Christian life and witness to be embodied in the world. The decisions one denomination makes about many theological matters will embody only one possible way in which those matters might be decided faithfully. That particular denomination realizes only one among the possible embodiments of the church. It depends on other denominations to embody other possible ways of deciding such matters, and only together can those denominations embody the fullness of the church.

Partial. It follows then that denomination is "partial" in that no denomination is ever the full embodiment of the church universal in this time. No denomination alone is the full breadth of the church. Denominations are built on decisions about matters of belief and practice, matters that faithful Christians might decide differently (and have). But no one denomination can have it both ways. Denominations, being partial, have to choose among the available possibilities (they are no different than congregations in this regard). Hence, denominations necessarily embody only part of the fullness of Christian life and witness. This is not a problem so long as denominations live in full acknowledgement of their own fragmentariness.

Permeable. Denomination is "permeable" in that denominations must be structured in ways that allow for movement in and out of any given denomination, and for movement on the part of the denomination itself. No denomination can make total, ultimate claims on its own members. There will be those who come to share the denomination's judgements about disputable theological matters that shape a particular denomination's life, and they should be welcomed in. There will also be those within a denomination who find themselves no longer sharing that denomination's judgements, and they should be permitted to leave. Further, any particular denomination may find its shared judgements changing over time.

Denomination and the Diversity to which God calls Us

At the heart of the ecumenical movement is a problem that has troubled political philosophers from Plato to the authors of the United States Constitution: the relationship between the one and the many, between the unity of the community and the diversity of its particular parts. The two concepts—unity and diversity—are symbiotic. "Unity" is meaningful only if it includes in one whole things that are unlike, and "diversity" is only diverse in relation to the other distinctive parts of a whole. So the question is one of emphasis or starting point. Do we say "Out of the many, one" (*e pluribus unum*) or "within the one, many?" Do we speak of unified diversity or diverse unity?[12]

The command that followers of Jesus Christ be one with Christ and thus also with one another is axiomatic in most contemporary Christian theology. What is less clear is the nature of and specific forms of diversity and unity to which we equally are called. And yet, "the two concepts—unity and diversity—are symbiotic".

The spectre of uniformity haunts discussions of the unity of the church. The denial that one who advocates unity is seeking uniformity runs as a leitmotif throughout ecumenical appraisals of unity.[13] Kinnamon notes this denial and its place in the ecumenical movement: "Already in 1927, at the First World Conference on Faith and Order, Archbishop Söderblom spoke of the goal as "unity in multiplicity"; and since that time, "unity does not mean uniformity" has been an axiom of the movement."[14]

As Kinnamon goes on to say, the issue is not diversity or no diversity. The issue in the life of the church is, *which forms of diversity cohere with that type of unity to which we are called*? (again, unity is symbiotically implicated in decisions about legitimate diversity.) "Thus, when ecumenists speak of the *problem* of unity and diversity, the diversity they have in mind is not so much that of race or sex, but of such things as church structure, styles of worship, and theological formulation. How much diversity on *these* matters is consistent with the unity we seek?"[15]

The ecumenical challenge is to specify the nature and texture of the diversity that lives in dynamic coherence with the unity to which the church is called. What particular forms and structures of diversity serve (at least potentially) the unity of the church? Which particular forms and structures of diversity break the unity of the church? The nature, the texture, of faithful diversity is rooted in Scripture and what Scripture teaches us about the character of human community rightly ordered to communion with the living God. The nature and texture of the diversified unity to which we are called is mapped in Scripture across at least these three characteristics: the superabundance of the divine work of creation and redemption; the under-determination of the divine instructions for the corporate ordering of the followers of Jesus Christ; and the finitude and creatureliness of human existence (social as well as individual), which means that human existence is necessarily shaped in structures that are finite (partial) and creaturely. These characteristics point to the affirmation that there are varieties of diversity to which God calls creation (including the followers of Christ individually and corporately). This call to diversity will shape the lives of Christians, as they are the church embodied.

Superabundance

The superabundance of God's work of creation is clearly expressed in Scripture (and plainly visible around us when we look and listen attentively). The account of creation in Gen. 1.1–2.3 traces the work of creation as the unfolding of increasing abundance and complexity. Other texts in the Old Testament, such as Job 38–41 and Psalms 104 and 48, carry forward attention to the theological importance of the superabundance of God's creating work.[16]

The superabundance of creation is realized in distinctive ways among human beings. There are, of course, multiple spectra of differences realized by individual human beings. At the level of social structures, the superabundance of God's work of creation also generates social bodies that embody and explore diverse realizations of the manifold possibilities of sociality generated by the Christian faith. This later aspect of superabundance is set forth forcefully in the account of the appearance and spread of the "generations" (generations that become the nations) in the early chapters of Genesis—particularly chs 5 and 10.

These chapters provide genealogies. The genealogies function structurally to tie the narrative of prehistory together as it moves from one event to the next. At the same time, the genealogies also show the increasing diversification of humanity. In each chapter God's blessing generates the rapid spread and diversification of the nations. Genesis 5 ties this outworking of peoples directly to the blessing that is an element of divine creation.[17] The genealogy in Genesis 10 makes the link between generations of descendants and the differentiation into nations explicit with its repeated summary, "These are the descendants of [Japheth/ Ham/Shem] in their lands, with their own language, by their families, in their nations." (here, v. 5, repeated with slight variation in vv. 20 and 31). As Claus Westermann comments, "As far as we know this is the first attempt in the history of humankind to conceive and define the basic elements of the entity "people." It arose from the theological impulse to express how the separation of humankind into people is grounded in the will and blessing of the creator."[18] What begins to emerge in these genealogies and the narrative of which they are a part is the rise of distinctive particularities within humanity, identities held in common by some, but not by all, distinctive social bodies made up of distinct individuals.

It is striking that these genealogies precede the story of Babel in Gen. 11.1–9. Interpreters of the Babel story often read it as a tale in which diversification is a punishment. Read in this way, the people attempt to build their way to heaven; their hubris, embodied in the tower project, is punished by the diversification of languages (God "confuses" their language). The people are scattered, and the scattering and diversification are their punishment. But there is another reading of this story, a better interpretation of its place in the context of Genesis 1–11 (and, indeed, of the rest of Scripture).

The story of Babel interrupts the flow of genealogies that both precede and follow it. In it sin is manifested by a human rejection of the divine command to "abound on the earth and multiply in it" (Gen. 9.7). Genesis 10 records human obedience to that command, hammered home by the repeated refrain "these are the descendants of . . . in their lands, with their own language(s), by their families, in their nations" (Gen. 10.5, 20, 21). Genesis 11.1–9 records disobedience to the divine command, a drive for monolithic incorporation of humans into a single project, built on uniformity. God intervenes into the project of Babel to undo a concentration of humanity that runs counter to God's blessing.[19] Following that undoing, the flow of generations and nations moves the narrative directly forward to Abram and Sarai, God's focusing the divine work through a particular nation among nations. The multiplicity of human languages serves God's purposes in creation.

This differentiation into peoples, nations and tribes is not only a feature of creation. It is also a feature of redemption. The story of God's scattering the peoples in Genesis 11, cutting off the false unity that led to the Tower of Babel project, is countered by the story of the coming of the Holy Spirit in Acts 2. The scattering of the peoples was sealed by the rise of different languages. In Acts 2 the miracle lies in the ability of the followers of Jesus to proclaim "God's deeds of power" in the languages of all the nations.[20] God's response to the rise of many languages is not to recreate "one language and the same words" (Gen. 11.1). There is one message of the Saviour communicated to the listeners in the listeners language.[21] This pattern is consistent with Scripture's affirmation that the divine act of creation generates a multitude of creaturely forms and a multitude of human ways of life (accompanied and supported by a multitude of languages) that find a place within God's redemptive purposes.

The expansion and differentiation of peoples and nations in Genesis 5, 10 and 11 finds its telos in Revelation 21 amid the new heaven and new earth, in the New Jerusalem. The glories generated by the nations (which are established out of God's blessing) are gathered in to God's new order. "I saw no temple in the city, for its temple is the Lord God the Almighty and the Lamb. . . . The nations will walk by its light, and the kings of the earth will bring their glory into it. . . . People will bring into it the glory and the honor of the nations." (Rev. 21.22, 24, 26) The nations have continued until the very end, and they have value ("their glory," "the glory and honor") to the end, value that will be drawn into the New Jerusalem with its new ordering of creaturely existence.[22] The diversity that has arisen within creation as the embodiment of divine blessing is part of the divine purpose for creation, and it is glory that will be preserved by God. Across the history that stretches from the Garden of Eden to the garden city, the New Jerusalem, there are values to be gained that can only be gained by the differentiation of the nations. God does not cast those values aside, but gathers them in. The divine pattern is not one of monocultures but of differentiation, of spaces created for the best realization of as full an array of particular goods as possible.

Scripture and tradition call us to unity. Christ's prayer for the church in John 17 is a particularly clear articulation of a theme found across the New Testament (e.g. 1 Cor. 12; Eph. 4.1–6). The unity to which these passages call us is symbiotically related to the diversity to which God also calls us, a diversity that has a texture as complex and wide-open as the glory of the nations.[23]

Under-determination of New Testament polity instructions

One of the most striking features of the New Testament is the spareness of its instructions (commandments) for shaping the ecclesial bodies into which Christians are gathered.

This spareness contrasts with the Old Testament. The Torah is replete with instructions for the shaping of the corporate body formed by the followers of the God of Abraham, Isaac and Jacob—so full of such instructions that the majority of the Torah continues to be a challenge for many Christians. The gathering and canonization of law and polity and regulation indicate a desire to assemble authoritative material that will provide as much determination as possible in the written materials that shape a corporate life.

The New Testament follows a different strategy. In the New Testament we find a gathering of narratives that display the life to be led in following Jesus, both for individuals and for the community gathered together in Christ and in pursuit of Christ in the world. There are passages that look to be imperatives for corporate life: "Bless those who persecute you; bless and do not curse them. Rejoice with those who rejoice, weep with those who weep. Live in harmony with one another . . . " (Rom. 12.14–17a) There are repeated instructions for specific individuals within congregations, having to do with their individual faithfulness to Jesus Christ and touching generally on the impact they are having on the larger congregation: "I urge Euodia and I urge Syntyche to be of the same mind in the Lord. Yes, and I ask you also, my loyal companion, help these women, for they have struggled beside me in the work of the gospel . . . "(Phil. 4.2–3). There are also more concrete instructions for the shaping of corporate life, which bear a resemblance to some of the instructions in the Torah: "The saying is sure: whoever aspires to the office of bishop desires a noble task. Now a bishop must be above reproach, married only once, temperate, sensible, respectable, hospitable, an apt teacher . . . " (1 Tim. 3.1–2) Yet these instructions have themselves been a source of significant controversy in the life of the church. They have required extensive interpretation, and they have received it.

Interpretation of such passages has been central to the long debate within the church about the existence and content of a "divine law" (*ius divinum*) specifying the ordering of the life of the church.[24] Disagreements about the right structuring of the church during the period of the Reformation hinged on disagreements about the content of the *ius divinum*.[25] In my own tradition it was long held that the *ius divinum* specified Presbyterian government as the right structure for the Christian church. That belief, however, no longer holds in my denomination.[26] Such controversy has arisen because of the fact that strong and divergent interpretations of the scriptural materials relevant to the ordering of the church can be worked out. Scripture is not indeterminate in these matters, but it is underdetermined.

The under-determination of the divine instructions (commandments) for shaping the ecclesial bodies into which Christians are gathered is tied to the superabundance, the plenitude of the created order. The divine instructions for shaping ecclesial bodies present a situation in which those instructions may be embodied in a variety of ways. Scriptural material that bears on the right ordering of the people of God is generative—it generates possibilities for the life of the church.[27]

The question at hand is, as always, at what point, and in what ways, does diversity become disorder? The burden of this argument is that there must be room for significant diversity in shaping life together—differing theological emphases, different ways of patterning the ministry of oversight, different realizations of the ministry. Denomination is a way in which room can be held open for these sorts of diversities, room that allows time during which to assay the claim of legitimacy for particular realizations of Christian life together that differ from those presently in existence.

Finitude and creatureliness

While human beings are blessed creatures, we remain creatures. As creatures, we are finite, limited in our ranges of knowledge, perception, openness, capacity for relationship. Our finitude is tied together with our embodiment. However widely our thinking may range, our bodies locate us in a particular place in space and time, partakers in and shaped by specific contexts.

Being such creatures, we require structures in which to live that are less than universal. We already acknowledge this, at least in part. No serious proposal disputes the legitimacy of congregations in which we gather in separate groups to live out the Christian faith in worship and in manifold other ways (catechesis/Christian education, mission, service in the world, interaction with the broader church). Our shared recognition of the necessity of local gatherings for worship and for communal life is a recognition of the nature of finite, creaturely existence.

Christians are called to be one with all other followers of Jesus Christ, but no individual Christian is capable of developing in a concrete form such oneness with all other followers of Jesus.[28] Unity with all other followers of Jesus Christ takes form in a particular pattern of relationship. Our relationships cannot extend universally. God can relate universally, we cannot. We require intermediary structures that provide finite creatures such as we are a way of living.

The knitting together of the universal and the local is a key feature of Christian faith. In an article in which he puts "the anthropological term . . . tribe" into play as a means of understanding ecumenism and, especially, the persistent problem of the reception of ecumenical dialogue, James Sweeney summarizes this key feature:

> The fundamental issue is a familiar one, the universal and the particular, and it lies at the heart of Christianity as a faith imbued with a universal vision yet sunk in the contingency of history, with a belief in the God who is one and transcendent and yet revealed in the man Jesus. The practice of this faith involves paradox. We must respect the necessary boundaries of the human while impelled to break out beyond them. Seemingly of two minds, this actually exhibits the elusive paradox of Christianity itself. Put concretely, the open community has its boundaries; and not simply as a concession to human frailty, but because the drive to oneness and universality will dissipate unless it is held and channeled in the visible, sacramental community of the faithful.

The church is universal; human beings are not. As Sweeney puts it, "The "tribe"has its place".[29] He notes:

> Church communities are socio-cultural creations as well as faith responses to the Word, and faith and culture cannot simply be separated out; faith must find cultural expression. In this sense, the "tribe"—the particular and distinct community—is not antipathetic but belongs to the Gospel, in the same way that in the Divine dispensation *one* chosen people, the Jews, and *one* man, Jesus, constitute the offer of *universal* salvation. The implication is that the ecumenical goal in discerning the shape of the church to come should be to enhance particularity, to cherish the maximum diversity of expression of authentic church order, not permit the minimum. Such idealism is also, paradoxically, the most realistic path to take since it respects actual church communities.[30]

The question is, at what level and in what forms do such limited gatherings of Christians become illegitimate? What intermediate structures between congregation and global church are permissible?

As noted above, that there are such intermediary structures is clear. Roman Catholicism includes national and regional conferences of bishops in which

bishops of a particular nation or region gather to reflect together on their particular context for ministry; its recognition of both religious orders and uniate
churches represents an acknowledgement of and an effort to accommodate the
need for intermediary structures. Orthodoxy includes autocephaly, which also
allows for responses to the particularities of regional contexts for ministry. Baptist congregations gather in associations that allow for contextualization and
the engagement of the particularities of specific contexts. Lutheran congregations live in patterns of commitment (denominations) that stretch both nationally and globally. The examples could be multiplied.

Global bodies formed within particular Christian traditions, such as the
Lutheran World Communion, arise, in many cases, because within those traditions the intermediary ecclesial structures are strong, but there has been a need
to find institutional forms that enable concrete ways of living towards the global,
universal reality of the church. Councils of churches embody the same impulse,
a movement through intermediary ecclesial structures towards the reality of the
church that is also universal.[31]

Such intermediary structures are necessary because humans are finite and
creaturely. The biblical witness is remarkable for its insistence that the divine
work among human beings moves towards universal ends through localized
means. In the story of the creation of earthly creatures, the first human is created
in a place that is not specified—simply somewhere on earth, a generic place
which is not identified and goes unnamed. Having created the first human in a
generic place, God immediately places that human being in a very specific place:
"And the Lord God planted a garden in Eden, in the east; and there he put the
man whom he had formed" (Gen. 2.8—Adam is formed and brought to life in
the preceding verse). Creatures are preserved during the flood by a very particular group of human beings, in a very concrete structure, a place that floats.
Redemption is worked for a created order broken by sin through a very particular people who spring from individuals. Across the rest of Scripture, God's commitment to achieving universal goals through particular persons and structures
carries this scandal of particularity forward.

A scandal that should not be a scandal. God works in the created order on a
creaturely scale, in creaturely dimensions.[32] Being finite and creaturely, we
human beings require finite and creaturely structures in which to live out our
faith. And it is clear that these structures are needed not only on a local scale but
on broader scales as well. Denomination, as noted above, provides such broader
structures. Denomination is one form of intermediary structure within the
church, alongside others (religious orders, uniate churches, autocephalous
churches). Denomination provides a form in which Christians can live their
affirmation that the church is more than their local congregation. In a denomination the reality of those others makes a particular claim that reaches into the

life of a congregation and opens that congregation to the substantive presence of brothers and sisters in the faith.

The finitude and creatureliness of ecclesial bodies lead to their dynamic character. Ecclesial bodies arise in particular moments, on the basis of particular insights or energies. And ecclesial bodies also fall away and cease to exist when the insights prove unable to continue to sustain the ecclesial body, when the energies dissipate and no new impulse arises to sustain the institutional structures that have grown up to carry these insights across time. Denomination provides one way of embodying this dynamism.

The Unity to which God calls Us

What then, on this account, of the unity of the church? What is the nature of the unity implied by this account of denomination? Is the church nothing more than a notion, or an eschatological concept? Is it the "church invisible", an ideal that stands beyond the mundane reality of actually existing church bodies? Is the church simply an aggregate of all the denominations and other ecclesial structures, heaped together?

It is not.

The church is indeed visible in the multitude of congregations, gathered in denominations. The church is visible in these bodies taken as a whole—both as they presently exist and as congregations and denominations have existed across time. The unity of the church is (or should be) visible in the relationships between these bodies. The *unity* of the church is made visible in the relationships they bear towards one another, particular sorts or varieties of relationships, specifically those that embody the contingent, intermediary, interdependent, partial and permeable nature of denominations and congregations. These relationships will find embodiment in an array of forms (councils, communions, covenants, multilateral and bilateral initiatives). The relationships will grow or fade away, abide or mutate, be rediscovered and renewed or remain constant.

Certainly, the relationships between these bodies will often obscure the unity of the church, either intentionally or inadvertently. Denominations are particularly prone to contradict unity by denying that the characteristic elements of denomination apply in their case. Denominations are constantly tempted to take the characteristics of the one true church upon themselves, in denial of their finitude and fragmentariness.

This is a complex and dynamic form of unity. It is not the tightly linked institutional unity that many of us find attractive. Over the last few decades there has been vigorous discussion of "reconciled diversity" as a way of understanding the unity to which we are called. The phrase is constructed in a way that makes diversity the substantive term, the noun; and unity, a modifier. I believe that what is proposed in this essay would better be called "articulated unity". This is a unity in which the relationships among ecclesial bodies will take an array of forms. Some ecclesial bodies will move towards organic, structural union—forming unions, or one will agree to be assimilated by another.[33] Other ecclesial bodies will form full communion agreements, which will provide formal links among denominations in complex patterns.[34] There will continue to be councils of churches of varying geographic scope. What is central across this web of relationships is their quality: the character of the relationships ecclesial bodies and their individual members have with one another.

Such unity is built and maintained with the arts of persuasion as its toolbox. Persuasion is not, perhaps, the longed-for ecumenical "killer app". But then, what better tools might we have? Let us remember that we (the church) have maintained our unity using other tools—especially coercion—and the results were, to put it euphemistically, unfortunate.

The ecumenical project is sometimes portrayed as a temporary program for reaching a goal—visible unity. The ecumenical movement in the twentieth century drew considerable energy from a clear belief that the denominations could be visibly united "in this generation" (to borrow a phrase from an equally energized movement of a slightly earlier period, the mission movement). Much of the sense of malaise and failure in the ecumenical movement over the last few decades is surely attributable precisely to the failure to arrive at the desired destination in this generation. The vision of unity proposed here implies that the work of ecumenical dialogue is not a temporary project for arriving at a destination, but is instead a permanent element of life for Christians and, especially, for the ecclesial bodies in which they are gathered together.

Conclusion

One of the theological issues that confronts us in assessing denomination is the issue of the limits of diversity within the church. How much room is there, within the church's unity, for differences in the structure and beliefs of groups of congregations? Denomination as a category embodies an affirmation that the church may be pluriform without undoing its unity. And surely that claim has good scriptural precedent. The story of God's dealings with humanity tells of one people made up of 12 irreducible tribes. The story of the Gospel is told irreducibly in four Gospels, four Gospels that were generated from and still reflect (as best our scholarship can see) four very different Christian communities which were living out the one faith in four very different ways.

The failure of denominations and theologians to provide a theological account of denomination represents a significant failing on the part of both groups. Denomination has become virtually an aporia in Christian life and thought. The account of denomination offered in this sketch may be judged less than fully successful. While it is entirely possible to turn away from the account I have sketched, we may *not* decline to offer *some* account of who we (and so many Christian sisters and brothers) are.

Notes

1 Some theologians dismiss denomination as nothing more than a sociological term, asserting that it is not properly theological. So Edwin Van Driel says, "The issue is that 'denomination' is not a theological but a sociological concept".Edwin Chr. Van Driel, "Church and Covenant: Theological Resources for Divided Denominations," *Theology Today*, 65, 4 (January 2009): 449–61. This is false, both historically and in current usage. Historically, the term "denomination" came into use among church leaders and theologians. It was then, much later, taken up by sociologists. Winthrop Hudson, in a 1955 article, traced the use of the term back to "the early years of the Evangelical Revival", citing John Wesley, Winthrop S. Hudson, "Denominationalism as a Basis for Ecumenicity: A Seventeenth Century Conception", *Church History* XXIV, 1 (March, 1955): 32–50; reprinted in Russell E. Richey, *Denominationalism* (Nashville, TN: Abingdon, 1977), pp. 21–42. (This collection has been reprinted: Eugene, OR.: Wipf & Stock, 2010.) Hudson's article makes it clear that denomination is rooted not only in sociopolitical realities, but in theological convictions as well. Hudson could equally well have cited Gilbert Tennent, a significant figure in the history of American Presbyterianism (the tradition in which both Van Driel and I now stand): "All Societies, who profess Christianity, and retain the Foundation-Principles thereof, notwithstanding their different Denominations and Diversity of Sentiments in smaller Things, are in Reality, but One Church of Christ . . . " Quoted in Leonard J. Trinterud, *The Forming of an American Tradition: A Re-examination of Colonial Presbyterianism* (Philadelphia: The Westminster Press, 1949), p. 132. Trinterud also notes that a draft of the first American Presbyterian Directory for Public Worship also speaks of other ecclesial bodies as "denominations." Trinterud, pp. 277–78. The intensive work of Philip Schaff on the topic of denomination is clearly theological. Nor is this merely a matter of past usage. For example, it is clear in the current *Book of Order* of the Presbyterian Church (U.S.A.) that "denomination" is interchangeable with "church" (see e.g. *Book of Order, 2009–2011*, Louisville, KY: Office of the General Assembly, 2009), G-15.0200.

2 Russell Richey's observations on this situation, offered in 1976, describe our present moment well: "In mainstream Protestantism . . . denominationalism is taboo. A topic best shunned. If comment is required, denunciation shows good taste and theological sophistication. It is not uncommon to find denominations and the fact of denominational divisions scathingly treated and blamed for the various ills in Protestantism." Russell E. Richey, "Denominationalism: A Theological Mandate," *Drew Gateway* 47 (1976–7): 93. Richey has edited or co-edited two volumes that have countered this

neglect—*Denominationalism* (see n. 1 above); Robert Bruce Mullin, and Russell E. Richey, *Reimagining Denominationalism: Interpretive Essays* (New York: Oxford University Press, 1994). Several of Richey's essays on denomination are to be printed in a forthcoming volume from Cascade Books of Eugene, Oregon.

3 Veli-Matti Kärkkäinen, *An Introduction to Ecclesiology: Ecumenical, Historical and Global Perspectives* (Downers Grove, IL: InterVarsity Press, 2002). Kärkkäinen is an ordained minister of the Full Gospel Churches of Finland (biographical information at   www.templeton.org/humble_approach_initiative/Pneumatology/participants/karkk.html; 22 February 2010).

4 See, e.g., Carl E. Braaten and Robert W. Jensen (eds), *Christian Dogmatics* (Philadelphia: Fortress Press, 1984) and Francis Schüssler Fiorenza and John P. Galvin (eds), *Systematic Theology: Roman Catholic Perspectives* (Minneapolis, MN: Fortress Press, 1991).

5 *The Constitution of the Presbyterian Church (U.S.A.)*, Part II, *Book of Order, 2009–2011* (Louisville, KY: The Office of the General Assembly, 2009), G-1.0100b. *The Book of Order* includes three parts: The Form of Government (G-), The Directory for Worship (W-), The Rules of Discipline (D-). Reference is by part, chapter, section and sub-section, and lettered paragraph (where necessary). E.g. G-1.0100b refers to "The Form of Government", chapter 1, section 1, lettered paragraph b. The *Book of Order* is available online at www.pcusa.org/oga/boo/boo-online.htm. [The PC(USA) is presently (Spring 2011) considering major revision of the *Book of Order*, which would change these citations.]

6 ibid., G-1.0400.

7 Examples of such institutions and agreements include the Councils of Churches at local, national and world levels; multi- and bilateral agreements such as the Porvoo or Meissen agreements; there are full communion agreements being made that create a web of interrelationships, such as *Called to Common Mission*, the full communion agreement between The Episcopal Church (TEC) and the Evangelical Lutheran Church in America (ELCA), alongside the *Full Communion Agreement* that established full communion between the ELCA, the PC(USA), the United Church of Christ and the Reformed Church in America.

8 The fluidity of religious commitment among Americans and the erosion of denominational loyalty was highlighted in the "U.S. Religious Landscape Survey" conducted under auspices of the Pew Forum on Religion and Public Life (cf. www.religions. pewforum.org/). Michael Root comments on this phenomenon, both that which is good and that which is bad about it, in "The Unity of the Church and the Reality of the Denominations," *Modern Theology* 9, 4 (October 1993): 385–401 (386–94).

9 I am grateful to Peter de Mey for articulating the importance of intermediary structures during discussion in November, 2009—though I may develop reflections on the reality of intermediary structures that vary from de Mey's own insights.

10 Which is not to elide the vigorous discussion within the Roman Catholic Church about the relative priority of the local church and the universal church, a discussion that was carried out in a public exchange between Walter Cardinal Kasper and the future Pope, Joseph Cardinal Ratzinger. For an account of this exchange, see Killian McDonnell, "The Ratzinger/Kasper Debate: The Universal Church and Local Churches", *Theological Studies* 63 (2002): 227–50.

11 One of the difficulties of ecumenical dialogue is the existence of differences over precisely such matters. There are elements of Christian belief and practice that have

a level of undecideability about them, matters in which the existing authoritative sources do not rule out all alternatives but one. In such matters, shall we foreclose some of the alternatives for faithful Christian belief and practice? On what basis, and to what purpose? It is part of the argument of this essay that to be a creature of the living God is to be presented with areas in which there are multiple possibilities for faithful living open to us, not all of which we can realize ourselves. Others may realize a different possibility than the particular possibility we are committed to realizing.

12 Michael Kinnamon, *The Vision of the Ecumenical Movement and How It Has Been Impoverished by Its Friends* (St. Louis, MO: Chalice Press, 2003), p. 51.

13 A few examples. Yves Congar, quoting John Paul II in an address to a Coptic delegation, 22 June 1979: "Unity—whether universally or on a local level—does not signify uniformity or the absorption of one group by the other." Congar, *Diversity and Communion*, trans. John Bowden (Mystic, CT: Twenty-Third Publications, 1985), p. 41. George Lindbeck, writing a few years later: "There is now, at least on paper, a consensus in the organized ecumenical movement that the God-willed unity of the church involves more than interdenominational cooperation and intercommunion between autonomous bodies divided in faith and order. This does not mean that uniformity is desirable. There may be great variations, as Vatican II also suggests, in practice, worship, organizational structures and doctrinal formulations, but the differences must be seen as compatible, they must be reconciled." George Lindbeck, "Two Kinds of Ecumenism: Unitive and Interdenominational", *Gregorianum* 70, 4 (1989): 649.

14 Kinnamon, *The Vision of the Ecumenical Movement*, p. 52.

15 Kinnamon, *The Vision of the Ecumenical Movement*, p. 52. This formulation is striking: diversity of worship styles? If a congregation has one worship service in traditional style and another in a contemporary style, does that break the unity of the church? If a parish has masses celebrated in, say, English, with traditional Anglo Roman Catholic worship music, alongside masses celebrated in Spanish, with culturally appropriate praise music, does that break the unity of the church? Presumably, the answer to these questions is, no. But what if across the street there is a Meeting House in which Friends have gathered to worship in the customary Quaker way? Does that break the unity of the church? If the two congregations acknowledge one another as sisters and brothers in the faith? Could the meeting of the Friends be brought into the Roman Catholic parish without substantially altering its pattern of worship and organization, so that it is still recognizably a gathering of Friends? Could the present arrangement, the two congregations meeting across the street, represent a legitimate diversity within the unity of the church?

16 Psalm 104.27 summarizes this line of thinking: "O Lord, how manifold are your works! In wisdom you have made them all; the earth is full of your creatures."

17 "When God created humankind, he made them in the likeness of God. Male and female he created them, and he blessed them and named them "humankind" when they were created." (Gen.5.1–2) To be a human creature is to be blessed by God and that blessing generates a humanity that is differentiated within its commonalities. See Claus Westermann, *Genesis 1–11: A Commentary*, trans., John J. Scullion SJ (Minneapolis. MN: Augsburg Publishing House, 1984), pp. 360–62, for an exploration of the theological importance of Genesis 5.

18 Westermann, p. 509.

19 "The purpose of God's intervention in v. 8 is to guard humanity against a danger that grows with its unity; and so there is no longer any opposition to Genesis 10. The human race exists in a plurality of peoples over the earth with an abundance of potential for development in individual peoples, cf. 10.5, 20, 31. This is what humanity is and this is what preserves it in being." (Westermann. p. 556)

20 There is debate among the commentators: was the gift at Pentecost given to the speakers (to speak in foreign languages) or the hearers (to hear the words in their own language). Richard Pervo argues for the view that the miracle takes place in the listeners, not in the speakers. Richard I. Pervo, *Acts: A Commentary* Hermeneia: A Critical and Historical Commentary on the Bible (Minneapolis, MN: Fortress Press, 2009), p. 64. Pervo points to a list of advocates of various positions in Joseph A. Fitzmyer, *The Acts of the Apostles: A New Translation with Introduction and Commentary* The Anchor Bible, 31 (New York: Doubleday, 1998), p. 239. Fitzmyer himself leans toward the miracle occurring in the speakers, enabling them to speak in foreign languages (236).

21 Lamin Sanneh takes up this very feature of the Christian Gospel in his exploration of the translatability of the Gospel. "Without a counterpart to the revealed Quran of Muslims, Christians transmitted their Scripture in the languages of other people, indicating thereby that these languages have a priority in the Christian scheme. This is more than just a tactical concession to win converts. It is, rather, an acknowledgement that languages have intrinsic merit for communicating the divine message. They are worthy of God's attention." Lamin Sanneh, *Whose Religion Is Christianity? The Gospel Beyond the West,* Grand Rapids, MI: William B. Eerdmans Publishing Company (2003), p. 100. Languages, in their diversity, are not only worthy of God's attention: they are part of the goodness of God's creation.

22 My understanding of these verses follows especially Kevin Park, "Nations will bring their glory" (a homily on Revelation 21.22–26), *Perspectives: A Journal of Reformed Thought* 19, 9 (November 2004): 24. Park's homily is available online: www.pcusa. org/re-formingministry/papers/parkhomily.pdf.

23 I consider unity more thoroughly below.

24 See, e.g. Avery Dulles, *A Church to Believe In: Discipleship and the Dynamics of Freedom* (New York: Crossroad, 1982), esp. chap. 6, pp. 80–102.

25 Dulles, *A Church to Believe In,* pp. 80, 82–87.

26 "This form of government is established in the light of Scripture to give order to this church [viz. denomination] but is not regarded as essential to the existence of the Church of Jesus Christ nor to be required of all Christians." *Book of Order,* G-4.0304 (portion in brackets added). A similar understanding can be found in the Confession of 1967 in its section on "Forms and Order". *The Constitution of the Presbyterian Church (U.S.A.). Part I: The Book of Confessions* (Louisville, KY: The Office of the General Assembly, 2002), 9.40.

27 Walter Cardinal Kasper suggests something similar for tradition and memory in the life of the church, speaking of "development and actualization" and "unresolved alternatives": "We should not imagine that we possess more of the Holy Spirit today than the church of the early church fathers and the great theologians of the early Middle Ages. *Anamnesis/memoria* is there a fundamental category. It does not in any way exclude vital development and actualization, but must also be understood as 'dangerous memory,' disclosing for us the unresolved alternatives within the tradition and thus liberating us from the spell and the blindness created by prevailing fashions and

plausibilities." Walter Kasper, " 'Credo Unam Sanctam Ecclesiam'—The Relationship between the Catholic and the Protestant Principles in Fundamental Ecclesiology" in *Receptive Ecumenism and the Call to Catholic Learning: Exploring a Way for Contemporary Ecumenism,* (ed.) Paul D. Murray, assisted by Luca Badini-Confalonieri (Oxford: Oxford University Press, 2008), pp. 84–5.

28 And of course, beyond Christians, there remains the command to love all people. Such love must be embodied in concrete relationships with and acts towards particular people who are beyond the boundaries of the church. Those relationships will also by their very nature require structuring in social bodies and institutions that are particular in their make-up and in their focus on some, but not all, others.

29 James Sweeney, CP, "Receptive Ecumenism, Ecclesial Learning, and the 'Tribe' ", in *Receptive Ecumenism and the Call to Catholic Learning: Exploring a Way for Contemporary Ecumenism,* (ed.) Paul D. Murray, assisted by Luca Badini-Confalonieri, (Oxford: Oxford University Press, 2008), p. 335. The term "tribe" is in many ways unfortunate for contexts other than anthropology: the overtones of "tribalism" are strong. But "tribe" need not be equivalent to "tribalism" any more than "universal" need be equivalent to "uniform". The issue is not with the words themselves but with our willingness (or unwillingness) to use them flexibly.

30 Sweeney, "Receptive Ecumenism": 341.

31 See Diane Kessler, and Michael Kinnamon, *Councils of Churches and the Ecumenical Vision*, Risk Book Series (Geneva: WCC Publications, 2000).

32 Even in a passage like the theophany in Isaiah 6, one is struck by the way in which God's being and presence is conceptualized in profoundly creaturely ways: " . . . and the hem of his robe filled the temple. Seraphs were in attendance above him; each had six wings . . . " The same pattern of conceptualization is present in the visions of heaven in the book of Revelation (e.g. Rev. 4–5).

33 British Methodism provides a dramatic example in the expressed willingness of the leaders of The Methodist Church of Great Britain to merge into the Church of England. See "A Pastoral Letter to the Methodist People from the President and Vice President of the Conference and the General Secretary", www.methodist-presandvp. blogspot.com/2010/02/pastoral-letter-to-methodist-people.html; accessed March 16, 2010.

34 As an example of such complexity, the Evangelical Lutheran Church in America is in full communion with both The Episcopal Church (TEC) and the PC(USA), but TEC and the PC(USA) are not in full communion with one another.

Chapter 2

DENOMINATION: AN ANGLICAN APPRAISAL

PAUL AVIS

First, we might ask why the term "denomination", which is endemic in talk about the churches, is as popular as it is—to the extent that a book is being put together about it! After all, "denomination" is not a biblical word or idea, nor is it a theological or ecclesiological term. It does not come down to us from the Christian tradition, and it has no specific theological content. "Denomination" does not tell us anything about the nature and mission of the Church of Christ and the place of the Church in the gracious purposes of God. All that makes me rather wary of it! If I want to speak theologically, I use theological language. If I want to speak sociologically, I use sociological language. "Denomination" is a sociological term and implies a sociological theory about the place of the churches in modern society. But, strangely enough, we find theologians and church leaders using this sociological term when they are speaking in a theological or ecclesiological register, and that seems unfortunate.

Let me come clean: "denomination" is not a word that I use. I do not refer to my own church, the Church of England, as a denomination, nor do I describe the Anglican Communion as a denomination. But neither do I refer to other churches by that term. It is not that I think Anglicanism is somehow protected from the language of denomination: I treat all other churches in the same way. It is not that I think that they are of Paul or Cephas or Apollos, while Anglicans are of Christ (1 Cor. 1.12)! I refer to all churches as churches and to the major expressions of Christianity as "Christian traditions". In so doing, I try to do justice to their view of themselves, and I pay them the courtesy of speaking of them as they would wish to speak of themselves. Where other churches openly refer to themselves, in their official documents or on their websites, as denominations, I think that is regrettable and that they have lost the plot. Churches should describe themselves in God-language, language that reflects something of the mystery of the Church considered as the body, the bride, the temple of Christ. Those whose role is to speak for the Church are bishops, priests or lay leaders, not sociologists: they should stick to their brief.

The Uses of "Denomination"

Nevertheless, the concept of a "denomination" has its uses and may be unavoidable in certain kinds of discourse. It recognizes the unique position of the churches in modern civil society—a society that is characterized by the radical differentiation and pluralization of institutions.[1] I say "differentiation" and "pluralization" deliberately, though these are not very elegant terms, rather than "difference" and "plurality", because the churches, like other institutions, are subject to a remorseless socioeconomic process that separates them out from each other and drives towards ever increasing specialization and plurality. This process is an aspect of the progressive complexification of modern "Western" society as a system. The process of complexification militates against what is held in common: in the case of the churches, shared beliefs and common structures. Each becomes a little system, or perhaps a sub-system, in a social ecology that supports many such entities but at the same time seems to hold them apart. Institutional religion shares the same fate as other institutions in a society characterized by a high degree of structural complexity: it too becomes differentiated out and institutionally distinctive.[2] It requires an institutional infrastructure with a bureaucracy to service it and a managerial ideology to legitimate it. The churches are specialized institutions, catering for particular spiritual and emotional needs and, in turn, reinforcing those needs by providing them with a conceptual and structural framework. Thus, the churches create specific ecclesial identities that tend to define themselves polemically over against other ecclesial identities. Although there are social and cultural differences between churches that exist side by side within one country, their differences are often not differences of fundamental Christian belief, but of structure, polity and governance—differences with regard to where authority is located and how it is exercised. It is these differences—over episcopacy, papacy, congregational autonomy, and so on—that are played up and that perpetuate division. We know who we are because we are not the other.[3]

It is arguable that, in postmodernity, the pluralism that was characteristic of modern society is steadily degenerating into sheer fragmentation. This perception seems to be borne out by the galloping multiplication of Christian churches, the proliferation of competing denominations, especially in the developing world. Given that there are now more than 34,000 separate Christian churches in the world, however small, denominationalism is here to stay![4]

The concept of denomination arises where a taxonomy of churches is employed. How does one particular Christian tradition compare with and relate to others that seem to sit alongside it? Denomination implies plurality: it hardly arises when there is not much with which to compare a particular tradition. In an overwhelmingly Roman Catholic country such as Poland, an overwhelmingly

Orthodox country such as Greece, or an overwhelmingly Lutheran country such as Norway, it does not make sense to refer to the Roman Catholic Church in Poland or the Orthodox Church of Greece or the Lutheran Church of Norway as "denominations". They are not one among many, except when they are placed in a global perspective—they are, to most intents and purposes, the church of the nation. I would define a denomination as a church that exists among a plurality of competing churches, where none of them is numerically dominant or enjoys a markedly privileged position.

The pluralism or pluralization of modern civil society may be regarded as a neutral phenomenon: no particular value judgement need attach to it. But since the plurality of churches only became possible when states legislated for religious toleration, value judgements soon began to impinge. To tolerate is to relativize, and to relativize is to privatize. Public doctrine cannot be relative without ceasing to be public doctrine: it is an ideological framework that is widely acknowledged. Private opinion is necessarily relative because it is infinitely diverse. So the pluralism of religion and of religious institutions is made possible through laws of toleration, but toleration implies relativization, and relativism is an ideological reality that corresponds to the private realm. States legislate for toleration only when they have to. On the part of the state, toleration is a compromise strategy for maintaining social cohesion and political unity, as an overarching framework within which a broad latitude of opinion and expression can be allowed. As Owen Chadwick puts it: "From the moment that European opinion decided for toleration, it decided for an eventual free market in opinion."[5]

The process of pluralization that was accelerated by toleration had the effect of relativizing religious belief, that is to say, of undermining the credibility of exclusive claims to provide salvation. The privatization of religious commitment means that "religious language, religiously based assumptions about the world and religiously legitimated moral principles have become the preserve of committed minorities, rather than being part of the taken-for-granted assumptions of society as such."[6] Privatizing religious belief and practice devalues it and helps to trivialize it. It becomes a matter of personal preference, of private predilection, to be viewed with a mixture of bemused scepticism and nervous apprehension.

Pannenberg has pointed to a crucial implication of pluralism and the consequent privatization of religious belief and practice: the fate of the integration of meaning.[7] Where the state actively sponsors pluralism through a policy of toleration (in its contemporary form, multiculturalism), public doctrine is reduced to a bare minimum; it becomes a skeletal framework, holding the ring, as it were, for competing versions of the good life. Public doctrine can no longer provide the key to the integration of meaning that human life craves. It ceases to legitimate a worldview, a religious faith. That role now devolves to the family: it is in the family unit and through family activities and mutual support within the family that an integration of meanings can be achieved, and nowhere else—the family or nothing. This is the silver lining of privatization. But is the nuclear family robust enough to serve this function? What happens when family life cannot stand the strain? Many pressures on the modern family render it incapable of fulfilling this moral and spiritual function on its own. Today, the family as an institution seems to be struggling.[8] What do we look for then? Is this the moment for the state to step in and to try to reclaim at least something of its previous role as the legitimator of social stability? (These are issues that as I write are figuring in the British General Election campaign of 2010, e.g. should marriage be recognized in the taxation system?). So denominationalism is made possible by religious toleration, but that is only possible at the cost of relativizing the claims that the denominations make for their beliefs. In turn, relativism plays into the radical privatization of religious belief and practice that typifies Western society today. This is the sting in the tail of denominationalism.

Denomination and Ecumenism

What is the relationship between denominationalism and the ecumenical movement? It seems to me that there are certain paradoxes in play here. Ecumenism presupposes a denominational structure to the Christian landscape; it is premised on a plurality of distinctive churches that subsist in a state of separation and competition that ecumenical dialogue seeks to overcome. But when ecumenism is successful it brings into prominence what the churches have in common, as well as sharpening the real remaining differences between them. Ecumenism needs denominationalism, even as it seeks to overcome it.

A glance at modern church history suggests that the rise of denominationalism and of the ecumenical movement went hand in hand and that there might be a causal link between them, even if after a short time lag. In Britain the heyday of denominationalism was probably the second half of the nineteenth century and the first half of the twentieth. Roman Catholics were a marginal minority (we are talking about Britain, not Ireland); the Church of England was at its zenith, and the nonconformist churches of England and Wales were also at the peak of membership and influence. Religious societies cut across the churches, bringing Christians together to make common cause for the sake of the Bible, missions, social amelioration and reform, and so on. Movements of religious consciousness, whether catholic or evangelical, created ferment within many churches, wherever they happened to begin—they reflected intellectual and cultural currents that were both broad and deep. It was in such circumstances that the first stirrings of Christian unity were felt. Ecumenism came out of strength, not weakness, and was bound up with the missionary imperative.

The formation of the Evangelical Alliance in 1846 to "associate and concentrate the strength of an enlightened Protestantism against the encroachments of Popery and Puseyism, and to promote the interests of a Scriptural Christianity" was a straw in the wind—a form of pan-evangelical ecumenism. The 1888 Lambeth Conference, taking its cue from the Protestant Episcopal Church of the USA (now The Episcopal Church), formulated the famous Lambeth Quadrilateral (Scripture, sacraments, creeds and a common ministry) as a basis for unity. After the interruption of the First World War, the 1920 Lambeth Conference issued its seminal *Appeal to All Christian People*, which generated an ecumenical momentum that continues to this day. Until the Second Vatican Council (1962–5) Roman Catholics were prohibited by the pope from participating in ecumenical activities. The claim to be the one and only instantiation of the Church of Christ precluded the minimal level of recognition accorded to other churches that is needed for dialogue and for local cooperation. In *Mortalium Animos* (1928) Pope Pius XI made precisely this connection: the (Roman) Catholic Church was "the one true Church of Christ". Therefore the way to unity was for separated Christians ("dissidents") to return to the fold and to submit completely to the papacy. "No one is in the Church of Christ, and no one remains in it, unless he acknowledges and accepts with obedience the authority and power of Peter and his legitimate successors."[9] So it was no accident that Vatican II simultaneously weakened the exclusive claims of the Roman Catholic Church (in the notoriously disputed phrase *subsistit in*: *Lumen Gentium* 23)[10] and committed Roman Catholics to work for unity. The Roman Catholic document that is most ecumenically generous in recognizing the ecclesial authenticity of other churches is Pope John Paul II's *Ut Unum Sint* (1995), and this is the encyclical that humbly and charitably asks for help from separated brethren in reinterpreting the papal office for an ecumenical age.[11]

Sometimes it is when we see ourselves as one church among others that we become disturbingly conscious of the disunity of the Church of Christ. With the realization that disunity is rampant and that schism is a sin comes the desire to work for reunion. The fact of denominationalism is a standing rebuke to the churches. It is eloquent testimony to the fact that they have failed—failed to heed the prayer and command of Christ and the apostles in the New Testament that the Church should be visibly one.[12] The divisions within the Church—of which denominationalism is perhaps the most blatant manifestation—raise the question of whether the Church actually exists on earth, or whether what we have is an inferior substitute, a quasi-church. Only a miracle of grace can preserve the Church on earth in the teeth of human drive to assert difference and to mark separation. We cannot be complacent about denominations. To acquiesce in denominationalism is to confess failure; to glory in it is a sickness.

On the other hand, the more that theological dialogue and local ecumenical cooperation reveal what the churches have in common, the more the exclusive or distinctive claims of each tradition are undermined. Denominations revel in being different; without difference they have no standing ground. Their rationale is that that they offer something different and something better—it used to be said, the only way of salvation. Why should we continue to champion the claims of our own tradition over against those of others once we have come to see that we are 90 per cent the same all the time? We hold a common faith, worship using very similar liturgical forms and experience a high degree of convergence even in the traditionally divisive areas of ministry and sacraments. Then we lose the will to go to the stake for our cause, our church. Denominational differences have been relativized, marginalized; they are not that important any more. What is to stop us joining together? What remains genuinely church-dividing? What possible excuse can there be for not uniting forthwith?

By the same token, denominational differences are played down when common issues cut across all the churches. Don't we all currently struggle with issues of funding and resources? Aren't we all tearing ourselves apart over homosexuality in the Church? Aren't we equally struggling to make our mission and evangelization effective in the face of secularist opposition and consumerist apathy? It makes sense to join forces. We are all in the same boat; we must sink or swim together. Are genuine differences about, say bishops or the pope, sufficiently important to prevent us pulling together? Unity in mission is not only a visionary ideal, but also a practical necessity.

It might seem that the interest goes out of ecumenism when it loses its sharp edges. Controversy is the lifeblood of theology, including ecumenical theology. Walter Kasper, President of the Pontifical Council for Promoting Christian Unity, believes that dialogue between the Roman Catholic Church and the other major Christian traditions has now moved beyond polemic: "it can happily be stated that some of the classic disputes, which were at the root of our painful divisions, have today been basically resolved through a new consensus on fundamental points of doctrine. In other disputed questions there is at least convergence, which has helped the dialogues to move beyond previous polemical stances, and has created a more relaxed ecumenical atmosphere in which an '*exchange of gifts*' has been enriching for both sides."[13] If only it were so! The timing of Kasper's book was unfortunate: it was published just as the storm broke over Pope Benedict XVI's overture to disaffected Anglicans in the Apostolic Constitution that provided for Anglican *Ordinariates*. Although it was presented as a pastoral response to the pleas of alienated Anglican traditionalists, the initiative was essentially an incitement to separation, to go out of communion with one's church, which is schism. That is the antithesis of all that the ecumenical movement stands for. Official Anglican responses at the time were muted and polite, albeit spoken through gritted teeth. Subsequent reflection has been tinged with bitterness. Ecumenism discovered that dialogue sometimes needs to be polemical after all.

The Church of England within the Anglican Communion

It would be rash to attempt to generalize about Anglicanism with regard to denominational identity and denominational consciousness. What may be true of the churches of the Anglican Communion generally may not be true of the Church of England, the most ancient—together with the Church of Ireland—of Anglican churches and historically the mother church of the Anglican Communion.

The Church of England may turn out to be the exception that proves the rule with regard to denominational identity. The Church of England is unique among Anglican churches in that it is the established national church. Some other Anglican churches are national churches, but the English Church is the only one that is still fully established by law.

A church that is strongly identified with the nation or the state (they are not necessarily the same) does not easily fit the category of denomination: it is *the* church, not *a* church, a defining expression of the Church in that context, not one of many competing claimants. The Church of England may be regarded as a "national church" *par excellence*, with its ministry extending back into the remote beginnings of the Middle Ages, together with its recognition in law and in the (unwritten) constitution as the *established* church. The Church of England is the only Anglican church that is fully or strongly established, though, since all churches are subject to the law of the land, and the precise relationship of any church to the law of the land is a matter of degree, some Anglican churches still retain certain vestiges of establishment.[14]

To start close to home, there is the instructive case of "The Church in Wales", disestablished in 1920, which retains some significant aspects of establishment, especially with regard to the occasional offices or *rites de passage*. Its clergy are obliged by law to baptize, marry and bury all parishioners for whom these ministries are requested. The name "The Church in Wales" makes a rather grand claim and is not indicative of a fully disestablished church, nor does it suggest that Welsh Anglicanism sees itself as one denomination among others. Its archbishop is called the "Archbishop of Wales" (not "*in* Wales"), a title that has strong overtones of territoriality and national identity. On these grounds alone, there is something to be said for the suggestion that the Church in Wales was "re-established" when it was "disestablished".

The Church of England may be the only fully established Anglican Church, but it is certainly not the only *national* Anglican church. Within the Anglican Communion many—though not all—churches (or provinces), especially those in the former dominions of the British Empire, see themselves as national churches, even when they are not the largest church and not established churches. A classical definition of the Anglican Communion, formulated by the 1930 Lambeth Conference of Anglican bishops from around the world, described it as "a fellowship, within the one, holy, catholic and apostolic Church, of those duly constituted dioceses, provinces, or regional Churches in communion with the See of Canterbury" that are characterized by their catholic faith and order and by the fact that they are "particular or national churches . . . bound together . . . by mutual loyalty sustained by the common counsel of the bishops in conference."[15] But are these national Anglican churches also denominations, even if they would not use that language about themselves? If we define a denomination as a church that exists among a plurality of competing churches, none of which is numerically dominant or enjoys a legal monopoly, we can ask whether a national church and even an established church can *also* be regarded as a denomination. First, let us apply this rough definition, with its criteria of numerical ascendancy and legal monopoly, to the Church of England, the church by law established in England.

The Church of England is the largest Christian Church in England. It has baptized more than 20 million of the population of 50 million. Although the numbers worshiping week by week (though in many cases not every week) hovers around the one million mark (about the same number as the Roman Catholic Church in England), its actual pastoral constituency of people who have a meaningful contact with the Church—through its numerous church schools, through Sunday School, youth groups, occasional offices and community events—is many times larger than this. It is the numerically dominant church in England, though not overwhelmingly so.[16]

The established church's legal monopoly was undermined as long ago as 1689 by the Act of Toleration, and then completely destroyed by the abolition of the Test and Corporation Acts and by the emancipation of Roman Catholics, in 1829–31. However, the Church of England still retains a number of legal and institutional privileges: for example in the areas of chaplaincy (prisons, hospitals, armed services, ancient schools and colleges), the General Synod's power to enact primary legislation so that church law is part of the law of the land, and the presence of twenty-six bishops *ex officio* in Parliament, in the House of Lords, and not least the role of the Sovereign as its Supreme Governor.

Given its numerical ascendancy and its legal privileges, should the Church of England be regarded as a denomination? One way of answering that question is to consult the Church of England's own understanding of itself, of its identity and mission. Here we might look for evidence to the General Synod and in particular to the House of Bishops within the Synod. As someone who has been closely involved with the General Synod for more than twenty years, first as an elected member and subsequently in a staff capacity, I am convinced that the Synod and the episcopate particularly does not see itself in denominational terms. The name "The Church of England" is taken quite literally. There is little sense of being simply one church seeking to take a role among a plurality of other churches. The Church of England in its national manifestation does not think of itself as one denomination among others. As an historic church, going back through the Reformation to the beginnings of Christianity in England and so to the Church of the Apostles, it simply sees itself as the Church. As the established Church, with a nationwide mission and ministry that is carried out at every level of national life, from the parochial, through the regional (diocesan) to the level of state (with reference to the Crown and parliament), it still sees itself as the Church of the English people. As a church that is both catholic and reformed, it sees itself not as a particular option among Christian churches, but as the authentic Church. To push the case even further in a politically incorrect direction, Anglicans in England really cannot see why the other churches are needed! Why cannot other Christians simply go along to their local parish church? All are welcome, none are turned away. No denominational foibles or eccentricities are rammed down people's throats. Surely there is nothing to offend Christians of goodwill here? There is nothing about the modern Church of England that should grate on the conscience of individuals, preventing them from joining in communion with it. Other churches do not have to defend themselves against the established Church—they are not persecuted. They do not need to be separate in order to preserve certain cherished insights that are thought to be missing from Anglicanism—the Church of England is a very broad church, where many varieties of belief and practice flourish unhampered. It would be a very exacting kind of Christian who could not find a niche somewhere in the historic church of the land. I suspect that that is not far from how many Church of England people think about their church in relation to the alternatives.

Now, if this characterization of the Church of England is broadly on target, we need to ask whether that church is deceiving itself. Has it come to terms with the radical pluralism of the religious scene in England? Has it faced up to its long-term decline? Has it got its head buried in the sand with regard to the actual numbers attending its services? Denominationalism is a reality that affects all churches in the developed West. To be in denial about prevailing tendencies towards denominational identity and denominational behaviour is ideological, a form of ecclesiastical false consciousness.

Although the Church of England may find the denominational descriptor distasteful and cling to some fading glory from its heyday in late Victorian, early

Edwardian England, when nearly three times as many stipendiary clergy served a population about half the size, the fact is that it sometimes behaves like a denomination. With the creation of the Archbishops' Council in 1999, there was a perceptible shift of the centre of gravity from the parishes and dioceses, where the church's ministry and worship were still deeply woven into the texture of English community life, especially in the countryside, to the national centre, with its executive board and its supporting bureaucracy located at Church House, Westminster. At about that time the Church of England centrally produced its own logo: it was making itself into a market brand. Until recently the telephone switchboard in Westminster answered calls with the words "The Church of England; how may I help you?" That was regarded as outrageous presumption by many in the parishes and at diocesan level, who believed that they and those like them, with their weekly round of worship and other activities centred on the parish churches, gathered together within the dioceses, were the Church of England.

On the other hand, there is much about the Church of England today that militates against a denominational understanding. Its Canons locate the centre of gravity in the diocese, defined as the community of word and sacrament gathered by the bishop and as the bishop's sphere of oversight, where he (at the time of writing it is still "he") is the chief pastor (Canon C 18). When Anglicans are being self-consciously ecclesiological they talk of the diocese as the local church. Through its constitutive parishes (more than 13,000 of them), it constitutes the Church of England on the ground. Again, the Church of England is unlike a denomination in that it does not have a membership roll. The Church of England does not keep a list of signed-up members. It has a Church Electoral Roll, but this is an instrument of church governance, not a comprehensive membership roll. The Church of England does not use the language of membership in a denominational sense. In its official documentation it refers to "members" in various contexts, but no unified meaning can be discerned here. The meaning of membership that is dominant in Church of England discourse is the Pauline idea of membership of the body of Christ through baptism (1 Cor. 12.13). The Catechism informs the candidate for Confirmation that in their baptism they were "made a member of Christ, the child of God, and an inheritor of the kingdom of heaven". Strictly speaking, all baptized parishioners who have not opted out are "members". And it is a moot point whether parishioners who have in fact chosen a different church have thereby ceased to be part of the Church of England. Of course, if they wish to have no truck with their parish church, give no cognisance to the parish priest, who is there to minister to all who are willing to receive that ministry, and generally renounce the Church of England and all her ways, it would be perverse to suggest that they were still within the Church in any meaningful sense—though I think we have to say that if they had been baptized by the Church of England, they would not be completely outside her borders. But if they have some involvement with the life of the parish and even occasionally attend their parish church, it would certainly make sense to see them as participating to some degree in the Church of England. But, as I say, the Church of England is not interested in making members for itself; what it is committed to is providing many different opportunities to maximize the participation of individuals and households in the life of grace in the Church, and then helping them to become committed disciples of Jesus Christ as they follow the path of Christian initiation through baptism to Confirmation and first Communion.

To sum up, the centre of gravity of the Church of England is found in its history, its national mission and its diocesan and parochial structure: these are not conducive to a denominational description. On the other hand, there are indicators of a shift to a more denominational consciousness within that church. We might say that the Church of England is balanced on the cusp of denominational identity, but it would be rash to predict which way it will fall—or whether it will continue to hover for some time to come. The congregationalist tendency within many parishes is pointing in a denominational direction, but the proliferation of "fresh expressions of church", for whom denominational issues are very marginal, is perhaps a countervailing trend.

When we look at worldwide Anglicanism we note that the more historic churches of the Anglican Communion do not define themselves, in their official ecclesiological discourse, as denominations, but as provinces or churches of a wider Communion and, above all, as belonging to the one, holy, catholic and apostolic Church of Jesus Christ. Unlike the Orthodox Churches or even the Roman Catholic Churches (notwithstanding Vatican II), in order to make this claim about themselves, Anglican Churches do not need to dismiss or devalue the claims of other churches; they do not need to make an exclusive claim for themselves or to unchurch others. By recognizing that others as well as themselves are true manifestations of the one Church, Anglicans give a special priority to the visible unity of the Church—an eschatological horizon in the light of which all denominational defensiveness and competitiveness must melt away.

Notes

1   Cf. the discussion in P. Avis, *A Church Drawing Near: Spirituality and Mission in a Post-Christian Culture* (London and New York: T&T Clark, 2003), ch. 3.
2   Cf. N. Luhmann, *The Differentiation of Society* (New York: Columbia University Press, 1982), esp. pp. 230, 248; T. Luckmann, *Life-World and Social Realities* (London: Heinemann Educational, 1983), esp. p. 130.

3 See the discussion in P. Avis, *Reshaping Ecumenical Theology: The Church Made Whole?* (London and New York: T&T Clark, 2010), esp. ch. 4, "The Hermeneutics of Unity".

4 See D.B. Barrett, G.T. Kurian, and T.M. Johnson, *World Christian Encyclopedia* (2nd edn, New York, Oxford University Press, 2001), pp. 3, 10.

5 O. Chadwick, *The Secularization of the European Mind in the Nineteenth Century* (Cambridge: Cambridge University Press, 1975), p. 21. See also W.K. Jordan, *The Development of Religious Toleration in England*, 2 vols (London: Allen and Unwin, 1932); Joseph Lecler, *Toleration and the Reformation* (London: Longmans, 1960).

6 H. MacLeod in F. Young (ed.), *Dare We Speak of God in Public?* (London: Mowbray, 1995), p. 4.

7 W. Pannenberg, *Christianity in a Secularized World* (New York: Crossroad, 1989), pp. 29–31.

8 Cf. S. Barton (ed.), *The Family in Theological Perspective* (Edinburgh: T&T Clark, 1996).

9 J. Neuner, SJ, and J. Dupuis, SJ (eds), *The Christian Faith in the Doctrinal Documents of the Catholic Church*, revised edn (London: Collins, 1983), p. 260.

10 W.M. Abbott, SJ (ed.), *The Documents of Vatican II* (London and Dublin: Geoffrey Chapman, 1966), p. 23.

11 For Anglican commentary on *Ut Unum Sint*, see House of Bishops of the Church of England, *May They All Be One* (London: Church House Publishing, 1997); M. Santer, "Communion, Unity and Primacy: An Anglican Response to *Ut Unum Sint*", *Ecclesiology* 3, 3, (2007): 283–95.

12 See further, P. Avis, *Reshaping Ecumenical Theology*, esp. ch. 10: "Forging Communion in the Face of Difference".

13 W. Kasper, *Harvesting the Fruits: Basic Aspects of Christian Faith in Ecumenical Dialogue* (London and New York: Continuum, 2009), pp. 197–98.

14 See further, N. Doe, *Canon Law in the Anglican Communion* (Oxford: Clarendon Press, 1998); P. Avis, *Church, State and Establishment* (London: SPCK, 2001).

15 1930 Lambeth Conference, Resolutions 48 and 49. R. Coleman (ed.), *Resolutions of the Twelve Lambeth Conferences 1967–1988* (Toronto: Anglican Book Centre, 1992), pp. 83–5. See further, P. Avis, *The Identity of Anglicanism: Essentials of Anglican Ecclesiology* (London and New York: T&T Clark, 2008).

16 See P. Avis (ed.), *Public Faith: The State of Religious Belief and Practice in Britain* (London: SPCK, 2003), esp. ch. 7, D. Voas, "Is Britain a Christian Country?"

Chapter 3

THE ECUMENICAL DIMENSIONS OF BAPTIST DENOMINATIONAL IDENTITY

STEVEN R. HARMON

My Baptist theological reflections on the ecclesiological category "denomination" are conditioned by two particularities: my specific Baptist identity as a member of the Cooperative Baptist Fellowship (CBF) and my vocational identity as an ecumenical theologian who has represented the Baptist World Alliance in bilateral dialogues with the Anglican Consultative Council and the Pontifical Council for Promoting Christian Unity, and as a member of the Commission on Faith and Order of the World Council of Churches. This chapter will therefore begin with a consideration of what the internal debate within the CBF about whether it is or should become a "denomination" reveals about broader Baptist perspectives on denominational identity. I will then explore the ecumenical possibilities of denomination as an ecclesiological category for Baptists.

The Cooperative Baptist Fellowship as "Denomination"

My Christian nurture from infancy onward, through baptism, to my discernment of a calling to vocational ministry, ordination, and theological education, took place within the denominational framework of the Southern Baptist Convention (SBC). By the time I enrolled as a divinity student at one of the SBC's official seminaries in 1989, however, the denomination was a decade into a bitter public struggle between well-organized political networks of "conservatives" and "moderates" over the control of its institutions and agencies.[1] By the end of my second year of seminary in 1991, Southern Baptist moderates had largely disengaged from these political efforts and formed the CBF as a network for fellowship among like-minded churches and individuals who perceived themselves as disaffected from those who now led the SBC, and for the support of emerging institutions and agencies that would provide alternatives for the key denominational services that the SBC had traditionally provided to local churches: theological education, mechanisms for the cooperative support of missions, literature for Christian education, denominational news media, and public advocacy for Baptist perspectives on matters of religious liberty and ethics. I soon identified myself with the CBF, and from 1998 to 2008 taught theology at one of its partner institutions of theological education, Campbell University Divinity School in Buies Creek, North Carolina.

Throughout the first decade of its existence the CBF engaged in a public debate over the manner in which it should differentiate itself from the SBC. The debate tended to be framed in terms of the question, "Is the CBF a denomination?" Some members of the CBF favored official "denominational" status in the hope that it would help CBF churches establish an identity separate from the SBC, which they believed no longer reflected or welcomed their version of Baptist identity. Others opposed it: some for the pragmatic reason that it would be too difficult for many churches to modify their long-cherished official associations with the SBC (though Baptist congregational polity does allow for multiple national denominational associations); others, because they identified "denomination" with the oppressive forms of institutional authority they had experienced in the SBC; and still others, because they contended that denominations were a thing of the past and were not viable in a postmodern world. Almost everyone involved in this debate regarded a denomination as an institutional organization that assumes a particular sort of bureaucratic structure. Furthermore, all assumed that, whatever its nature, there should be some sort of identifiable entity beyond the local church, comprising other local churches and individuals committed to similar convictions about Baptist faith and practice.

From 1991 to 1995, the CBF "denominational question" surfaced in business sessions at annual CBF General Assembly meetings and in news articles and op-ed pieces in Baptist media. In 1995, CBF Moderator Patrick Anderson appointed a five-member committee charged "to study the CBF denominational question" with the understanding that the committee would not bring a specific recommendation but rather a report that would "raise our level of conversation and understanding about issues involved in CBF becoming or not becoming a separate convention".[2] (Many Baptists with historic connections to the SBC prefer the designation "convention" to "denomination" or "church" when referring to trans-local associations of Baptists at the national level, owing to the reference of "convention" to the group of representatives of local congregations who convene each year in annual session, in contrast to a permanent bureaucratic or hierarchical structure. The CBF "denominational question" was therefore frequently framed in terms of whether the CBF should be understood as a convention distinct from the SBC.)

In response to this charge the committee commissioned several position papers on the issue by CBF-affiliated theological educators, ministers, and laypersons;

interpreted the results of an earlier survey of the CBF constituency conducted by its Coordinating Council; and solicited letters from all who wished to express and elaborate their opinions on the matter. The final report of the committee was issued prior to the 1996 CBF General Assembly in the form of a 141-page book that included a summary of the input from surveys and letters, along with the full text of the twelve position papers. In keeping with the charge given the committee, the report made no specific recommendation, and accordingly, the CBF took no action on it other than disseminating it. The denominational issue continued to be discussed in the aftermath of the report's publication, especially as the CBF took steps to begin endorsing military and hospital chaplains.

For the purposes of this essay, the collection of position papers solicited and published by the CBF special-study commission provides the best window into the theological dimensions of the question of denominational identity among Cooperative Baptists. Some of the report's authors discerned clear advantages to self-identifying as a denomination or convention.[3] Others identified denominational status with oppressive forms of institutionalism that would inevitably betray the principles that gave birth to the CBF, and urged against becoming a denomination. Carolyn Blevins cited, in summary, H. Richard Niebuhr's contention in his 1929 book *The Social Sources of Denominationalism* that denominations "tend to: compromise with the world, accommodate to the caste system, seek primarily to preserve themselves, and be influenced by culture more than they influence culture". Blevins granted that those identified with the CBF have principles worth preserving, but contended that replicating the features of modern American denominations might prove to be the worst possible way of preserving the distinctive gifts of this expression of Baptist identity.[4] Yet other contributors recognized the need for the CBF to establish an identity of its own but cautioned against making this move too swiftly in light of significant recent shifts in attitudes towards denominations in American Christianity.[5]

A paper representing this last category, "On Being a Denomination: CBF and the Future" by Nancy T. Ammerman, offered in my judgment the best-developed historical, sociological, and theological analysis of the CBF denominational question among the papers collected in the report.[6] Her categories for interpreting the functions of a denomination and their relation to CBF denominational identity provide an ideal point of departure for my own observations and proposals regarding denomination as a Baptist ecclesiological category.

Ammerman proposes four senses in which trans-congregational patterns of ecclesial life function as denominations.

First, denominations may be identified as "agencies," "through which we do missions and from which we get the goods and services that help us do the work of our local churches".[7] Inasmuch as the CBF has from its inception established partnership networks with agencies that support and send missionaries; provide graduate–professional theological education; publish literature in support of programs of Christian education in local churches; offer access to denominational news media; voice Baptist convictions about religious liberty and other ethical concerns in the public square; and assist the ministries of local churches in other ways, despite the disavowals of denominational status quoted above, the CBF has long functioned as a denomination in the sense of agency, though in ways that Ammerman labels "postmodern denomination".[8]

Second, a denomination functions as a "specific religious tradition that binds us to one another"[9]—i.e. a theological identity rooted in the convictions and practices that distinguish Baptist communities from, say, Lutheran or Reformed or Catholic ones. Despite the aversion of many in the CBF to doctrinal specificity, Ammerman insists that the CBF must embrace this aspect of denominational identity as well:

> In Baptist life, theology belongs to the people, and this moment of crisis has offered us a reason to ask theological questions. We pride ourselves on being non-creedal, but what do we believe? What do we want to teach our children about why they should be Baptist? What do we contribute to the larger body of Christ? What ways of being Christian and ideas about God are uniquely treasured by us?[10]

This way of portraying the inescapably theological dimensions of denominational identity parallels the definition of the the church's doctrinal task offered by the late Baptist theologian James William McClendon, Jr.: "a church teaching as she must teach if she is to be the church here and now".[11] Baptists who identify with the CBF are far from agreed on the content of what it is that their church must teach, but Ammerman insists, "Still we need ways to talk about what we believe. . . . In many ways, to be Baptist is simply to participate in the conversation about what it means to be Baptist".[12] The latter stress on what it means to participate actively in the ongoing formation of a religious tradition is reminiscent of Alasdair MacIntyre's definition of "a living tradition" as "an historically extended, socially embodied argument, and an argument precisely in part about the goods which constitute that tradition"[13]—a connection to which this essay will return in its proposal for a more intentionally ecumenical understanding of Baptist denominational identity. The third and fourth senses of denominational identity defined by Ammerman likewise have something in common with MacIntyre's description of the "living tradition" that is central to the life of various types of institutions, including denominations: denominations have "cultural identities" that consist in their external perceptions by the larger culture as well as in their own internal cultural life, and they are "social institutions" that conform to the way a certain species of social-organizational life is ordinarily constructed.[14] This essay will return to possibility of developing Ammerman's categories of Baptist denominationalism in a more explicitly MacIntyrean direction in connection with my own proposals for an ecumenical construal of denomination as an ecclesiological category for Baptists.

Although the CBF officially continued to disavow the "denomination" label, it did find it necessary to claim a distinct organizational identity separate from the SBC in connection with its 2001 application for membership in the Baptist World Alliance (BWA), the Baptist counterpart to the Lutheran World Federation and other world communions. When the CBF was asked to elaborate its case for membership, it formulated a rationale for its distinction from the SBC that exemplified all four meanings of "denomination" in Ammerman's typology. The BWA Membership Committee initially deferred action on the application, requesting from the CBF further evidence that it was not an "integral part" of any other BWA member body, in this case, the SBC. In 2002, the CBF Coordinating Council voted to acknowledge officially that the CBF had "separated ourselves from the structures and organization of the SBC, and have a distinctly diverse understanding to the SBC of what it means to be an organized body of Baptist churches and individuals in covenant relationship,"[15] and in 2003, the BWA General Council voted to accept the application. In addition to this declaration of separate identity, the Coordinating Council response listed "twenty indications that we are no longer integral to the SBC," among which the following are germane to this reflection on what "denomination" means for Baptists:

4. We have our own annual assemblies that routinely draw 3,000 to 5,000 of our constituents, at which we elect leadership, pass budgets and conduct business.
6. We have substantial organizational documentation, including a Constitution and Bylaws, which clearly establishes our unique and separate identity.
7. We have our own organizational structure, including a board of directors, formal annual budgets, and a large group of employed staff and office buildings.
8. We have organized autonomous states and regions with their own boards of directors, formal budgets, employed staffs, and office buildings.
9. We own and operate our own missions sending agency, foundation and a benefits board with over 300 participants.
10. Our 140 missionaries are in partnership with other autonomous entities worldwide as representatives of the CBF.
12. We have over 150 partnering churches that have no formal membership in the SBC.

13. We have planted over 50 churches that partner only with CBF at the national and international level.
14. We are recognized as an official endorsing body for chaplains and pastoral counselors by the US Armed Forces Board; national pastoral care, counseling and education organizations; and other viable entities. . . .
15. We are recognized as a non-governmental organization (NGO) by the United Nations and have participated as such on the world stage.
20. We are recognized by numerous U.S. Baptist state conventions as a legitimate national Baptist body, including Virginia, Texas, and North Carolina, each of which offers a channel for its churches to give to CBF through its state budget.

Yet after this list, which reflects the traditional features and functions of modern North American denominations, the response insists, "Though fully independent of the SBC or any other union, we do not declare that we are a denomination or convention. . . . We have chosen instead to define ourselves as a 'fellowship,' which means that we are 'a Baptist association of churches and individuals' in partnership for the advancement of God's Kingdom". As of the writing of this essay on March 24, 2011, the "Frequently Asked Questions about CBF" portion of the official CBF website concludes with the question, "Is CBF a denomination?" and provides this answer: "CBF is not a denomination but rather a fellowship of churches and Christians"[16]—one that nevertheless embodies Ammerman's description of denomination as agency, religious tradition, cultural identity, and social institution.[17]

The Ecclesiality of Baptist Denominations

Barry Ensign-George's definition of denomination in Chapter One of this volume as "a structured entity between congregation and church" that "is a contingent, intermediary, interdependent, partial and permeable embodiment of the church" likewise largely applies to the self-understanding of CBF as a "fellowship", even if the CBF and its constituent churches and individuals do not claim to be a denomination. This application requires a significant qualification, however. For while many Baptists have affirmed the existence of an "invisible" universal church inclusive of all who belong to Christ, they have also tended to regard only the local congregation as the "visible" expression of the church.[18] Thus, for most Baptists a "denomination," or its functional equivalent, will be conceived of as an entity between the (visible) local church and the (invisible) universal church.

Cooperative Baptists and other sorts of Baptists do regard their form of trans-local fellowship as "contingent." They hold the local congregation to be the necessary form of life together in Christian community and typically assume the universal church as a spiritual given. But they view denominational structures as connections that the local church may maintain with intentionality as long as the denomination is serving the congregation's needs, but that the local church may ignore, supplement with other structures for trans-local connections, or dispense with entirely when the denomination is no longer perceived to be of service to the life of the congregation. Yet it must be conceded that many Baptists manifest a triumphalistic perspective on Baptist identity that regards it as anything but contingent: the Baptists have most consistently restored the New Testament church, it is thought, and denominations will no longer be necessary when other denominations recognize this and embrace Baptist principles themselves.[19] Whenever Baptist identity is conserved as an end in itself in order to preserve for perpetuity a distinctively Baptist pattern of faith and practice that is not regarded as a temporary way-station en route to the full visible unity of the universal church, Baptist denominational identity ceases to be contingent.

Therefore, there are aspects of Baptist conceptions of denominational identity that do not lend themselves easily to Ensign-George's characterization of denominations as "intermediary" between the local congregation and the church universal. Yet in the case of the CBF, this functionally denominational form of Baptist trans-local connections does make available to its constituents various means of connection with the rest of the church. The CBF is now a member body of the BWA through which CBF partnering congregations and individuals are linked in fellowship with Baptists who belong to other Baptist denominational bodies internationally as well as in the United States. Though not an official member body of the National Council of the Churches of Christ in the USA (NCCCUSA) or the World Council of Churches (WCC), it is a member of Christian Churches Together, and individual members of the CBF have served on commissions of the NCCCUSA and the WCC. Some other Baptist denominational bodies, such as the Baptist Union of Great Britain and the American Baptist Churches, USA (formerly the Northern Baptist Convention) have been official members of the WCC since its inception.[20]

While Baptist congregational polity does imbue the Baptist denominational tradition with a strongly independent spirit, and while it is true that many Baptist congregations declare themselves to be Independent Baptist churches and do not belong to any form of trans-local fellowship, Baptists have, from their seventeenth-century origins, also embodied an associational principle that qualifies their congregational independence as an interdependent congregationalism. In this more connectional dimension of Baptist ecclesiology, the independence of local congregations is not absolute. Local Baptist congregations are interdependent in their relations with one another, not only in local associations but also in various national and international associations of Baptists. When seven local Baptist congregations in London together issued the *London Confession* of 1644, they explained their interdependence in discerning the mind of Christ for their faith and practice in this fashion:

> [B]ecause it may be conceived, that what is here published, may be but the Judgement of some one particular Congregation, more refined than the rest; We doe therefore here subscribe it, some of each body in the name, and by the appointment of seven Congregations, who though wee be distinct in respect of our particular bodies, for conveniency sake, being as many as can well meete together in one place, yet are all one in Communion, holding Jesus Christ to be our head and Lord; under whose government wee desire alone to walke, in following the Lambe wheresoever he goeth; and wee beleeve the Lord will daily cause truth more to appeare in the hearts of his Saints . . . that so they may with one shoulder, more studie to lift up the Name of the Lord Jesus, and stand for his appointments and Lawes; which is the desires and prayers of the contemned Churches of Christ in London for all Saints.[21]

The rule of Christ in the local congregations in the plural therefore has implications for the efforts of any single local congregation to discern the mind of Christ, and vice versa. Together in their mutual relations they seek to walk under the government of Christ, seeking from him a fuller grasp of the truth, as one ecclesial communion—a communion which, it was hoped by these early Baptists, might extend beyond Baptist churches in association to include all the saints. Baptists do not always conceive of this interdependence as involving non-Baptists, but the interdependence embodied in Baptist forms of denomination has openings for trans-denominational expressions of interdependence that can be more fully exploited by Baptists who regard the visible unity of all Christians as an ecclesial good.

Despite the previously noted Baptist triumphalism that has surfaced in the tradition now and then, few if any Baptists would argue that their denomination is the full historical manifestation of the church. The strained historiographical apologetic of "Landmark" Baptists did seek to make the case that Baptists can trace a lineage of direct succession through pre-Reformation sectarian movements all the way back to the baptism of Jesus by John the Baptist,[22] but in the main, Baptists regard Baptist denominational identity as a partial embodiment of the church—even if many Baptists may consider some denominations as more partial than others in their approximation of the fullness of the church. Most Baptist conceptions of denomination are likewise permeable, with respect both to membership and to denominational mutability. It would be hard to conceive of a more permeable denomination-like configuration than the self-description of the CBF, for example. Even so, the reluctance of some Baptist congregations to recognize the baptisms of other communions when members of those churches present themselves for Baptist church membership can render Baptist denominationalism less permeable, and many Baptists at all points on the theological spectrum will consider the modification of what they regard as essential Baptist distinctives to be a betrayal of the Baptist heritage rather than something that contributes to its improvement.

In what sense can Baptists affirm denomination as an "embodiment" of the church? While Baptists do not regard a denomination as *ekklēsia* proper in the sense of the church local or universal, Baptist ecclesiology can admit that denominations are ecclesial to the degree that they participate in the qualities of church. Indeed, in a somewhat paradoxical manner, Baptist "gathered church" ecclesiology is, at least in theory, able to grant a substantial degree of ecclesiality not only to various forms of denominational trans-local associations of Baptists but even to ecumenical gatherings, for all of these embodiments of the church are instances "where two or three are gathered in my name" (Mt. 18.20 New Revised Standard Version [NRSV]) for the purpose of bringing their common life under the lordship of Christ. British Baptist theologian Paul Fiddes has made such connections between the location of the church in the gathered congregation and the embodiment of the church in various forms of trans-local fellowship:

> The liberty of local churches to make decisions about their own life and ministry is not based in a human view of autonomy or independence, or in selfish individualism, but in a sense of being under the direct rule of Christ who relativizes other rules. This liberating rule of Christ is what makes for the distinctive "feel" of Baptist congregational life, which allows for spiritual oversight (*episkopē*) both by the *whole* congregation gathered together in church meeting, and by the minister(s) called to lead the congregation. . . . Since the same rule of Christ can be experienced in assemblies of churches together, there is also the basis here for Baptist associational life, and indeed for participating in ecumenical clusters.[23]

The late Mennonite theologian John Howard Yoder made a similar point about the possibilities of free church ecclesiology for envisioning an ecumenical gathering as a gathered community under the lordship of Christ that gathers for the purpose of seeking his rule in the community:

> This view gives more, not less, weight to ecumenical gatherings. The "high" views of ordered churchdom can legitimate the worship of a General

Assembly or a study conference only by stretching the rules, for its rules do not foresee ad hoc "churches"; only thoroughgoing congregationalism fulfills its hopes and definities whenever and wherever it sees "church" happen.[24]

From the standpoint of Baptist and other expressions of Free Church ecclesiology, the embodiment of the church in the local congregation is the normative expression of church, but it is not the whole church.[25] This local embodiment of the church in its fullness is one in which gatherings of members from multiple congregations—and from other associations of local congregations, perhaps even from those belonging to other Christian communions—may participate. A denomination is ecclesial, though not an *ekklēsia* in Baptist perspective.

Baptist Denominational Identity and the Ecumenical Future

It would be easy to attribute the formation and perpetuation of Baptist denominational entities to a self-serving concern for the preservation and transmission of the Baptist tradition to future generations. Those who formed the CBF were certainly motivated in part by the concern that their perspectives on Baptist identity would no longer be inculcated by the institutions of the SBC. Denominations do have the legitimate function of serving as bearers of a religious tradition (cf. the second category in Ammerman's typology), and this function need not always be self-serving. It can be directed towards the end of the visible unity of the church, and the Baptist associational impulse has at its best suggested surprisingly ecumenical dimensions of Baptist denominational identity. Baptists form various types of trans-local fellowships partly out of the recognition that no local congregation possesses in and of itself all the resources it needs for becoming a community of faithful disciples. The local congregations are interdependent in their efforts to fulfill the mission of the church—perhaps beginning with those of like faith and order, but potentially extending this recognition to those belonging to other denominations. Interestingly enough, the CBF's closest approximation of a declaration of separate identity as a Baptist denomination, made even as it was disavowing the term, came in an effort to have a channel for wider ecumenical connections with other Baptists worldwide via the BWA (Baptist World Alliance), the world communion through which Baptists relate at the international level to other communions (e.g. through its delegations to the joint commissions of bilateral ecumenical dialogues and other forums for ecumenical encounter). Walter Shurden, a Baptist historian who wrote one of the position papers solicited by the CBF Special Study Commission, contended that the CBF should seek denominational status in part so that it would have its own representation in the BWA.[26]

In my opinion, only the end of the full visible unity of the church justifies the continued separate ecclesial existence of Baptist denominational identity. When continued denominational existence becomes an end in itself, it perpetuates the division of the church. If visible unity in the sense envisioned by the New Delhi definition is to be achieved,[27] there must be both an inter-confessional contestation of faith and order and an inter-confessional exchange of gifts. This can happen only when the denominations see themselves as lacking something essential to what it means to be "church" as long as they remain separated from full communion with the other churches—an insight that is most easily gained from participation in the ecumenical contestation of the matters of faith and order that currently preclude full communion—and it can happen only when the other churches are able to receive the distinctive gifts that each denomination has to offer the rest of the body of Christ. "Receptive ecumenism" therefore complements conciliar Faith and Order ecumenism as an ecumenical paradigm within which it may be envisioned that an embrace of thick denominational identity can contribute to the quest for the visible unity of the church rather than the solidifying of its divisions.

Some older approaches to ecumenism created Baptist resistance to institutional expressions of the quest for Christian unity, such as the WCC, by giving the impression that the price of visible unity would be the surrender of some of the things held most dear by each church. A newer approach to ecumenical engagement, however, is gaining traction in the international ecumenical community. "Receptive ecumenism" is an approach to ecumenical dialogue in which the communions in conversation with one another seek to identify the distinctive gifts each tradition has to offer the other and could receive from the other with integrity.[28] This paradigm for ecumenical engagement was given expression by Pope John Paul II in his 1995 encyclical on ecumenism *Ut Unum Sint*: "Dialogue is not simply an exchange of ideas. In some ways it is always an 'exchange of gifts.' " (§ 28).[29] Some bilateral dialogues, such as that between the Roman Catholic Church and the World Methodist Council, have worked towards concrete proposals for the exchange of ecclesial gifts.[30] Yet, as an international conference on receptive ecumenism held at Durham University (in the UK) in 2006 defined the enterprise, "the primary emphasis is on learning rather than teaching. . . . each tradition takes responsibility for its own potential learning from others and is, in turn, willing to facilitate the learning of others as requested but without dictating terms and without making others' learning a precondition to attending to ones' own".[31]

The starting place for this receptive ecumenical learning is the denomination as a bearer of a religious tradition, one of Ammerman's categories for the function of denominations. If the denomination is the bearer of a living tradition in the MacIntyrean sense, it will be a contested one. Thus, Ammerman suggests that "to be Baptist is simply to participate in the conversation about what it means to be a Baptist"[32]—in other words, to participate in the argument about the good that constitutes the Baptist tradition. This intra-confessional contestation can help Baptists discover the aspects of the catholicity of the church that are uniquely preserved within the Baptist tradition so that they know what it is they have to offer as gift, as well as what they might need to receive in the exchange of ecclesial gifts.

Despite their contingency, the denominations are the primary means by which the argument about the goods that constitute the living tradition of the church has been historically extended and socially embodied. The different denominational traditions are the historical extensions of the arguments within the larger tradition of the church catholic that led to their separate existence, and they are therefore the pathways along which we must travel in re-engaging those arguments en route to ecumenical convergence. The *Joint Declaration on the Doctrine of Justification* (JDDJ), for example, could never have resulted from the reconsideration of theological propositions alone.[33] Its differentiated consensus was possible only because, for four decades, representatives of the Lutheran and Catholic traditions traveled together back through their respective historical extensions of this sixteenth-century argument, and thus were able to contest their contemporary differences in a way that clarified the teaching of both communions and drew them closer together, at least on this matter. The JDDJ likewise illustrates the socially embodied nature of this contestation. It was undertaken not by a random assortment of Christian theologians who happened to have adopted either Catholic or Lutheran positions on justification, irrespective of the denomination to which they belonged, but rather by theologians who were formed by the social embodiments of those traditions and who also participated over time in the particular socially embodied institution that is a joint ecumenical commission.

Only the existence of the trans-local denominations makes it possible for the local churches and their individual members to participate in the contestation of their own tradition and in the contestation between the denominational traditions necessary for progress towards the visible embodiment of the spiritual unity of the church universal. This argument reveals not only differences and openings for convergence between them, but also the location of the universal church's dispersed gifts and the possibilities for their exchange. Denominations serve the end of visible unity when they foster within and without the denominational tradition both the contestation of divisions and the reception of gifts across the current divides. Even if Cooperative Baptists and some other Baptist unions eschew the label "denomination," their trans-local forms of ecclesial association are their gateway to engagement with the non-Baptist churches, so "that they may become completely one" (Jn. 17.23 NRSV).

Notes

1 For historical and sociological studies of the controversy in the SBC, see Bill Leonard, *God's Last and Only Hope: The Fragmentation of the Southern Baptist Convention* (Grand Rapids, MI: William B. Eerdmans, 1990); Nancy T. Ammerman, *Baptist Battles: Social Change and Religious Conflict in the Southern Baptist Convention* (New Brunswick, NJ: Rutgers University Press, 1990); David T. Morgan, *The New Crusades, the New Holy Land: Conflict in the Southern Baptist Convention, 1969–1991* (Tuscaloosa, AL: University of Alabama Press, 1996); and Barry Hankins, *Uneasy in Babylon: Southern Baptist Conservatives and American Culture* (Tuscaloosa, AL: University of Alabama Press, 2002). For a "moderate" recounting of the conflict and the genesis of the Cooperative Baptist Fellowship and related institutions, see Walter B. Shurden (ed.), *The Struggle for the Soul of the SBC: Moderate Responses to the Fundamentalist Movement* (Macon, GA: Mercer University Press, 1993); cf. idem, *Not an Easy Journey: Some Transitions in Baptist Life* (Macon, GA: Mercer University Press, 2005), pp. 248–303. Histories of the conflict written from the perspective of the ultraconservatives are Jerry Sutton, *The Baptist Reformation: The Conservative Resurgence in the Southern Baptist Convention* (Nashville, TN: Broadman & Holman, 2000), and James Hefley, *The Conservative Resurgence in the Southern Baptist Convention* (Hannibal, MO: Hannibal Books, 1991).

2 W. Randall Lolley, Eileen R. Campbell-Reed, Pope A. Duncan, Pete Hill, and Nancy A. Thurmond (eds), *Findings: A Report of the Special Study Commission to Study the Question: "Should the Cooperative Baptist Fellowship Become a Separate Convention?"* (Atlanta, GA: Cooperative Baptist Fellowship, 1996), p. vi. For fuller historical accounts of the formation and development of the CBF, see Walter B. Shurden, "The Cooperative Baptist Fellowship", ch. 11 in *The Baptist River: Essays on Many Tributaries of a Diverse Tradition*, (ed.) W. Glenn Jonas, Jr. (Macon, GA: Mercer University Press, 2006), pp. 241–68; Pamela R. Durso, *A Short History of the Cooperative Baptist Fellowship Movement* (Brentwood, TN: Baptist History and Heritage Society, 2006).

3 E.g. Kenneth Chafin, "Traveling New Roads", ch. 7 in *Findings*, (ed.) Lolley and others, pp. 69–76. Whereas Chafin's case for separate denominational identity has in mind the features and functions of the "convention" as established by the SBC, Samuel S. Hill's paper "A Discussion of Whether the Cooperative Baptist Fellowship Should Become a Separate Convention of Baptists" (ch. 10, pp. 93–102) argues for envisioning a more "radical" form of Baptist communal life "through embracing the dialectical relationship between a world-affirming theology and a change-minded heartbeat. It ought to be doctrinally better defined, its standards firmer. It must resist the temptation to make freedom its watchword, since freedom is a second-order concept. It ought to refuse 'buying into' 'modern' forms of organization and efficiency, to live more locally and less centrally. I urge that it endeavor to live with a quiet and firm appreciation of such radical stances as pacifism and a simple lifestyle ethic" (p. 102).

4 Carolyn DeArmond Blevins, "Cooperative Baptist Fellowship: Denominational Move Unwise at This Time", ch. 4 in *Findings*, (ed.) Lolley and others, pp. 41–48; cf. Will D. Campbell, "A Personal Struggle with Soul Freedom (Excerpted)", ch. 6, pp. 61–67.

 5 E.g. William L. Hendricks, "Cooperative Baptist Fellowship: Some Reflections", ch. 8
   in *Findings*, ed. Lolley and others, pp. 77–84; Bill J. Leonard, "Perspectives on Baptist
   Denominationalism: Anticipating the Future", ch. 11, pp. 103–11.
 6 Nancy T. Ammerman, "On Being a Denomination: CBF and the Future", ch. 2 in
   Findings, ed. Lolley and others, pp. 21–31. The CBF Special Study Commission also
   found Ammerman's treatment definitive and elected to place it first among the position papers published in the report, arranging the remainder alphabetically by
   authors' surnames.
 7 Ammerman, "On Being a Denomination", p. 22.
 8 Ammerman, "On Being a Denomination", p. 24.
 9 Ammerman, "On Being a Denomination", p. 25.
10 Ammerman, "On Being a Denomination", p. 26.
11 James Wm. McClendon, Jr., *Systematic Theology*, vol. 2, *Doctrine* (Nashville, TN:
   Abingdon Press, 1994), pp. 23–24.
12 Ammerman, "On Being a Denomination", p. 27.
13 Alasdair MacIntyre, *After Virtue: A Study in Moral Theory*, 2nd edn. (Notre Dame,
   IN: University of Notre Dame Press, 1984), p. 222.
14 Ammerman, "On Being a Denomination", pp. 27–30.
15 Cooperative Baptist Fellowship, "Response to the Membership Committee of the
   Baptist World Alliance by the Coordinating Council of the Cooperative Baptist Fellowship".
   Online: www.thefellowship.info/Files/About-Us/BWADocument.aspx.
16 Online: www.thefellowship.info/About-Us/FAQ.
17 Interestingly, Ammerman illustrated the manner in which denominations conform
   to social expectations for what organizations of a certain type "look like" by citing
   the state's criteria for what constitutes a denomination, implemented in the
   credentialing of military chaplains by the Pentagon—which happens to be part of
   indication number 14 in the CBF response to the BWA Membership Committee.
   The Pentagon considers the CBF a separate denomination, so the CBF invokes this
   as evidence that it is not integral to the SBC, even while denying that it is a
   denomination.
18 According to the Particular Baptist *Second London Confession* (1677/89), ch. 26.1,
   "The Catholick or universal Church, which (with respect to internal work of the
   Spirit, and truth of grace) may be called invisible, consists of the whole number of the
   Elect, that have been, are, or shall be gathered into one, under Christ the head
   thereof" (William L. Lumpkin, ed., *Baptist Confessions of Faith*, rev. ed. [Valley
   Forge PA: Judson Press, 1969], p. 285). Likewise, the General Baptist *Orthodox
   Creed* (1678–9) appropriated three of the four Nicaeno-Constantinopolitan *notae
   ecclesiae* in confessing in Article 29, "there is one holy catholick church, consisting
   of, or made up of the whole number of the elect, that have been, are, or shall be
   gathered, in one body under Christ, the only head thereof" and in article 30, " . . . we
   believe the visible church of Christ on earth, is made up of several distinct congregations, which make up that one catholick church, or mystical body of Christ" (Lumpkin, ed., *Baptist Confessions of Faith*, pp. 318–19).
19 E.g., the ch. on "Baptists and Christian Union" (ch. 14) in E. Y. Mullins, *The Axioms
   of Religion: A New Interpretation of the Baptist Faith* (Philadelphia: American Baptist Publication Society, 1908), pp. 221–34. The Baptist triumphalism evident in that
   ch. takes full flight in ch. 16, "The Contribution of the Baptists to American Civilization", and ch. 17, "Baptists and World Progress".

20 James Leo Garrett, Jr., *Baptist Theology: A Four-Century Study* (Macon, GA: Mercer University Press, 2009), pp. 595–96, has compiled a list of Baptist unions that have held membership in the WCC from the reports of WCC assemblies from 1948 through 1998. In addition to the Baptist Union of Great Britain, the American Baptist Churches, USA, and three historical African American unions—the National Baptist Convention, the National Baptist Convention of America, and the Progressive National Baptist Convention—this list includes the following as full member bodies: Baptist Union of Western Congo, Episcopal Baptist Community (Democratic Republic of Congo), Native Baptist Church of Cameroon, Union of Baptist Churches of Cameroon, Nigerian Baptist Convention, Bangladesh Baptist Sangha, Baptist Union of New Zealand, China Baptist Council, Myanmar Baptist Convention, Samavesam of Telugu Baptist Churches (India), Jamaica Baptist Union, Baptist Union of Denmark, Baptist Union of Hungary, Evangelical Christian–Baptist Union of Russia (formerly the USSR), union of Baptist Congregations in the Netherlands, and Baptist Convention of Nicaragua. Three additional unions have held associate member status: Baptist Union of El Salvador, Bengal–Orissa–Bihar Baptist Convention (India), and Evangelical Baptist Union of Italy.

21 *London Confession* (1644) pref. (Lumpkin, *Baptist Confessions of Faith*, pp. 155–56).

22 For a historical overview of the development of this approach to Baptist historiography (to which no recognized Baptist historian today holds but which has continued to exert some popular influence among some Baptists), see James Edward McGoldrick, *Baptist Successionism: A Crucial Question in Baptist History* (ATLA Monograph Series, no. 32; Metuchen, NJ: Scarecrow Press, 1994).

23 Paul S. Fiddes, *Tracks and Traces: Baptist Identity in Church and Theology*, Studies in Baptist History and Thought, vol. 13 (Milton Keynes: Paternoster, 2003), p. 6.

24 John Howard Yoder, *The Royal Priesthood: Essays Ecclesiological and Ecumenical*, (ed.) Michael G. Cartwright (Grand Rapids, MI: William B. Eerdmans, 1994), p. 236.

25 In conjunction with the German Union of Free Evangelical (Baptist) Churches, the Baptist World Alliance sponsored the Symposium on Baptist Identity and Ecclesiology in Elstal, Germany, 21–24 March 2007, that addressed the question "Are Baptist Churches Autonomous?" Among the five affirmations agreed upon by the 60-plus conference participants were these two: "That for Baptists, the local church is wholly church but not the whole church", and "That our local churches and Conventions/Unions are participants in the one church that God has called into being as we anticipate the full revelation of the children of God" (available online at www.bwanet.org/media/documents/Elstal%20Statement-mar07.pdf). The former affirmation closely echoes the dictum of Reformed ecumenist Jean-Jacques von Allmen ("L'Église locale parmi les autres Églises locales", *Irénikon* 43 [1970]: 512).

26 Walter B. Shurden, "A Solicited Letter to the Study Commission", ch. 13 in *Findings*, (eds) Lolley and others, p. 126.

27 "Report of the Section on Unity", in *The New Delhi Report: The Third Assembly of the World Council of Churches, 1961* (New York: Association Press, 1962), p. 116: "We believe that the unity which is both God's will and his gift to his Church is being made visible as all in each place who are baptized into Jesus Christ and confess him as Lord and Savior are brought by the Holy Spirit into one fully committed fellowship, holding the one apostolic faith, preaching the one Gospel, breaking the one bread, joining in common prayer, and having a corporate life reaching out in witness and service to all and who at the same time are united with the whole Christian fellowship

in all places and all ages, in such wise that ministry and members are accepted by all, and that all can act and speak together as occasion requires for the tasks to which God calls his people".

28 See Paul D. Murray (ed.), *Receptive Ecumenism and the Call to Catholic Learning: Exploring a Way for Contemporary Ecumenism* (Oxford: Oxford University Press, 2008).

29 John Paul II, *Ut Unum Sint* ("On Commitment to Ecumenism"), May 25, 1995. Online: www.vatican.va/holy_father/john_paul_ii/encyclicals/documents/hf_jp-ii_enc_25051995_ut-unum-sint_en.html.

30 The Joint International Commission for Dialogue between the World Methodist Council and the Roman Catholic Church, *The Grace Given You in Christ: Catholics and Methodists Reflect Further on the Church* (Lake Junaluska, NC: World Methodist Council, 2006).

31 Quotation from a briefing document distributed to conference participants in Walter Cardinal Kasper's foreword to *Receptive Ecumenism and the Call to Catholic Learning*, (ed.) Murray, p. vii.

32 Ammerman, "On Being a Denomination", p. 27.

33 Lutheran World Federation and Roman Catholic Church, *Joint Declaration on the Doctrine of Justification* (Grand Rapids, MI: William B. Eerdmans, 2000).

Chapter 4

THE LUTHERAN CHURCH: CHURCH, CONFESSION, CONGREGATION, DENOMINATION

GESA ELSBETH THIESSEN

From Postage Stamp to World Religion: An Initial Search for a Definition of "Denomination"

Consulting Wikipedia on the term "denomination", one finds the following: "Any name can be considered a "denomination" of the thing being named".[1] Some subheadings follow: "Denomination (currency), denomination (postage stamp), protected designation of origin, a protected product name, usually by region of production." With such relevant information, I check on "religious denomination", and am told that it includes the Christian, Jewish, Islamic, Hindu and Buddhist denominations. Informed that a "religious denomination" basically might be any religion under the sun, I move to Wikipedia's offering on "denominationalism": "the division of one religion into separate groups, sects, schools of thought or denominations". Getting closer.

So then, onto Wikipedia's "List of Lutheran Denominations". Several hundred Lutheran Churches appear, spanning all continents, including illustrious ones of which I have never heard.[2] I do not even start to check all these websites because I do intend, and the editors would insist, to finish the article before the end of the first century of the new millennium.

Finally, the website of the Lutheran World Federation (LWF), headquartered in Geneva, lets the interested reader know that the LWF

> is a global communion of Christian churches in the Lutheran tradition. Founded in 1947 in Lund, Sweden, [in the aftermath of the Second World War] the LWF now has 140 member churches in 79 countries all over the world representing over 68.5 million Christians. . . . LWF member churches confess the triune God, agree in the proclamation of the Word of God, and are united in pulpit and altar fellowship. The LWF confesses one, holy,

catholic, and apostolic church and is resolved to serve Christian unity throughout the world.[3]

What Constitutes the "Church"? Luther and the Augsburg Confession

In Luther's pre-Enlightenment time the word denomination was as yet unheard of in ecclesial and ecclesiological contexts. Luther speaks about the "church", "congregation", and "holy Christendom":

> Thus the word Kirche (church) means really nothing else than a common assembly, and is not German by idiom, but Greek (as is also the word ecclesia); for in their own language they call it kyria, as in Latin it is called curia. Therefore in genuine German, in our mother-tongue, it ought to be called a Christian congregation or assembly (eine christliche Gemeinde oder Sammlung), or, best of all and most clearly, holy Christendom (eine heilige Christenheit).[4]

Luther urged his followers *not* to name their Church after him. We should call it the "Christian Church", not the "Lutheran Church", a fact which adherents of the Lutheran confession have happily and consistently ignored. Luther with his strongly christological theology would have wished that Christians would always refer to Christ; it is His Church to which we belong. With Luther's aim of reforming the *whole* church, naming a church after a reformer would have meant polarization, division and exclusion. Indeed, for Luther this would have been a contradiction in terms.

According to him, the church, then, is not a place of power, a hierarchy or a building, but primarily the gathering (congregation) of believers around Word and sacrament.[5] The *Augsburg Confession's* definition of what constitutes the church is minimal:

> Article VII: Of the Church. Also they teach that one holy Church is to continue forever. The Church is the congregation of saints, in which the Gospel is rightly taught and the Sacraments are rightly administered. And to the true unity of the Church it is enough to agree concerning the doctrine of the Gospel and the administration of the Sacraments. Nor is it necessary that human traditions, that is, rites or ceremonies, instituted by men, should be everywhere alike. As Paul says: "One faith, one Baptism, one God and Father of all", etc. (Eph. 4.5–6).

Article VIII: What the Church Is. Although the Church properly is the congregation of saints and true believers, nevertheless, since in this life many
hypocrites and evil persons are mingled therewith, it is lawful to use Sacraments administered by evil men, according to the saying of Christ: "The
Scribes and the Pharisees sit in Moses' seat", etc. (Matt. 23.2). Both the
Sacraments and Word are effectual by reason of the institution and com-
mandment of Christ, notwithstanding they be administered by evil men.[6]

Church, Confession, Congregation, Denomination – An Attempt to Clarify Terms in English and German-speaking Contexts

In a way, the term "denomination" intrigues. It intrigues when one starts to
actually think about it, which is something one usually does not do. Quite the
contrary; in theology and church life we take this term for granted; we use it
frequently and with considerable ease. The ease of use, it seems to me, is due to
a mostly comfortable – and occasionally uncomfortable – vagueness regarding
its meaning and implications. Using this term signifies above all a key notion in
(post)-Enlightenment modernity, namely tolerance. Tolerance is essential to the
life of denominations and denominationalism, as it has come to connote the
peaceful coexistence of different Churches, notably in North America.[7]

"Denomination" is not a specifically theological or ecclesial word; yet, more
often than not, it is used as an equivalent for "Church". In Wikipedia's "List of
Lutheran *denominations*", several hundred "*Churches*" are listed.[8] So, why does
Wikipedia choose the title "List of Lutheran denominations" when, in fact, in
what follows, it would be just as appropriate to call it "List of Lutheran
Churches?" In this case, the words seem synonymous.

Denomination as a term is prevalent in English-speaking contexts. It can be
used in German, but rarely. The website of the Evangelical Church in Germany,
the "Evangelische Kirche Deutschlands" (EKD),[9] contains a small theological
dictionary. The word "denomination" is explained thus: "Latin and English
term for church mainly used in Great Britain and USA, and which in Germany
has "Konfession" as its equivalent."[10] However, while this definition goes some
way to explain the term, it is not quite as straightforward as the explanation
above might imply. There are some differences in meaning between "Konfession"[11]
as used in German and "denomination". Checking up on "Konfession" on the
same website, one reads that the word "Konfession" today is generally synonymous with "Church". Thus: Denomination = Confession = Church? Yes, and
sometimes no. "Konfession", the EKD website tells us, includes the "great Christian Confessions" – "Protestants (Lutherans, Reformed, Anglicans), Catholics,
Orthodox and Pentecostal Churches".

The word "*Konfession*" in its original meaning implies that churches are based on confessions of faith (*Bekenntnisse, Glaubensbekenntnisse*).[12] The Lutheran Church has been a strongly confessional Church. Its numerous writings are held in the *Lutheran Book of Concord* (1580).[13] Yet, the term "denomination" today not only refers to churches or communions that regard themselves as explicitly confessional (Catholic, Anglican, some Reformed, and Orthodox), but also includes new Pentecostal Churches and other ecclesial communities, and sometimes, it is even used for other religions, as we saw earlier. The term "denomination" is thus used in considerably broader contexts than what "Konfession" originally and customarily would imply. Essentially, then, denomination can indicate both the worldwide Lutheran (Anglican, Reformed, etc.) Church/Confession and actual regional Lutheran (Anglican, Reformed, etc.) Churches.

Recently, I was made aware of a further simple, yet important aspect of common linguistic usage.[14] Apparently, when a North American is asked to which *denomination* s/he belongs, the person will answer Lutheran, Catholic, Episcopalian, and so on. In a German-speaking context one would ask, however, to which *Church* they belong, and only rarely (usually in official documents) to which *confession*. In this case denomination, confession and church would thus be equivalent. It further seems that, when North Americans are asked to which *Church* they belong, what is usually meant is the *local congregation*, that is, the actual local church in one's village or city of residence. In German one would ask to which *community/congregation* (*Gemeinde*) a person belongs. Here may be the most significant difference in terms of the usage of "church", "denomination", "confession" and "congregation" in the respective Anglo/American and German contexts.

Barry Ensign-George comments that "denomination" is a "middle term" between "church" and "congregation".[15] In a Lutheran context this would appear to mean that all the local Lutheran Churches as well as some mergers and Lutheran church fellowships are denominations, for example the Evangelical Lutheran Church in Tanzania, Evangelical Lutheran Church in America (ELCA) and the "Vereinigte Evangelish-Lutherische Kirche Deutschlands" (VELKD).[16] Despite some significant differences in church practice, liturgy, and especially in theological, social and ethical convictions, ranging from the far "left" to the far "right", Lutheran Churches broadly adhere to the Lutheran Confessions (Konfession). Metaphorically speaking, the Bible, Creeds, and The Book of Concord constitute the fundamental confessional stem, while the denominations (local/regional churches or church fellowships) are the branches. At the same time, when we speak of the "Lutheran denomination", what is, in fact, meant more often than not is the stem, that is the Lutheran Konfession, or the worldwide Lutheran Church. Therefore, it seems, denomination, can imply both: the Lutheran Church/Confession as such, as well as regional churches or affiliations of churches. Thus, while I agree with Ensign-George that denomination frequently constitutes a "middle term" between congregation and church and that denominations are "a primary mode of trans-congregational structure and life within the church today", it is obvious that the term denomination not only connotes regional Churches, but also the worldwide Lutheran Church/ denomination/confession.

Denominationalism: Voluntarism, Tolerance, Diversity, Confusion

The lack of precision concerning definitions of and clear distinctions between the terms "denomination", "confession" and "church", is likely to remain into the future. This problem of confused terminology seems to be further underpinned by Ensign-George when he notes how denominations are "unable to provide compelling accounts of their own existence", having "no meaningful internal coherence". Or, as Charles Long, professor emeritus of Religious Studies, University of California, points out, denomination/denominator is most commonly "thought of in terms of a mathematical metaphor".[17] He, like most other scholars who have reflected on the concept of "denomination",[18] also notes the vagueness regarding the self-understanding of denominations:

> [T]he denomination, is expressive of a seemingly endless proliferation of religious orientations that do not fit neatly into the older Troeltschian classification of church-type and sect-type . . . [T]he religious body as a denomination simply suggests that aspects of religion are common without having to give any definition as to what this entails . . . It is a way of having a religion without being forced to say what it is.[19]

Denominations are a particular North American phenomenon. They arose during the Enlightenment and developed in the context of a democratic, capitalist, and pluralist society and culture.[20] Denominations emerged on a voluntary basis, which presupposes and implies tolerance as well as a sense of purpose.[21] Not only have they proliferated in North America, but the boundaries between them are apparently becoming ever more fluid with the result that people are ever more confused as to what is constitutive of their own denomination.[22] Thus church members increasingly switch denominational affiliations, also referred to as "church shopping". This seems to be particularly the case when people relocate and have to find a new local congregation. For example, an Episcopalian/Anglican or even Catholic church in a local neighborhood with a broad outlook and an ecumenical atmosphere might provide a welcome "home" for a newly arrived Lutheran, who might find that her or his local church is too far away, or might not find him- or herself on the same wavelength as the new local congregation and their way of worship, or may simply dislike the local Lutheran pastor. While this "switching" seems to be far more prevalent in the United States, it is evident also in the European context, although not at all as strongly. Also, of course, there is a much greater denominational variety in the United States. One would suggest that the fact that churches in North America are independent of the state, that is, that Americans do not have to pay church tax as is required in Germany, for example, would contribute to a sense of independence and flexibility when one is choosing a local congregation.[23]

Such "switching" has both positive and negative implications. On the positive side, the flexibility of moving from one denomination to another obviously reflects the modern sense of tolerance, which fostered the emergence of denominations as well as the ecumenical movement over the last century and our age of pluralism. As prejudices against and misinformation about other denominations recede, and as the ecumenical quest creates attitudes of increasing openness and curiosity, it does not surprise that followers of Christ are more ready to join other congregations which they find congenial to their own religious outlook and experience. Of course, this raises the issue of denominational double-belonging as such, and as a possible stage towards church unity. On the negative or, at least, more problematic side, this openness to dual or even multi-belonging will increase confusion about and challenge one's theological/ecclesiological convictions and tradition and thus one's denominational identity. While many believers tend to have somewhat vague ideas about Christian faith in general and the history and fundamental beliefs of their own (and other) denominations in particular, such knowledge becomes even more blurred and puzzled in our contemporary contexts of cultural, ethnic and religious plurality.

And yet, when one actually consults, not the ecclesiological literature, but the websites of denominations/churches, the sense of confusion and apparent inability to provide accounts of themselves are countered by the churches' mission statements and their eagerness to say who they are. In fact, many church websites are very informative and clear. Today these websites are a significant source of mission, as they are often the first point of contact and reference for a prospective new church member. For anyone who cares to know about Lutheran Churches (and I imagine the same applies to other denominations), the respective church website will usually display as one of the first of its links "Who we are" or "What we believe". I have checked various such websites, and it is obvious that the churches take great care in presenting what they see as constitutive of their faith tradition and history. Despite the differences in their outlooks and traditions, for all Lutheran Churches this will include: adherence to the Bible, the Apostles', Nicene and Athanasian Creeds, the Augsburg Confession, Luther's

Small (and Large) Catechism, and the other writings contained in the Book of Concord. This is the – very considerable – confessional basis.[24] In praxis, however, the vast majority of Lutherans (including theologians!) has never read all, or even just a few, of these works. Moreover, we now live in a world that has radically changed since the sixteenth century, and Lutheran Churches have developed and revised some of their teachings.

One imagines that the same discrepancy between a clearly laid out theological/confessional basis and a prevalent lack of knowledge of one's own tradition is equally apparent in other denominations.

Denominations and their Internal Divisions

A further difficulty for denominations attempting to present a clear understanding of themselves today is the awareness of increasing intra-denominational divisions. While a concept of what it entailed to be a Lutheran, Anglican, Roman Catholic or Presbyterian was a more clear-cut exercise until the early twentieth century, such clarity no longer exists. A manifestation of this is the denominational double or multi-belonging mentioned above. Indeed, a "liberal" Catholic and a "liberal" Lutheran may share more common ground today than a liberal member and a deeply conservative member of the same Church. Similar scenarios are found in other denominations, including the Catholic Church, where divisions between right/conservative/fundamentalist and left/liberal are increasingly felt, even though these terms, of course, are flawed in themselves. Indeed, one needs to be aware that these (polarizing) outlooks – or clichés – are (often far too) general, and many nuanced convictions can be found in between.

In the context of the Lutheran Churches, this relatively recent problem is noted by several Lutheran writers. As Christa Klein remarks:

> Coincidental with the loss of interest in American Lutheran history is the division of Lutherans on the future course of American Lutheranism. . . . Lutherans were wracked by the same tensions, albeit to a lesser degree, that absorbed most other denominations. The political right and left, theological liberalism and strains of fundamentalism, the charismatic movement and the rise of managerial styles of leadership all found nourishment in American Lutheranism.[25]

Not Quite the Same: European and North American Lutherans

Reading the various contributors to *Lutherans Today, American Lutheran Identity in the 21st Century* as well as other writers who have reflected on Lutheran history in the United States,[26] a European would be rather struck by the diversity of Lutheran groupings and, in particular, of theological viewpoints which developed in North America, including significant tendencies towards Pietism, biblical fundamentalism and Puritanism.

Mark Granquist of Luther Seminary in St Paul, Minnesota, comments that Lutheranism in the United States is largely a story of "synodical mergers and the march to ever larger and more complex denominational structures".[27] While in the mid-nineteenth century "over one hundred synods" existed in "twelve major groupings", "today 95 percent of the 8.5 million American Lutherans are members of the two largest denominations, the Evangelical Lutheran Church in America (5.1 million members) and the Lutheran Church–Missouri Synod (LCMS) (2.6 million members)" as well as the "Wisconsin Evangelical Lutheran Synod (400.000 members)". "A dozen or so of very small Lutheran groups", mostly "dissenters from previous mergers" can be added.[28] Granquist points out that mergers have been regarded as the work of the Holy Spirit, uniting Christians of Lutheran confession, but that such a romantic view of Lutheran denominational history is "greatly flawed", as it does not take into account the numerous problems and costs associated with mergers, leading to "hard feelings and disenchantment" and exposing "theological and ecclesiastical cracks that are endemic to American Lutheranism".[29]

While divisions and new alignments are no strangers to European Protestant Churches and, particularly, in the fellowship of Churches of the EKD, either, differences in theological outlook among German Lutherans would generally not be as striking as they have been in North America. In Germany, a small independent Lutheran Church, the Selbständige Evangelisch-Lutherische Kirche (SELK) exists with about 36,000 members. It is regarded as "conservative", with a strong emphasis on the Lutheran confessional writings, and with certain elements that are closer to traditional Catholic teachings, such as its understanding of ordination (a modified understanding of *in persona Christi*), of the role of personal and communal confession, belief in the non-ordination of women, and refusal of intercommunion with "mainstream" Lutherans. The SELK has links with the Lutheran Church–Missouri Synod (LCMS), the Lutheran Church in Lithuania and the Lutheran Church in Latvia. But, given its very small membership, it plays an insignificant role in Germany. Most Germans would hardly know that it exists. However, it has to be said that in this Church, too, theological and ecclesiological differences make themselves felt. For example, it appears that many of its members would like to see women ordained and are unhappy with the Church's links to the LCMS.

What makes the SELK significant to our theme is its historical origin. It emerged from the "Old Lutherans", i.e. those who, in the 1830s and 1840s, refused to join the Prussian Union decreed by Friedrich Wilhelm III in 1821,

which was a union of Protestant and Reformed Churches in Prussia. In disagreement over the new liturgical agenda (book of worship) which the King had
ordered, many Lutherans dissented, especially over the issue of the Eucharist.
They felt that the real presence in the Eucharist was no longer proclaimed. This
dissent led to their suppression, and, in turn, many, in search for religious freedom, emigrated to North America and Australia, where they founded new
Lutheran denominations. While mainline European Lutherans today might be
puzzled about how such denominations as the LCMS could emerge, it is these
historical events as well as the history, theological outlook and ecclesial organization of Scandinavian Churches, including certain Pietist leanings, which
explain the rise of the Missouri Synod and similar Lutheran Churches in North
America.

The Emergence of North American Lutheran Churches as Denominations

Most North American scholars who have dealt with denominations and denominational history remark that these were seen as somewhat embarrassing sub-
jects by scholars working in universities. In modern, scientific, open, ecumenical
university environments, writing about one's tradition was regarded as irrelevant, parochial, defensive, lacking in objectivity and thus not a subject for
proper scholarly engagement.[30] Yet, the need for proper scholarly works on
denominational histories with attention to developments in contemporary historiography has repeatedly been noted.[31]

Jaroslav Pelikan – one of the foremost twentieth-century historians of Christianity, a Lutheran and later a member of the Orthodox Church – in an article
entitled, "American Lutheranism: Denomination or Confession?" (1963),
attempted to make some predictions about the future of American Lutheranism.
He noted that a "foliation of theological diversity within some sort of confessional unity" was "closer to the tradition of Lutheranism than is the identification of confessional unity with uniformity that many Lutherans in this country
[United States] would regard as normative".[32] And he points out that American
Lutheranism had been influenced both by its ethnicity, being almost exclusively
Nordic, and "by a Pietism that could be either confessionally rigid or confessionally indifferent without surrendering its distinctive character".[33] This
strengthening of Pietist traditions which had been brought from Europe was not
limited to the Lutheran Churches in the United States, but became determinative for a "large part of the rest of American Protestantism". Pelikan emphasizes
that the "coalescence of Puritanism and Pietism" was a hugely neglected area of
enquiry in North American church history. Thus someone who knows Lutherans

from only a European perspective or from the "generalizations about it by Ernst Troeltsch and Karl Barth" would be surprised indeed at how "Puritan and theocratic" Lutheran Churches in the United States could become. However, he concludes that American Lutheranism would predictably "adapt itself ever more completely to its American Protestant environment during the coming decades, and that eventually, for better or for worse, it will become a denomination".[34] This is an interesting and a slightly puzzling conclusion. The very last words would imply that, up to this point Pelikan, and others for that matter, would have regarded the Lutheran Church in America in terms of being a "confession" or "church", but not yet as a denomination. What exactly he understands by "denomination" he does not specify, but what it might imply appears to be captured indirectly in his insistence that Lutherans "have nothing to lose but our [their] isolation".[35] This is a rather important point, and one that is consistently echoed by others, such as Todd Nicholl, Christa Klein, Mark Noll, regarding Lutheran history in North America – its noted "isolation" and "difference". Becoming a "denomination" essentially would imply being challenged by, and living in close dialogue with, other denominations, rather than pursuing an inward-looking attitude of seclusion and separation. Pelikan points out that North Americans Lutherans had indeed learned much and changed through their encounter with other denominations. However, these positive developments were concurrent with more negative ones. As Pelikan remarks, "at least a confessional isolationism kept its contact with the fathers if not with the brethren, but this new denominationalism runs the risk of following the most shallow contemporary fads in the church even while it still stands off reciting its formulas of discord".[36] Thus the "most damaging feature of such denominationalism" could be that it might drain "Lutheran theological vitality". Pelikan urged that Lutherans in the future be "faithful to the text and open to modern thought". They should take seriously their relationship to other denominations, especially the Catholic Church to which they have a "special responsibility"; and they should become "simultaneously more Catholic and Reformed" instead of seeking only Lutheran unity by clutching their "confessions desperately to . . . [their] breast", thus losing "both Catholic substance and Protestant principle".

Denomination with a Difference

In his important article "The Lutheran Difference", Mark Noll, professor of history at the University of Notre Dame, writes that impressions about US Lutherans, can be "wildly contradictory".[37] When traced through some of their own memoirs and literature, American Lutherans could be seen as "mildly exotic", "tragic"or "interesting", but above all, as "on the fringe".[38] However, as a social group, they appear to have been "pretty ordinary": mostly middle class, voting predominantly Republican (this may have changed in the 2008 presidential election), with 80 per cent of Lutherans living in the Midwest.

Most Lutherans emigrated to North America later than members of other mainline Protestant churches, notably between 1840 and World War I, which saw the influx of over 5 million Germans and almost 2 million Scandinavians.[39] Two distinct aspects were hugely influential in shaping their identity – hanging on to their old-world languages and having a strong confessional basis. "Gottes Wort und Luthers Lehr' vergehen nie und nimmermehr."(God"s word and Luther's teachings will never ever pass away.) This was the motto of *Der Lutheraner*,[40] a Lutheran journal founded by C. F. W. Walther in 1844.[41] Such triumphalist language, which might occasion a smile today, evidences the sense of pride and religious identity that Lutherans brought to the new world. Despite such strong confessional belonging, Noll observes that, as a social group, Lutherans have been largely "inconspicuous" in the United States, almost surprisingly so he maintains, given their strong cultural-theological background, ranging from Luther, Melanchthon, the "irenic" Book of Concord, to Bach, Kierkegaard and Bonhoeffer.[42]

Holding on to their confessions and language, Lutherans were "insulated from American life for a long time".[43] These two elements made them "different". Interestingly, both Todd Nicholl and Mark Noll challenge American Lutherans to make a specifically Lutheran contribution to America. For example, despite their large numbers, with nearly "four times as many Lutherans as Episcopalians, nearly three times as many as either Presbyterians or Jews, and almost as many as Methodists",[44] Lutherans have been seriously under-represented in American national politics. Noll wonders whether the ELCA may have something "authentically Lutheran to contribute", noting at the same time Klein's conclusions about "denominational leaders fleeing from distinctive Lutheran doctrines like two-kingdom theology in their haste to be relevant to . . . American life" as not being encouraging. While one can sympathize with those who find the two-kingdom theory problematic (it has also suffered the grossest misinterpretations), it is indeed a real question and a challenge whether Lutherans in the United States and Canada – and elsewhere – can offer something distinct and beneficial to contemporary faith and society – distinct in being specifically Lutheran, beneficial in that it must be of wider ecumenical, theological, social and political significance.

The mergers of the Lutheran Church of America (LCA) and the American Lutheran Church (ALC), which led to the creation of the Evangelical Lutheran Church of America (ELCA), is seen as a mixed blessing; it has been remarked that Lutheranism thereby lost some of its distinctiveness.[45] Noll makes several suggestions about what elements in Lutheran teaching have relevance in the future: history as being important to faith; taking a long view of history, which might protect against excessive fluctuation and instability; a rightly interpreted two-kingdom theory; a "noble theological tradition"; the theology of the cross;[46] the "Lutheran gift of ambiguity" – "the paradoxes . . . *simul justus et peccator*, Law [sic] and gospel as two sides of the same thing".[47] Significantly, he notes: "Rarely have American Christians considered Luther's tension with culture, which saw him committed to Christian activity, but always with the sharpest reservations."[48] In the face of Naziism and other totalitarian or exploitative and unjust cultures, including neo-capitalism and its deep failures, Luther's call for Christian cultural involvement *and* critical distance may indeed still have something to say to Western civilization! Nicholl observes that Lutherans may have resources to be explored for mission in "the contemporary United States", in modern politics, understanding of faith, science and liberal education, church order and ministry.[49]

Conclusion – Being part of the body of Christ

The history of Lutherans in North America emerges as being shaped by many strands, struggling to find unity – and not always quite succeeding – while also being ecumenically minded, and becoming a denomination(s) alongside others. Synods, splits and mergers are part of it. From a European Lutheran perspective, the fact that two large Lutheran denominations (ELCA and LCMS) exist side by side is perhaps strangest of all. In addition, over the last forty years, a "dramatic growth of parachurch groups, renewal movements and caucuses within and on the edges of denominational life" has happened across North America, and Lutherans are no exception.[50] This is a sign of the diversification among and across denominations, including an accommodation of the "seeker culture", the growing pick-and-choose à-la-carte way of living one's faith within a denomination while also getting involved in movements and events of other denominations and faith groups.

Is the Lutheran Church a denomination? Obviously yes. Yet, the idea of "denomination", while recognizing the church's diversity, implies, as Ensign-George argues, partiality and permeability vis-à-vis the one, holy, catholic and apostolic church of Christ which most of those belonging to denominations confess at worship each Sunday. Nor is the word "denomination" much used when Lutheran Churches refer to themselves. In the German context, where there are essentially two large churches (EKD and the Catholic Church), the term is not used at all, even though in the last decade there has been a rise of small independent Churches and trans-denominational movements in Germany and other parts of Europe.

Lutheran Churches worldwide refer to themselves as *Church*. Mark Hanson, presiding bishop of the ELCA, in his article "The Future of Denominations: Asking Uppercase Questions", rightly points out that the word "denomination" is not found in the Bible; rather, it is a "phenomenon of history and context".[51] According to him, denominations are needed, but not as competitors in the supermarket of religion with institutional survival as their primary aim. With reference to his colleague, Charles Miller, Hanson declares that "'whither denominations' is a lowercase question, while the question of the mission to which God calls us is the uppercase question. . . . What kind of church serves God's mission in the world today?"[52] This is what essentially matters. For Hanson, the biblical images of the vine and branches and being members of the one body of Christ are powerful pointers towards understanding that mission – the body metaphor being "the classic illustration of unity in diversity".[53] And so he notes the danger of denominations defining themselves by issues that divide them – thus dividing the body of Christ – rather than seeking to focus on the "gospel, faith and mission that unite them". Hanson therefore suggests that Lutheran identity should be thought of "in terms of what we bring as *a part of* the body of Christ, even as we are open to receiving the gifts of others".[54] Like Nichol and Noll, he emphasizes that the strengths of Lutheran faith lie in "justification by grace through faith"; "the priesthood of all believers"; "the freedom of the Christian"; and, in particular, its paradoxical, dialectical emphasis – law *and* gospel, simul justus *et* peccator, "creation as good *and* fallen", Jesus "human *and* divine, crucified *and* risen", "God hidden *and* revealed", and "faith *and* reason in healthy tension". These are gifts that Lutherans can bring to the whole body of Christ, the church universal.

Hanson's remarks echo those of Wolfgang Huber, presiding bishop of the EKD, when he advocates an "ecumenism of profiles" (*Ökumene der Profile*). Huber asserts that while Churches must not replace consensus ecumenism (*Konsensökumene*) by an ecumenism which emphasizes difference (*Differenzökumene*), it is part of our ecumenical task to live our faith through denominational belonging and living its strengths.[55]

Naturally, every denomination has its own strengths and can offer these to fellow Christians. Is it, however, realistic to think, that denominations will be only too eager to adopt the strengths of other denominations as their own? Indeed, how do we assert that something is a "strength" or "weakness" in the first place? Who can judge? In an ideal world, one can imagine that the strong points of each denomination would be ascertained, and then the churches would agree to all of them, and then, finally, the one church, wholly reformed, would result, denominations would cease, and we would be one church again. The reality, however, with the existence of hundreds of denominations, including the Catholic and Orthodox Churches, and the world of ecumenism itself disparate and wholly unclear about which model of church unity to adopt, looks very different. While the unity of the one church of Christ must always remain our (eschatological!?) hope and aspiration, it seems that denominations are here to stay for a while to come.

But focusing on the ecumenical aim of unity – a unity in diversity – could we envisage that denominations might be cherished as *local/regional Churches*, and that Churches will increasingly recognize each other as *church*, agree on fundamentals, including the full acceptance of each other's ministries, enjoying altar and pulpit fellowship? Differentiated consensus agreements, such as the Porvoo Agreement, may be a good guide to such unity in diversity.

There are voices who speak of the possible demise of the mainline denominations. Indeed, they may be threatened by the rise of Pentecostal churches and new ecclesial movements. In the face of this, Hanson asks:

> How will those called to serve denominations respond to the growing evidence that people in this culture seek meaning in life, want faith to matter, and seek to be part of a church that makes a difference not only in their lives but also in the life of the world?[56]

If churches cannot answer such questions and give convincing witness to their faith and confessions in the social, religious, intellectual and ethnic contexts in which they find themselves, then there is little hope or reason that they should survive.

Luther's dictum "[a] Christian (wo/man) is the most free lord of all, and subject to none; a Christian (wo/man) is the most dutiful servant of all, and subject to every one" may be a starting point, not just for Lutheran denominations but all those who believe in the one, holy, catholic and apostolic church. To bring something of the radical message of God's kingdom of love into this world surely must remain the task of, and the bond between, all Christian denominations, into the future.

Notes

1 http://en.wikipedia.org/wiki/Denomination; accessed 8 June 2009.
2 http://en.wikipedia.org/wiki/List_of_Lutheran_denominations; accessed 8 June 2009.
3 www.lutheranworld.org/Who_We_Are/LWF-Welcome.html.
4 M. Luther, *The Large Catechism* ("The Apostles' Creed", Art. 3), in (trans.) F. Bente and W.H.T. Dau, *Triglot Concordia: The Symbolical Books of the Ev. Lutheran Church* (St. Louis, MO: Concordia Publishing House, 1921). Online: www.iclnet.org/pub/resources/text/wittenberg/luther/catechism/cat-10.txt; accessed 29 June 2009.

5 Timothy J. Wengert, "Introduction", in Paul Rorem (ed.), Lutheran Quarterly Books, *Harvesting Martin Luther's Reflections on Theology, Ethics, and the Church*, (Grand Rapids, MI and Cambridge, UK: Eerdmans, 2004), p. 15.

6 "Augsburg Confession", in Bente and Dau (trans.), *Triglot Concordia*, Online: www.iclnet.org/pub/resources/text/wittenberg/concord/web/augs-007.html and www.iclnet.org/pub/resources/text/wittenberg/concord/web/augs-008.html; accessed 29 June 2009.

7 Cf. David R. Carlin, "The Denomination Called Catholic", *First Things*, 77 (1997): 18–21.

8 Emphases in italics are mine.

9 "Following the war, in 1948, the German regional churches adopted a constitution and formed the Evangelical Church in Germany (EKD). A fellowship of Lutheran, Reformed and United churches, the EKD is a public-law corporation, as are its member churches." "The territories of the 22 EKD member churches correspond in many cases to the borders of the kingdoms, dukedoms and principalities of the Napoleonic era and are a vestige of the much older *cujus regio, ejus religio* principle, that is, "whose rule, their religion". The Federal Republic of Germany is comprised of 16 federal Länder or states. Their borders do not coincide with those of member churches." www.ekd.de/english/4247.html; accessed 8 June 2009.

10 "Lateinische und englische Bezeichnung für Kirche, die hauptsächlich in Großbritannien und in den USA anzutreffen ist, in Deutschland gleichbedeutend mit Konfession gebraucht wird" www.ekd.de/lexikon/denomination.html; accessed 9 June 2009.

11 "Der Begriff Konfession (lat.: Bekennen des Glaubens; Bekenntnis) wird heute meist als Synonym für Kirche gebraucht. Die großen christlichen Konfessionen bilden Protestanten (Lutheraner, Reformierte, Anglikaner), Katholiken, Orthodoxe und Pfingstkirchen." www.ekd.de/lexikon/konfession.html; accessed, 9 June 2009.

12 Cf. David R. Holeton, "'Religion without Denomination? The Significance of Denominations for Church and Society': Some Reactions," *Communio Viatorum*, 44 (2002): 38–44 (38).

13 *The Book of Concord: The Confessions of the Evangelical Lutheran Church*, 2nd edn, (eds) Robert Kolb, Timothy J. Wengert, and (ed. and trans.), James Schaffer (Augsburg Fortress, 2001). The Book contains the Apostles' Creed, Nicene Creed, Athanasian Creed, the Augsburg Confession, the Apology [Defense] of the Augsburg Confession, the Smalcald Articles, the Treatise on the Power and Primacy of the Pope, the Small Catechism, the Large Catechism, and the Formula of Concord. The final words in the Book read: "Since now, in the sight of God and of all Christendom [the entire Church of Christ], we wish to testify to those now living and those who shall come after us that this declaration herewith presented concerning all the controverted articles aforementioned and explained, and no other, is our faith, doctrine, and confession, in which we are also willing, by God's grace, to appear with intrepid hearts before the judgment-seat of Jesus Christ, and give an account of it; and that we will neither privately nor publicly speak or write anything contrary to it, but, by the help of God's grace, intend to abide thereby . . . " (*Solid Declaration of the Formula of Concord*, XII, 40).

14 A North American friend conveyed this information.

15 Barry Ensign-George, "Denomination as Ecclesial Category: Sketching an Assessment", in this volume.

16 The VELKD, member of the EKD, comprises eight Lutheran regional Churches: Bayern, Braunschweig, Hannover, Mecklenburg, Nordelbien, Sachsen, Schaumburg-Lippe, Thüringen. For more information, see www.velkd.de/2.php; accessed 3 July 2009.

17 Charles H. Long, "The Question of Denominational Histories in the United States: Dead End or Creative Beginning", in *Reimagining Denominationalism, Interpretive Essays*, (eds) Robert Bruce Mullin, and Russell E. Richey (New York/Oxford: Oxford University Press, 1994), p. 102.

18 See the articles included in Robert Bruce Mullin, Russell E. Richey (eds) *Reimagining Denominationalism, Interpretive Essays*.

19 Long, "The Question of Denominational Histories in the United States", in *Reimagining Denominationalism*, pp. 101–2.

20 Russell Richey, "Denominationalism", in *Dictionary of the Ecumenical Movement*, Second Edition, (eds) N. Lossky et al. (Geneva: WCC Publications, 2002), pp. 294–96 (294–95).

21 Richey, ibid., p. 295.

22 Cf. Robert Wuthnow, *Christianity in the Twenty-first Century, Reflections on the Challenges Ahead* (New York: Oxford University Press, 1993), pp. 24–29.

23 I thank Martin Sauter, Head of Church Council, Lutheran Church in Ireland, for his comments and observations.

24 A rather interesting Lutheran website is the following: www.lutheranchurch-canada. ca/CTCR/LCC-ELCIC.pdf. "Where Canada's Lutherans stand" consists of two texts running parallel to one another, issued by the Lutheran Church–Canada (which is close to the LC–Missouri Synod) and the Evangelical Lutheran Church in Canada (close to the ELCA). In these texts both Churches describe their church organizations, present a confession of faith, and include summary accounts on various church positions – mission statements, ecclesiology, sacraments, worship, ecumenism, homosexuality, abortion, and so on.

25 Christa Ressmeyer Klein, "Lutherans, Merger and the Loss of History", *The Christian Century*, 2–9 (January 1985): 18–20 (19–20). See also Richard Cimino who, like Klein, and with reference to R. Wuthnow, remarks on the inner divisions in the ELCA. "The Evangelical Catholics: Seeking Tradition and Unity in a Pluralistic Church", in *Lutherans Today, American Lutheran Identity in the 21st Century*, (ed.) R. Cimino (Grand Rapids, MI and Cambridge, UK: Eerdmans, 2003), pp. 81–101 (96). Robert Wuthnow, *The Restructuring of American Religion* (Princeton, NJ: Princeton University Press, 1988).

26 Edited by R. Cimino (Grand Rapids, MI and Cambridge, UK: Eerdmans, 2003).

27 Mark Granquist, "Word Alone and the Future of Lutheran Denominationalism", in *Lutherans Today*, (ed.) R. Cimino, pp. 62–80 (62).

28 Granquist, ibid.

29 Granquist, ibid., pp. 62–63.

30 Several writers refer to this problem, for example some of the contributors to *Reimagining Denominationalism, Interpretive Essays*, (eds) R. B. Mullin, R. E. Richey, including Nancy T. Ammerman, Christa Klein, R. Richey. See also C. E. Tygart and Norman N. W. H. Blaikie from a sociological perspective: C. E. Tygart, "On the Inadequacies of the Utilization of the Concept of "Denomination" in the Explanation of the Position of Clergy on Social Issues", *Journal for the Scientific Study of Religion*, 15, 1 (1976): 87–90; N. W. H. Blaikie, "Comment", *Journal for the Scientific Study of*

Religion, 15, 1 (1976): 79–86 (79), "In spite of the fact that the concept "denomination" (or religious affiliation) has been extensively used in all types of sociological research, little advance appears to have been made in its theoretical elaboration and empirical specification".

31 Henry Warner Bowden, "The Death and Rebirth of Denominational History", in *Reimagining Denominationalism*, pp. 17–30.

32 Jaroslav Pelikan, "American Lutheranism: Denomination or Confession?", *The Christian Century*, 25 (December 1963): 1608–10 (1608).

33 Ibid.

34 Ibid.

35 Pelikan, ibid., 1609.

36 Pelikan, ibid., 1609.

37 Mark A. Noll, "The Lutheran Difference", *First Things*, 20 (February 2002): 31–40 (31).

38 "Perhaps the shy Norwegian bachelor farmers populating Lake Wobegon Lutherandom symbolize Lutheran reticence about itself." R. Cimino, "Introduction", in *Lutherans Today*, (ed.) R. Cimino, ix–xiv (x).

39 Noll, ibid., p. 32. Germans were the largest ethnic group in the United States.

40 This was a newsletter written entirely in German and published in St. Louis, MO.

41 Noll, "The Lutheran Difference", *First Things*, 20 (2002), p. 32.

42 Noll, ibid., 33.

43 A comment by Winthrop Hudson, in his book *American Protestantism* (1961), quoted in C. R. Klein, "Denominational History as Public History: The Lutheran Case", in *Reimagining Denominationalism*, pp. 307–17 (307).

44 Noll, "The Lutheran Difference", *First Things*, p. 33.

45 Noll refers to a comment by Peter Berger. Cf. Noll, ibid., p. 36.

46 Cf. Noll, ibid., pp. 37–40.

47 Noll, "Americans Lutherans Yesterday and Today", in *Lutherans Today*, pp. 3–25 (21). See also Todd Nicholl, "The Lutheran Venture and the American Experiment", *Word and World*, 12, 2 (Spring 1992): 162, "An often uncritical acceptance of nineteenth-century confessional theology and the twentieth-century pre-occupation with denominational affairs, mergers, and an increasingly retrospective ecumenism has severely limited the American Lutheran imagination."

48 Noll, ibid.

49 Cf. Nicholl, "The Lutheran Venture and the American Experiment", pp. 159–64.

50 Cimino, pp. x–xi.

51 Mark S. Hanson, "The Future of Denominations: Asking Uppercase Questions", *Word & World*, 25, 1 (Winter 2005): 7–14 (7).

52 Hanson, ibid., p. 9.

53 Hanson, ibid., pp. 10–11.

54 Hanson, ibid., p. 12.

55 Wolfgang Huber, "Was bedeutet Ökumene der Profile?", Lecture delivered at the symposium, "Ökumene der Profile" der Evangelischen Kirche im Rheinland, Düsseldorf, 29 May 2006. Online: //www.ekd.de/ausland_oekumene/48728.html; accessed 14 July 2009.

56 Hanson, "The Future of Denominations", p. 12.

Chapter 5

UNITED METHODISM:
ITS IDENTITY AS DENOMINATION

RUSSELL E. RICHEY

The first statements that The United Methodist Church (UMC) makes about itself constitute it as a denomination which recognizes its place amid the family of Christian churches and is vocationally committed to Christian unity. The "Preamble" to "The Constitution" reads:

> The church is a community of all true believers under the Lordship of Christ. It is the redeemed and redeeming fellowship in which the Word of God is preached by persons divinely called, and the sacraments are duly administered according to Christ's own appointment. Under the discipline of the Holy Spirit the church seeks to provide for the maintenance of worship, the edification of believers, and the redemption of the world.
>
> The church of Jesus Christ exists in and for the world, and its very dividedness is a hindrance to its mission in that world.
>
> The prayers and intentions of The United Methodist Church and its predecessors, The Methodist Church and The Evangelical United Brethren Church, have been and are for obedience to the will of our Lord that his people be one, in humility for the present brokenness of the Church and in gratitude that opportunities for reunion have been given.

The first three articles in The Constitution, following the Preamble, declare the two predecessor churches to be one, identify the church's new name, and specify that the doctrinal statements of the Evangelical United Brethren (EUB) and Methodists are now those of the UMC. Then follow two more denominationally orienting affirmations:

> Article IV. Inclusiveness of the Church—The United Methodist Church is a part of the church universal, which is one Body in Christ. . . .

Article VI. Ecumenical Relations—As part of the church universal, The United Methodist Church believes that the Lord of the church is calling Christians everywhere to strive toward unity; and therefore it will seek, and work for, unity at all levels of church life: through world relationships with other Methodist churches and united churches related to The Methodist Church or The Evangelical United Brethren Church, through councils of churches, and through plans of union and covenantal relationships with churches of Methodist or other denominational relations.[1]

Similarly, when the UMC makes a mission statement, it does so in ecumenical terms. In Part III, "The Ministry of All Christians", the *Discipline* begins to describe "The Mission and Ministry of the Church" in this fashion:

Section I. The Churches

¶ 120. *The Mission*—The mission of the Church is to make disciples of Jesus Christ for the transformation of the world. Local churches provide the most significant arena through which disciple-making occurs.[2]

The UMC does not seem to employ the word "denomination" with any great frequency in identifying itself. The *Discipline* contains two longish histories, one an overview of organizational developments; the other, of doctrine. The former does begin calling the UMC a "new denomination" and later mentions "denominational structure" and "denominational leadership". Otherwise, that and the doctrinal survey seem to prefer to employ the word "church" or "churches" for the UMC and its predecessor bodies.[3]

Such preferences for words other than "denomination" for self-description seem to have been typical for Methodists from the point of their organization as a distinct church in 1784 to the present. For instance, when Bishops Thomas Coke and Francis Asbury annotated the *Discipline* in 1798 and provided extensive commentary on Methodism and Methodist practices, they used the word "church" on 84 pages and the word denomination once (in 187 pages total). The one usage came in their defense of Methodist strictures concerning "the carnal diversions of the world". They said, "These diversions have been pronounced *by the spiritual ministers of Christ*, of all denominations in all ages, as inconsistent with true religion. . . . "[4] Such use of the word "denomination" when referencing other or the multiplicity of religious bodies seems to have been common. In his 360-page *Short History of the Methodists*, Jesse Lee, Methodism's first historian, put the words "any", "other" or "no" before "denomination(s)," using the latter to refer to bodies other than the Methodists.[5] Ezekiel Cooper, who held various prominent offices, including head of the Methodist Book Concern produced a 230-page biography of Asbury in which he twice used the word "denomination", mentioning "the ministry of every denomination" and "different denominations of christians". The word "church" or "churches" is to be found on 84 pages and often several times in each place.[6] This usage, which I do think is typical within Methodism, indicates a preference for other terms in self-description but implicitly locates Methodism as one denomination among others. That double statement—accenting one's own denominational identity but conceding one's place within the array of denominations—I take to be a key aspect of denominationalism. And in sustaining such a tension, I believe, Methodism has embodied and perhaps even typified the denominational principle.[7] That embodiment continues in the UMC as the above self-definition in the quotations indicates.

The Denomination

The denomination I believe to be a creature of modernity; a religious institution; a body with identifiable boundaries and leadership; a constellation (though not necessarily precise, specific and unchanging) of practices, beliefs, values and membership standards; a voluntaristic or willed religious entity which nevertheless understands itself to possess all the necessary marks or characteristics of religious integrity in the tradition with which it identifies itself.[8] Each of these criteria deserve brief elaboration, and I start at the end and work backwards.[9]

By that last criterion, a denomination like United Methodism presents itself as fully and properly church, as possessing all that is essential in the Christian tradition to be "church", as just as "Christian" a church as any other. That some Christian movements, including both the Orthodox and Roman Catholic Churches, do not recognize United Methodism as fully church but as only "separated brethren", to use the Catholic judgment, upsets a few Methodists, but most could care less. United Methodists understand themselves to be church. Hence the resort to church terminology throughout the *Discipline*. And being recognized as fully and properly "church" by another denomination is a threshold for full Eucharistic union, a goal now in bi-lateral conversations. Contests and disagreements over this criterion of integrity differ among Christians and will differ even more in the various other religious traditions (think Reform and Orthodox Judaism, the Nation of Islam and Shia and Sunni Muslims, and so on).

As voluntaristic or willed, the denomination names itself, denominates itself, so as to function in a religiously pluralistic competitive environment, an environment which permits it to exist, to present a public face, and to garner adherents. It needs, therefore, some measure of societal recognition of religious freedom and of a civil policy of toleration. Denominations flourish, of course, in the United States, where the First Amendment effectively makes every religious body, including the Roman Catholic Church, into a denomination. But denominations have prospered as well in European societies which continued an established church but allowed dissenting bodies to function in the public realm.

Two subsidiary but very important characteristics of a denomination often follow from its voluntaristic or willed nature. Claiming one's willed character and recognizing the reality that other denominations are so constituted encourages one religious body to concede the validity and integrity of others and to grasp that it will prosper only if it cultivates and encourages adherence and adherents. Implicit in denomination's voluntarist or willed nature, then, are civility and even an ecumenical spirit and a missionary style. The latter point may be obvious, but the former, advanced years ago by Winthrop Hudson, is no less important.[10] The above quotations from the UMC *Discipline* illustrate current commitment to an ecumenical and missional self-understanding. Below I will show both to have been characteristic of Methodism from its organization as a church in 1784. Both the missional/missionary and the ecumenical/civil characteristics represent tendencies of the denominational style and are not uniformly or invariably present or accented. One does not have to think hard to name denominations which are neither civil nor ecumenical, and some degree of mainline Protestantism's decades of decline has to do with the dampening of its missionary spirit. Nevertheless, the claiming or evidencing of a movement's voluntaristic, willed, missionary and ecumenical nature remains an important indicator of denominational identity and style. And by functioning in relation to such indicators, a denomination makes an implicit theological statement about both itself and other movements that it recognizes as denominations. So Christian denominations and denominationalism offer, implicitly if not explicitly, a branch, vine or body theory of the church. Methodists, Presbyterians or Lutherans are, then, one branch, connected to the vine which is Christ.

By its constellation (though not necessarily precise, specific and unchanging) of practices, beliefs, values and membership standards, a denomination positions itself in the religious marketplace and defines something of a niche for itself. In the competition and free-for-all, certainly between and among Protestants, denominations have tended to emphasize the differentiating and distinguishing aspects of this constellation. On the stump one touted the (relatively) unique doctrinal emphasis, baptismal practice, clergy-deployment pattern, understanding of ministry, authority system. Circuit riding and camp meetings for Methodists, immersion for Baptists, presbytery for the Reformed became signatures. Leaders would at times recognize and affirm that much of what it meant to be Christian was shared, but they put a premium on the coherence of their own practice, belief, authority system, ethos and values, a coherence that knit the distinctive and the shared or common together. So in the UMC *Discipline* today, the section on "Our Doctrinal Heritage" begins with "Our Common Heritage as Christians" and "Basic Christian Affirmations" before adumbrating "Our Distinctive Heritage as United Methodists" and "Distinctive Wesleyan Emphases".

To characterize a denomination as a body with identifiable boundaries and leadership is to insist that it can be mapped, its members counted, its headquarters marked, and its present leadership named. There are mega-churches, with greater human, technological and financial resources than some denominations. There are media, virtual, or otherwise-packaged ministries with more adherents. There are para-church movements with a greater presence across the country. There are single-purpose, caucus or reform impulses with more drive and better political connections. There are spiritual practices and mystical impulses whose literature is far more likely to be found in an airport bookshop. There are churches, sects and ethical systems that make more forceful claims to be the sole possessor of truth or revelation. The denomination differs from all of such forms of American religiosity in its effort to be, with its buildings, its practices, its headquarters, its literature, its leadership, and its members, all that defines a church—word, sacrament, order (or comparable touchstones for other religions). So, United Methodism, in the first paragraph of its Preamble, offers that classic Reformation definition of "church" and places itself within the church universal.

In institutionalizing itself, the denomination announces itself as a religious or an ecclesial entity, organized and ordered to persist over time, and intending its own self-perpetuation. It makes some provision for training and authorizing new leadership; it sets about producing literatures and sacred texts; it secures property in accord with appropriate laws; it incorporates or otherwise safeguards itself as a societally recognized entity; and in every way, it behaves as though it will be around until the end of time. When two or more denominations come together, as did the Methodists and the Evangelical United Brethren (EUB), the new body goes through the process of reconstituting itself for the long haul. The denomination names itself in relation to its tradition (for Protestants, the Christian tradition); it locates itself in the longer saga of God's working with God's people; it identifies its special place in this longer (Christian or other) story; and so it creates for itself, and recognizes itself as having, a history. Producing its history is one signal that a movement is acquiring denominational status.

For the above reasons, I view the denomination as a creature of modernity. The Christian church and other religious movements have looked and behaved differently in other times and places. And the denomination's viability for the future, by the estimation of a number of commentators, remains far from certain. Some who make that latter call and posit a post-denominational stage of American religious organization, do so by equating the denomination with its recent main-line expression as a corporate, nationally centered, top-down managed, program-packaged entity. That bureaucratized organizational pattern does seem to be waning. Whether denominations will disappear and America no longer be a denominational society is less sure. Denominations cohered, programmed, and promoted themselves differently, and they looked different in earlier periods. And in each period a characteristic denominational style tended to run across the spectrum. Furthermore, as one denominational period yielded to the next, the group of denominational players who set the dominant style also tended to grow. Marginal but dynamic denominations of one period often found a place and were yielded a place in the inner cohort of denominations and denominational leaders. So Methodists, a disdained and marginal body in the early nineteenth century, gained national visibility during and after the Civil War, and became players in religious agenda-setting in the twentieth century. Something of the same renego-tiation of insider/outsider boundaries seems to be taking place now, as evangelical and mainline Protestants jostle over place and power in the public sector.[11]

Methodism: Catholic and Wesleyan

From their establishment in 1784 as the Methodist Episcopal Church (MEC), the successor American Methodist bodies have typically lived with the tension or paradox characteristic of denominationalism more generally. They have in one moment affirmed their place in the larger Christian community, their catholicity, their unity with other Protestants in common cause. In the next moment they have accented their Wesleyan peculiarities. The tension can be seen in the name chosen for the new church, a name apparently not selected by John Wesley or the two superintendents (bishops) Thomas Coke and Francis Asbury, but from the floor in the course of the 1784 Christmas Conference. Theirs was to be a surrogate Episcopal Church, one of two successors to colo-nial Anglicanism. The Methodist **Episcopal Church**, like the Protestant **Episco-pal Church**, adopted the Church of England's threefold order of bishops, elders and deacons. The MEC employed Wesley's revised form of the *Book of Com-mon Prayer* for its rituals. It confessed with an Americanized and shortened "Articles of Religion". And by its middle and last name, it connected itself through Anglicanism to the whole of the Christian tradition. The first name, of course, identified the new church with Wesley's movement.

Two other terms used frequently by Methodists in self-identification capture this tension—"connection" and "Zion". The former word continues in self-descriptive use to this day and carries important ecclesiological implications for United Methodism. The *Discipline*, for instance, includes a section entitled "The Journey of a Connectional People", now a brief two paragraphs in length. In 1988 and 1992, the *Discipline* featured a several-page treatment under that title which proclaimed United Methodism a connection of shared vision, memory, community, discipline, leadership, mobilization and linkage. Each of these motifs was expounded theologically and historically.[12] Notwithstanding its current shorter and less theologically expansive treatment, the term continues to be important in United Methodist gatherings and publications as an expressive self-descriptive. The second term, "Zion", did not continue in common usage much past the Civil War. Methodist use of both "connection" and "Zion" deserve a few words of elaboration.

John Wesley had used the term "connection" to identify the movement for reform of the Church of England, which he led. So the early American Methodists followed suit. Their minutes from 1773 to 1784 bore the title "Minutes of Some Conversations between the Preachers in Connection with the Rev. Mr. John Wesley", which was carried over into the first *Discipline* in 1784 when, with Wesley's blessing, ordinations and ecclesial provisions, the American Methodists became a church.[13] The minutes of the first conference, that of 1773, proceed in the curious question-and-answer format that Wesley adopted and illustrate the coherence of the movement in loyalty to him.

The following queries were proposed to every preacher:

1. Ought not the authority of Mr. Wesley and that conference, to extend to the preachers and people in America, as well as in Great-Britain and Ireland?

   Answ. Yes.

2. Ought not the doctrine and discipline of the Methodists, as contained in the minutes, to be the sole rule of our conduct who labor in connection with Mr. Wesley in America?

   Answ. Yes.

3. If so, does it not follow that if any preachers deviate from the minutes, we can have no fellowship with them till they change their conduct?

   Answ. Yes.

The following rules were agreed to by all the preachers present:

1. Every preacher who acts in connection with Mr. Wesley and the brethren who labor in America, is strictly to avoid administering the ordinances [sacraments] of baptism and the Lord's supper.

2. All the people among whom we labor to be earnestly exhorted to
    attend the church [Church of England], and to receive the ordinances
    there; but in a particular manner to press the people in Maryland and
    Virginia to the observance of this minute.[14]

The term "connection"[15] became thereafter a standard way of designating
Methodism and, implicitly, of recognizing the source of its important commitments, emphases, practices and beliefs. When recognizing membership, Methodists spoke of being in connection. And to this day, full identity as clergy is
being in "full connection".

At the 1784 Christmas Conference in Baltimore, the Methodist Episcopal
Church organized itself with Wesleyan resources, transforming his "Large Minutes" into their first *Discipline* and continuing their connection with him by
explicit commitment:

Q. 2.   What can be done in order to the future Union of the Methodists?

A.   During the life of Rev. Mr. Wesley, we acknowledge ourselves his Sons in
        the Gospel, ready in Matters belonging to Church–Government, to obey
        his Commands. And we do engage after his Death, to do every Thing
        that we judge consistent with the Cause of Religion in *America* and the
        political Interests of these States, to preserve and promote our Union
        with the Methodists in *Europe*.

They adapted what might be termed the Wesleyan mission statement for the
new nation and gave themselves a large missional mandate:

Q.4.   What may we reasonably believe to be God's Design in raising up the
        Preachers called *Methodists*?

A.   To reform the Continent, and to spread scriptural Holiness over these
        Lands.[16]

The ecumenical or catholic note is muted but captured in the relative openness
to participation by non-Methodists provided in the guidelines for communion.

Q. 44. Are there any Directions to be given concerning the Administration of
        the Lord's Supper?

2.   Let no Person who is not a Member of the Society, be admitted to the
        Communion without a Sacrament-Ticket, which Ticket must be changed
        every Quarter. And we empower the Elder or Assistant, and no others,
        to deliver these Tickets.[17]

In 1816, for reasons that are not evident in the General Conference *Journal*, the editors were instructed to go through the *Discipline* and substitute the word "church" where the term "connection" had previously appeared. A similar substitution was ordered for the word "society", which had been the Wesleyan term for the local expression of "church". A probable motivation was the Methodist desire to represent their "connection", their "denomination", as fully and properly church, to reiterate a point made earlier. But again, the term "connection" remained immensely popular as one that identified Methodists across the Western world as one body, institutionalized in distinctive ways in the British and American orbits, but sharing common loyalties to touchstones Wesleyan. So, also in 1816, when American Methodists began specifying a particular set of doctrines and books on which ministers would be examined, the list of both was strongly Wesleyan. The theological list consisted of what Methodists term "the evangelical doctrines" and the book list of Wesley's own writings, of Methodist apologists, or of general writings, several of which Wesley himself had abbreviated in his *Christian Library* or made use of in his own writings.[18]

The term "connectional" therefore pointed to American Methodism's Wesleyan distinctives. The Biblical word "Zion" functioned in a comparably popular idiomatic fashion to locate Methodism within the great story of God's drama with God's people(s). In the annual *Minutes* appeared a question that elicited responses in the popular idiom. Quest. 11 read "Who have died this year?" The entry for John Dickins, the first head of publications for the church, recounted his considerable services to the Methodist cause and proclaimed that "His works shall praise him in the gates of Zion".[19] Frequently, where one might expect Methodists to speak about "our church" or "our denomination", they spoke instead of Zion or "our Zion". The word locates Methodism in relation to not only the historical Israel and the long saga of God's redemptive acts but also to the future, to the eschatological New Jerusalem. Itinerating Bishop Francis Asbury, for instance, rode into North Carolina in 1795 and observed:

> This country improves in cultivation, wickedness, mills, and stills; a *prophet of strong drink* would be acceptable to many of these people. I believe that the Methodist preachers keep clear, both by precept and example; would to God the members did so too! Lord, have pity on weeping, bleeding Zion![20]

So, identifying Methodism with the people of God, the corporate, trans-congregational reality of God's chosen ones, the claim to be part of Zion legitimated a dynamic, redemptive, quasi-political self-understanding and orientation to the world and to the American continent. As their mission statement proclaimed (see above), they would "reform the Continent" and "spread scriptural Holiness over these Lands". They were about making this new nation into a Zion.

For Zion they labored; to Zion they belonged. So when one of the African American churches organized itself, it denominated itself the African Methodist Episcopal **Zion** Church, and its members continue to refer to it as "Zion". Asbury noted in 1789, "The number of candidates for the ministry are many; from which circumstance I am led to think the Lord is about greatly to enlarge the borders of Zion".[21] In a letter of 1792 he affirmed, "I feel myself uncommonly moved to believe the Lord will give peace to his church, and great prosperity to his Zion this year".[22] James Haw reported on a Kentucky revival of 1789, "Good news from Zion—The Work of GOD is going on rapidly in the new Western world".[23] Ezekiel Cooper spoke of going "Zionward".[24] When, in 1818, Methodists launched their magazine, *The Methodist Magazine*, which in its various iterations continues to the present, they did so in the trust "the work will be found both useful and entertaining to the real friends of Zion". The next year, 1819, they launched the Missionary and Bible Society with an appeal to "the friends of Zion".[25] The address delivered by the bishops to the 1824 General Conference spoke of "the prosperity of our Zion" and asserted "the borders of our Zion have been enlarged".[26] The editor, historian, college president and denominational spokesperson Nathan Bangs would later speak of the "building up our Zion as on a hill"[27] or write "the history of our Zion".[28]

Methodists had no patent on the use of the word "Zion" or application of it to the church or use of it in self-description. Protestants who read the Old Testament in terms of the New generally applied such Biblical terms to their new Israel. For that reason, in their use of it, Methodists made an important statement about their ecclesial citizenship. They identified themselves with the longer saga and larger reality of the church. So the 1804 MEC General Conference sent greetings to the British Conference and took notice of missions in Ireland and Wales, "Whenever we hear of the prosperity of Zion, and of the success of the Gospel of our Lord Jesus Christ, it gives us a pleasure far superior to our powers of expression". So Freeborn Garrettson, looking back over the Methodist history he had experienced, reflected the early Methodist understanding of Zion as embracing:

> I love Zion, for she is my chief joy.—I pray for the militant church wherever scattered, or of whatever sect; but I engaged to confined myself to the people with whom I have lived, and for whom I have spent the prime of my life.[29]

Historical yet eschatological, geographic yet missional, organizational yet dynamic, Zion connected Methodists with the totality of God's redemptive activity. Zion claimed the sacred past and the eschaton. It required territory and purpose. It prescribed order and action. Zion united Methodists with God's people throughout the whole history of redemption, with other Protestants fulfilling God's purpose in their own day, and with the new Jerusalem to come. Asbury made those connections in his year-end meditations for 1802:

> My general experience is close communion with God, holy fellowship with the Father and his Son Jesus Christ, a will resigned, frequent addresses to a throne of grace, a constant serious care for the prosperity of Zion, forethought in the arrangements and appointments of the preachers, a soul drawn out in ardent prayer for the universal Church and the complete triumph of Christ over the whole earth.[30]

Here Asbury might have used connection where he employed Zion, and Zion where he spoke of the universal Church and the millennium, but no matter, as these words implicated one another.

A Catholic Spirit

The impetus in 1816 to substitute the conventional term "church" for the Wesleyan words "society" and "connection" might well have come from Nathan Bangs, who in so many ways pressed Methodism to be fully a church and claim its rightful place within the family of Protestant denominations. If so, if Bangs was the motion-maker, he modestly did not credit himself in his four-volume *A History of the Methodist Episcopal Church*, which went through twelve editions and remains an invaluable source for understanding early American Methodism.[31] Arguably the most important figure in Methodist history after the death of Bishop Francis Asbury in 1816, Bangs had established himself as Methodism's chief spokesperson with apologetical works that appeared in 1815 and 1816. Others followed in 1817 and 1820. As their titles indicate, Bangs defended Methodist doctrine against Calvinist critics, and Methodist polity and episcopacy against Episcopalians: *The Errors of Hopkinsianism Detected and Refuted, The Reformer Reformed, An Examination of the Doctrine of Predestination,* and *A Vindication of Methodist Episcopacy*.[32] In 1820, Bangs became the MEC book agent, head of the Methodist Book Concern, whose responsibility was to oversee the publishing and distribution enterprise of the denomination. Thereby he became editor of *The Methodist Quarterly Review*, the church's first successful magazine (which, with some short breaks, continues to this day).[33] In 1826, Bangs launched the *Christian Advocate* (New York), soon making it the most widely circulated newspaper in the nation. He founded and headed the Methodist

Missionary Society, led in the creation of the Course of Study to train ministers, pressed for the establishment of colleges, served briefly as president of the church's premier institution, Wesleyan University, and certainly would have been elected to the episcopacy if he had indicated an openness to serve. In 1837, Bangs published *An Original Church of Christ*,[34] a theological/historical treatise and another of his apologetical works, one aimed at legitimating Methodist polity, the church's first book-length effort at ecclesiology. That Methodists actually do ecclesiology has been an open question from other churches and even among Methodists. In the 1960s, Methodism's premier theologian, Albert Outler, queried, "Do Methodists Have a Doctrine of the Church?" In this much-cited essay, the first in a volume that was dedicated to precisely that question, Outler responded with a yes and no.[35] Another Methodist, L. Harold DeWolf, proclaimed less ambiguously: "There has never been an official Methodist doctrine of the church excepting the brief and very general statements in the Articles of Religion and the General Rules. . . . To this day such a Methodist doctrine remains unformulated". Durward Hofler concurred: "There is no Wesleyan doctrine of the church as such, for John Wesley unlike John Calvin did not undertake a systematic compilation of his theology or his ecclesiology".[36] These folk surely had not read Bangs's *Original Church of Christ*.

Here Bangs translated the idiomatic connection and Zion into conventional theological terminology, sustained the tension between particularity and catholicity, and provided Methodism with a denominational self-understanding. He drew on John Wesley's important sermon, "A Catholic Spirit",[37] which, like much of the Wesleyan corpus, conceptualized the Methodist reform impulse as being integral to the Church of England and hospitable to faithful Christians everywhere. A sequence of statements from Bangs should illustrate how his fidelity to Wesley worked then to provide Methodists with every reason to prize their own doctrine, order and practices but to understand their mission as one shared with others.

> We believe, indeed, that God has made the Methodists, unworthy as they may be, instruments of reviving and spreading pure Christianity among mankind. We believe that the evangelical labors of Wesley, his coadjutors and followers, "have provoked very many" "to love and good works", and that thereby gospel light, love, and holiness have been extensively diffused among the different orders of Christians. . . . With all those who are engaged in the solemn work of converting the world to Jesus Christ, we wish most heartily to co-operate, that we may unitedly carry on the warfare against the "world, the flesh, and the devil" (Bangs, 381).

> Now that efforts are making to spread the gospel of our common salvation to the ends of the earth, by the united instrumentality of all denominations of evangelical Christians, why should the breach be widened between any of them, by the utterance of those things which tend naturally to alienate

affection? . . . It is much more important, in my estimation, to exemplify the purity of true religion in our doctrine, spirit, and conduct, than it is to contend for mere forms and ceremonies (Bangs, 23).

Indeed, the grand principle of Methodism from the beginning was, to lay fast hold of the cardinal doctrines of Christianity, with a determination never to unloose the hold, and then to adopt all those means to diffuse them among mankind, which the developments of time and circumstances should dictate to be necessary and expedient (Bangs, 367).

It is the wish of the present writer, that while we rally around our own standards, maintain our own peculiarities, and "contend earnestly for the faith once delivered unto the saints", as we understand it, we should needlessly give offence to none, but conform our love toward all men. It is possible, I think, to cleave to our own institutions, and yet exercise a catholic spirit toward all those who love our Lord Jesus Christ in sincerity. It is possible, indeed, to rise to that height in Christian experience, to be absorbed in the spirit of divine love, and so ardently drawn forth in quest of immortal souls, as to lose sight of sectarian differences and partialities, and to be wholly taken up in the more paramount interests of the Redeemer's kingdom (Bangs, 381).

In these passages, Bangs insisted that Methodists from Wesley's day forward honoured his exhortation to cleave to its own denominational charism but exercise a catholic spirit. He understood Methodism's evangelistic enterprise to be about spreading the gospel of our common salvation. That united instrumentality of evangelical Protestants rested on a common embrace of the cardinal doctrines of Christianity. The shared faith, in turn, oriented the collectivity of Protestant churches towards the kingdom, the foundations of which were to be laid in America. Confident in Methodism's place in that millennial enterprise and in a Christian unity that transcended differences, Bangs implicitly understood denominationalism, the reality of a denominationally divided Protestantism, to be yet conformed to God's purposes. Missing here but present elsewhere in Bangs's account is the conferral of ecclesial significance on a Christian America. Putting Methodism's catholic denominationalism in a civil religious context would become more common in the Methodist historians who followed Bangs, a tendency reinforced by secular canons of historiography.[38]

A Concluding Note

Methodists then and United Methodists today, as the immediately above and initial quotations indicate, conceive of their purposes in American society not only as capitalizing on their unique strengths, style and commitments but also as joining them with the like-minded of other religious bodies. Methodists did and United Methodists do live and embody the characteristics of denomination-alism—a religious institution; a body with identifiable boundaries and leader-ship; a constellation (though not necessarily precise, specific and unchanging) of practices, beliefs, values and membership standards; a voluntaristic or willed religious entity which nevertheless understands itself to possess all the necessary marks or characteristics of religious integrity in the tradition with which it iden-tifies itself; and certainly, willing and able to function under the game rules of modernity and of American constitutional and legal arrangements.

So, Methodism, in its various denominational configurations, has behaved very much like a denomination, though it has chosen to employ other terms than "denomination" in self-identification and self-description. However, vari-ous closely related factors have led United Methodists increasingly to imagine themselves as no longer just a North American denomination but a global church. When their imaginations run away with them, these United Methodists even invoke comparisons with Roman Catholicism. The official website, which maps annual conferences, carries a banner proclaiming "United Methodism is Global". And indeed, United Methodism does have a significant presence in Africa and the Philippines and in smaller conferences throughout Europe, including Russia. In other regions, particularly in Latin America and Asia (espe-cially in Korea), the mission conferences of United Methodism's predecessor churches opted for independence when given that choice. But among those that remained constitutive parts of now United Methodism are large and fast grow-ing conferences in Africa. And recently, the million-plus-member Cote d' Ivoire church, a denomination birthed by British Methodism, aligned itself with United Methodism. Similar betrayals of long-established comity agreements with British Methodism and its daughter churches have occurred because of large-scale immigration, with relocated African United Methodists creating UMC congre-gations in contexts in which, by theory and custom, they would join British Methodist churches and learn to sing familiar Charles Wesley hymns to strange tunes.

With its membership continuing to decline in North America, then, United Methodists have become eager to affirm themselves a worldwide connection. The Council of Bishops, whose membership includes episcopal leaders from outside the United States (in what are now termed "central conferences"), has led the way in understanding the church to be a global entity. The heads of boards and agencies have followed suit. And the 2008 General Conference, mindful of the fact that it and much of the structure of the church behaved as though United Methodism were only American, even with ever-more central conference delegates present, authorized the creation of a committee to study "the Worldwide Nature of the Church". That 20-member committee, hard at work at the time of this writing, will issue a report and recommendations for the 2012 General Conference. Currently the committee is pursuing questions like "How should United Methodists live more justly and equitably into the reality of the worldwide Church?" and "What holds us together as United Methodists?" A working paper offers a hint at their answer and an emerging ecclesiological nuancing of the Wesleyan/Methodist rubric of connection:

> Connectionalism has been one of the distinctive marks of Methodism, for which local authority or freedom does not mean total independence but interdependence. United Methodist Churches in all regions need one another for mutual affirmation, correction, and transformation. Through mutual accountability and holy conferencing, they are to help and support each other to authentically embody and boldly proclaim the gospel in their own respective context.[39]

Is a church with a third of its membership outside North America a denomination? Does it consider itself one? What is it?

Notes

1 *The Book of Discipline of The United Methodist Church–2008*, pp. 21–23. (Hereinafter, references to a *Discipline* or *Minutes* or *Journal of General Conference* will be rendered with the short title *JGC* for the latter, the name of the church and the year; so, *Discipline*/UMC 2008, p. 21. *The Book of Resolutions of The United Methodist Church*, produced quadrennially after each General Conference and now a massive volume, contains a large number of ecumenical resolutions, commitments, overtures and enabling actions illustrating and affirming Methodism's century-long investments in the various twentieth-century efforts at Christian union and, more recently, at inter-religious relations. These, too, particularly the ecumenical rather than the inter-religious statements, affirm denominational identity ecumenically.

2 *Discipline*/UMC 2008, p. 87.

3 "Historical Statement" and "Our Doctrinal Heritage", *Discipline*/UMC 2008, pp. 9–20, 41–59 (9 and 20).

4 *The Doctrines and Discipline of the Methodist Episcopal Church in America, with Explanatory Notes by Thomas Coke and Francis Asbury* (Philadelphia, PA: Henry Tuckniss, 1798; reprint: Rutland, VT: Academy Books, 1979), p. 142. The word is not used at all in the 212 pages of *The Doctrines and Discipline of the Methodist Episcopal Church in America, Revised and Approved at the General Conference held at Baltimore . . . 1792 to which are added, the Minutes of the General Conference . . . 1796*, accessed online in Early American Imprints, Series 1, no. 32472.

5 Jesse Lee, *A Short History of the Methodists, in the United States of America* (Baltimore: Magill and Clime, 1810), accessed online in Early American Imprints, Series 2, no. 20536.

6 Ezekiel Cooper, *The Substance of a Funeral Discourse on the Death of the Rev. Francis Asbury* (Philadelphia 1819), pp. 208, 170, accessed online in Early American Imprints, Series 2, no. 47725.

7 On that point and for a different way to come at the concerns of this project, see Russell E. Richey "Methodist Creation of the Denomination", in Richey (ed.), *Doctrine in Experience: A Methodist Theology of Church and Ministry* (Nashville, TN: Kingswood Books/Abingdon, 2009), pp.182–200.

8 I have elaborated these points in several essays, most recently in "Denominations", in *The Companion to Religion in America,* (ed.) Philip K. Goff (Oxford: Wiley-Blackwell, 2010) pp. 90–104.

9 Compare the criteria identified by one of the co-editors of this volume, Barry Ensign-George in "Denomination as Ecclesiological Category: Sketching an Assessment". He offers "five characteristics of denomination, understood as a structured entity between congregation and church. Denomination is a contingent, intermediary, interdependent, partial and permeable embodiment of the church".

10 Winthrop S. Hudson, "Denominations as a Basis for Ecumenicity: A Seventeenth Century Conception", *Church History*, 24 (1955): 32–50, and also in Richey (ed.), *Denominationalism* (Nashville, TN: Abingdon Press, 1977), pp. 19–42.

11 The argument of this paragraph I set forth at length and various ways in "Institutional Forms of Religion", in Charles H. Lippy and Peter W. William (eds), *Encyclopedia of the American Religious Experience: Studies of Traditions and Movements*, 3 vols (New York: Charles Scribner's Sons, 1988) I, pp. 31–50; *Reimagining Denominationalism*, of which I was co-editor and co-author with R. Bruce Mullin, (New York: Oxford University Press, 1994); "Denominations", in *The Blackwell Companion to Religion in America*, and "Denominationalism", in Charles H. Lippy and Peter W. Williams (eds), *Encyclopedia of Religion in America, 4 vols.* (Washington D.C.: CQ Press, 2010) I, pp. 541–51.

12 *Discipline*/UMC 1992, section 112, pp. 111–14; *Discipline*/UMC 1988, section 112, pp. 116–18. In 1996, General Conference reduced that section to two very short paragraphs, replacing it, in effect, by an extended discussion of "Servant Ministry and Servant Leadership". *Discipline*/UMC 1996, sections 109–16, pp. 109–12. See *Discipline*/UMC 2004, p. 90; *Discipline*/UMC 2008, pp. 90–91.

13 The title of the first *Discipline* was *Minutes of Several Conversations Between The Rev. Thomas Coke, LL.D., The Rev. Francis Asbury and Others, at a Conference, Begun in Baltimore, in the State of Maryland, on Monday, the 27th of December, in the Year 1784. Composing a Form of Discipline for the Ministers, Preachers and Other Members of the Methodist Episcopal Church in America* (Philadelphia 1785).

14 *Minutes of the Methodist Conferences, annually held in America from 1773 to 1784, inclusive.* (Philadelphia: Printed by Henry Tuckniss; sold by John Dickins, 1795), 1773: (5)–7. Compare the more standard *Minutes of the Annual Conferences of the Methodist Episcopal Church, for the years 1773–1828* (New York: T. Mason and G. Lane for the Methodist Episcopal Church, 1840), p. 5.

15 Richey, "Methodist Connectionalism", in Richey (ed.) *Doctrine in Experience*, pp. 159–81. See also especially the first and last of the United Methodism and American Culture series, Russell E. Richey, Dennis M. Campbell and William B. Lawrence (eds), *Connectionalism: Ecclesiology, Mission, and Identity*, UMAC, I (Nashville, TN: Abingdon Press, 1997); *The People(s) Called Methodist: Forms and Reforms of*

Their Life, UMAC, II (Nashville, TN: Abingdon Press, 1998); *Doctrines and Discipline*, UMAC, III (Nashville, TN: Abingdon Press, 1999); and *Questions for the Twenty-First Century Church*, UMAC, IV, (Nashville, TN: Abingdon Press, 1999); and Richey, *Marks of Methodism: Practices of Ecclesiology*, UMAC, V, (Nashville, TN: Abingdon Press, 2005). Chapters in the latter cover connectional and catholic as two of four marks of a Methodist practice of church, the other two being disciplined and itinerant.

16 *Minutes of Several Conversations Between the Rev, Thomas Coke, LL. D., the Rev. Francis Asbury and others, at a Conference, Begun in Baltimore, in the State of Maryland, on Monday, the 27th of December, in the Year 1784.* (Philadelphia: Charles Cist, 1785), pp. 3–4.

17 Ibid., 17.

18 See the typescript minutes of the Baltimore Conference for 1817, pp. 99–100, courtesy of Edwin Schell of that conference, for one of the first such listings. More readily available is the largely identical Course of Study approved by the 1824 New York Conference, MEC, *Methodist History*, 10:1 (October, 1971), pp. 61–62. "A course of reading and Study for the Candidates for the ministry of the Methodist Episcopal Church". The holy Scriptures saith "Study to shew thyself approved unto *God*, a work man that needeth not to be ashamed, rightly dividing the word of truth, and to hold fast the form of sound words; which thou hast hear of me in faith and love, which is in Christ Jesus, & to give attendance to reading, to exhortation, to doctrine". It is recommended to those preachers who are entering into the ministry, to study, and make themselves acquainted with the following points, so as to give Satisfactory Answers in their examination:

1. The General depravity & Corruption of the human heart
2. The doctrine of redemption by Christ—including the doctrine of General attonement [sic.]
3. The Nature of repentance toward God
4. Justifycation [sic.] by faith
5. The direct Witness of the Spirit
6. Holyness [sic.] of heart and life
7. The divinity of rewards & Punishments
8. The Doc't. of perseverance
9. Baptism
10. The resurrection from the dead
11. The eternity of rewards and Punishments
12. The nature of the Church government esp. our own

In order to obtain a necessary knowledge [sic.] on those points, we recommend the reading the following books, viz.—

1. The holy Scriptures
2. The Methodist dicipline [sic.]
3. Wesley's Sermons
4. His notes
5. His Answer to Taylor on Original sin
6. Fletcher's appeal

    7. Saints rest by Baxter
    8. Laws serious call
    9. Portrait of St. Paul
    10. Smith's Lectures on the Sacred office
    11. Rollins Antient [sic.] History
    12. Josephus' Antiquities
    13. Newton on the prophecies
    14. Fletchers Checks
    15. Cokes Commentary & Benson's
    16. Bensons Sermons
    17. Wood dictionary
    18. Mosheam Church History or Mr. Wesleys
    19. Wesley Philosophy
    20. Locke on the understanding and Duncans Logick.

19 *Minutes of the Methodist Conferences, 1773 to 1813* (New York, 1813), p. 205. The line from Dickins appeared in italics in the original.

20 *The Journals and Letters of Francis Asbury*, (ed.) Elmer T. Clark, 3 vols (London: Epworth Press; Nashville, TN: Abingdon Press, 1958), II, p. 46. The entry is 30 March 1795. Hereinafter the reference to the 3-volume set is "JLFA".

21 JLFA, I, p. 606, July 31, 1789.

22 JLFA, III, p. 109, Jan. 1, 1792. The term seems to be something of an evangelical commonplace, a useful way of connecting one's own religious efforts and body with the larger reality of the church. It certainly was not unique to Methodists nor to North Americans. It recurs through the hymnody of evangelical Protestantism. This discussion does not assume Zion to be a Methodist distinctive. We are only concerned with how Methodists used the term. Incidentally, it may have functioned for early Methodists, before the formal organization of the church in 1784, as a useful euphemism, allowing them to leave "church" to the Anglicans but to claim through its Biblical antecedent all the essentials of church. Joseph Pilmore, for instance, uses the term "Zion" frequently for the spiritual reality brought into being by the Methodists and reserves the word "church" for Anglicanism and Anglican buildings. For his references to "Zion" see *The Journal of Joseph Pilmore*, (eds) Frederick E. Maser and Howard T. Maag (Philadelphia: Historical Society of the Philadelphia Annual Conference, 1969) pp. 32, 37, 38, 67, 73, 74, 91, 101, 102, 108, 109, 110, 111, 127, 158, 179, 189.

23 *The Arminian Magazine*, II, p. 202, "An Extract of a Letter from James Haw, Elder . . . to Bishop Asbury".

24 George A. Phoebus, *Beams of Light on Early Methodism in America* (New York: Phillips & Hunt, 1887), p. 9.

25 Nathan Bangs, *A History of the Methodist Episcopal Church* (4 vols. New York, 1860), III, pp. 73, 90.

26 Bangs, III, p. 262.

27 Bangs, II, p. 39.

28 Bangs, III, p. 64.

29 JLFA, III, p. 287. Freeborn Garrettson, *Substance of the Semi-Centennial Sermon before the New York Annual Conference* (New York, 1827).

30 JLFA, III, p. 372, 28 December 1802.

31 Nathan Bangs, *A History of the Methodist Episcopal Church*, 12th edn, 4 vols. (New York: Carlton & Porter, 1860).

32 *The Errors of Hopkinsianism Detected and Refuted* (New York, 1815); *The Reformer Reformed: Or A Second Part of the Errors of Hopkinsianism Detected and Refuted* (New York, 1816), *An Examination of the Doctrine of Predestination* (New York, 1817) *A Vindication of Methodist Episcopacy* (New York, 1820).

33 Of its current form, the on-line digital *Methodist Review*, I am one of two co-editors.

34 I am using the second or 1840 revised edition of Bangs (New York: T. Mason and G. Lane) and providing page references after each long quotation.

35 "Do Methodists Have a Doctrine of the Church?" in *The Doctrine of the Church*, (ed.) Dow Kirkpatrick (New York: Abingdon, 1964), pp. 11–28. But see Scott J. Jones, *United Methodist Doctrine: The Extreme Center* (Nashville, TN: Abingdon Press, 2002); Ted A. Campbell, *Methodist Doctrine: The Essentials* (Nashville, TN: Abingdon Press, 1999); Thomas C. Oden, *Doctrinal Standards in the Wesleyan Tradition* (Grand Rapids, MI: Francis Asbury Press of Zondervan Publishing House, 1988); Thomas A. Langford (ed.), *Doctrine and Theology in The United Methodist Church* (Nashville, TN: Kingswood Books/Abingdon Press, 1991); W. Stephen Gunter et al., *Wesley and the Quadrilateral: Renewing the Conversation* (Nashville, TN: Abingdon Press, 1997); Scott J. Jones, *John Wesley's Conception and Use of Scripture* (Nashville, TN: Kingswood Books/Abingdon Press, 1995); Walter Klaiber and Manfred Marquardt, *Living Grace: An Outline of United Methodist Theology*, translated and adapted by J. Steven O"Malley and Ulrike R. M. Guthrie (Nashville, TN: Abingdon Press, 2001); Kenneth J. Collins, *John Wesley: A Theological Journal* (Nashville, TN: Abingdon Press, 2003); and my *Marks of Methodism: Theology in Ecclesial Practice*, UMAC 5 (Nashville, TN: Abingdon Press, 2005).

36 "The Doctrine of the Church" in *Methodism*, (ed.) William K. Anderson (Cincinnati and elsewhere: Methodist Publishing House, 1947), p. 217. Durward Hofler "The Methodist Doctrine of the Church", *Methodist History* 6 (October 1967): 25.

37 "A Catholic Spirit", *The Works of John Wesley*, 2, *Sermons* 2, (ed.) Albert C. Outler (Nashville, TN: Abingdon Press, 1985), pp. 79–95.

38 See Richey, *Methodist Connectionalism: Historical Perspectives* (Nashville, TN: General Board of Higher Education and Ministry, UMC, 2009).

39 "Core Principles Team Report", 28 March 2010, the Worldwide Nature of the Church Study Committee.

Chapter 6

ORTHODOXY ON DENOMINATION

ELENA VISHNEVSKAYA

The Orthodox position on "denomination" has been succinctly expressed by the prominent Orthodox theologian John Meyendorff: "[T]he Orthodox Church is neither a "sect" nor a "denomination" but the true Church of God. This fact defines both the necessity and the limits of our involvement in ecumenism".[1] Undeniably, the idea of denomination is foreign to the Orthodox self-understanding. The Orthodox Church sees herself as representing the fullness of God's truth and revelation in the original "one, holy, catholic, and apostolic church". Thus, to the Orthodox, the term "denomination" is oxymoronic: a divinely ordained whole cannot be compromised; fragments cannot claim ontological validity:

> The Orthodox have always believed—and have said so at ecumenical gatherings—that the Orthodox Church is the One Church of Christ to which Christ promised that "the gates of hell will not prevail against it" (Matthew 16:18). This promise of Christ would be meaningless if the Church were to be "divided". Thus we believe that the "oneness" of the Church is still with us—in Orthodoxy.[2]

The apostolic succession and tradition are at the very root of the Orthodox faith: the same gospel has been proclaimed since the days of the Apostles by the pastors who trace their descent by unbroken succession from the Apostles and, through them, from Jesus Christ, himself. The Orthodox Church is, therefore, the continuation of the Church established by Christ and the Apostles. Unsurprisingly, the Orthodox find the term "denomination" objectionable, as it betrays, to them, a certain measure of ecclesiological relativism. The reality of the Church, as the Orthodox conceive it, is inimical to any talk of denomination.

It comes as no surprise that the Orthodox churches have been accused of "a sense of superiority in their confidence of apostolic fidelity".[3] A frequently cited example of such an attitude is "the refusal of the Orthodox to practice "intercommunion":

> [I]t is assumed that they are another confessional body which regards itself as superior compared with the rest. In this situation it becomes difficult for the Orthodox to point to an ecclesiology so radically different from that assumed by the other members of the WCC. It is difficult to show in this context that to belong to a confessional body is not the ultimate thing in the Church and that the Orthodox Church regards itself as *the* Church not on a confessional basis but on the basis of the fact that it identifies itself with the eucharistic community in what it regards as its proper and saving form.[4]

Back in 1844, Alexei Khomiakov, one of the brightest religious minds of Russia, argued in *The Church Is One* that the Church should not be criticized for what may appear as pride on account of her self-designation as "Orthodox" or "Holy". There will come a day when the Church will have pervaded the world and nations will have entered into her bosom. Then the name "Orthodox", as well as all local distinctions, will recede into the past.[5] Another influential Russian theologian, Sergei Bulgakov, wrote that the Orthodox Church considers herself the authentic Church enjoying the fullness and purity of truth in the Spirit. The Church's stance towards other confessions follows as a corollary of this self-understanding. To Bulgakov, pluriform confessional reality is an injury to the unity of a Church that wills to see the whole of the Christian world as Orthodox. Bulgakov disavows the spirit of proselytism, imperialism or pride—it is self-evident to him that the truth is one and whole. Bulgakov writes that Orthodoxy constitutes the only answer to the knotty issue of Christian unity. The entry into the Orthodoxy will resolve and put to rest any problems encountered by individual confessions. After all, Orthodoxy is not one of many—it represents the Church herself, in the plenitude of truth. Hence the goal behind the Orthodox involvement in the ecumenical movement—to witness to the truth and faith embodied in the Orthodox Church.[6]

Early on in the history of ecumenism, some Greek Orthodox theologians expounded that "the Orthodox Church participates in the ecumenical movement with the clear consciousness that she is the Una Sancta, a conviction that could not be affected or diminished in any way whatsoever by this participation".[7] Those who held dear this conviction exemplified two differing positions—pro and con respectively—on the Orthodox membership in the World Council of Churches (WCC).[8] The involvement of the Orthodox Church in ecumenism is to this day a matter of much debate among the Orthodox; the volume of this debate has been augmented by the Russian Orthodox Church, which joined the WCC in 1961. Some Orthodox seem willing to negotiate the central tenets of their faith to win the acceptance of their ecumenical counterparts, while others regularly implement extreme anti-ecumenical propaganda to sow seeds of strife and conflict in the Orthodox Church. John Meyendorff observes:

> Unfortunately, Orthodox thought in the matter is too often polarized between two equally wrong positions: "open" relativism and "closed" fanaticism. The first accepts a naïve Protestant idea that it is sufficient to forget about "doctrines" and practice "love" to secure unity. The second fails to recognize the authentically Christian values of the West, which Orthodoxy simply cannot reject, if it wants to be faithful to the fullness of Christian Truth.[9]

In the second half of the twentieth century Orthodox participation in the ecumenical movement received an energetic endorsement from the Russian theologian Georges Florovsky, who was one of the first Orthodox theologians to appreciate the ecclesiological otherness of the various participants in the ecumenical conversation. Florovsky proposed regarding the catholicity of the Church as embracing the value of both Eastern and Western ecclesial ways of being. In the words of Florovsky's admirer Metropolitan John Zizioulas, "there is, in other words, some kind of ecclesiality beyond the canonical borders of the Orthodox Church".[10]

In "The Limits of the Church", Florovsky points out a problematic tension present in the thought of Cyprian of Carthage, the African theologian of the third century. In the *Unity of the Catholic Church,* Cyprian insists on the absolute lack of grace in the sectarian milieu. For Cyprian, schism is an intentional breaking away from the divinely instituted family or the severing of ties with the fountainhead of grace. Thus, the church is the only proper locus for the sacraments—outside the church, the sacraments lose their efficacy.[11]

Florovsky notes that "the historical influence of Cyprian was continued and powerful", while "the practical conclusions of Cyprian have not been accepted and supported by the consciousness of the church".[12] The way the church has lived out her faith shows that the sacraments are not contained by the canonical borders—the sacraments are operative even "outside the church". The sacraments receive their unique raison d'être from the Holy Spirit, who accomplishes "the extension of the [church's] mystical territory even beyond the canonical threshold".[13] Pneumatological in origin and nature, the church transcends what appear to be rigid canonical divisions. Therefore, Florovsky challenges St. Cyprian's idea of the concurrence of the canonical and charismatic borders of the church.

Florovsky also considers Augustine's insight into the correlation between the church and the sacraments which was brought into relief in the Donastist controversy. Arguing against the Donatist position, which maintained that the administration of and participation in the sacraments are the prerogative of the virtuous and the blameless, the Latin bishop espouses Christ as the objective guarantor of the validity of the sacraments, regardless of the subjective state of those involved in the sacramental mystery. Thus, "[t]he actuality of the sacraments celebrated by schismatics signifies for Augustine the continuance of their links with the church".[14] Florovsky regretfully admits that "there has not yet been a creative appropriation of Augustine's conception" in the Orthodox Church.[15]

Predictably, Florovsky's views did not win scores of adherents in Orthodox circles. The applicability of the word "Church" to non-Orthodox bodies is still vehemently disputed among the Orthodox. Some Orthodox refuse to identify non-Orthodox bodies as churches, while other Orthodox seem more agreeable to the use of the term, as long as it is understood as a self-designation employed by the non-Orthodox families.[16] Perhaps this explains why the Orthodox have found the Toronto Statement by the central committee of the WCC very congenial to their understanding of the ecumenical relations: "[M]embership [in the WCC] does not imply that each church must regard the other member churches as churches in the true and full sense of the word".[17] Accordingly, the 1991 Report of an Inter-Orthodox Consultation of Orthodox WCC Member Churches, "The Orthodox Churches and the World Council of Churches", reads: "[T]he Toronto Statement remains as an essential criterion for our participation and membership in the WCC".[18] Commenting on the famed document, Russian Bishop Hilarion Alfeyev remarked in an interview:

> If we call one Protestant community or another a "church", which in our point of view has lost all the main traits of church-ness, then it is only because this community calls itself a church. Among the members of the WCC there are more than a few such groups, which in our view long ago lost the fundamental properties of church-ness or which never possessed them in the first place. We are speaking here of such properties as apostolic succession of the hierarchy, the mysteries, faith in the reality of the Eucharist, etc.[19]

The ostensibly haughty attitude towards other Christian families has long dismayed the larger ecumenical community and contributed to the deterioration of trust between the Orthodox and the rest of the Christian world. Many Orthodox clergy and scholars have expressed regret over the unfortunate alienation between East and West. Metropolitan John Zizioulas, for instance, reprimands

the Orthodox for "a growing self-consciousness of difference or even superiority over the Barbarian West".[20] In an attempt to avoid further estrangement
between the Orthodox and non-Orthodox, the Primates of the Orthodox
Churches delivered a message on 10 October 2008, which affirmed the intent of
the Orthodox Church "to continue, despite any difficulties, the theological dialogues with other Christians".[21] The difficulties, however, have continued to
prove formidable. One of the stumbling blocks in the way of reaching ecumenical concord has been the concept of denomination, which appears fundamental
to the Western theological landscape, while highly objectionable to the Orthodox Church.

In an attempt to clarify and validate the term "denomination", the Protestant
scholar Ensign-George identifies several criteria that may be helpful in drawing
the contours of denomination. First, the scholar considers contingency as he
locates the birth of denomination in time and space. According to Ensign-
George, "denomination is not a necessary pattern of Christian life together"
since the origin of denomination can be traced to "a particular moment".

The Orthodox would agree with Ensign-George that the Church "arose in a
particular time and place"; that is, ecclesiality is a historical actuality: "[T]he
church is external, visible, and orderly, having structures, offices, and ministries".[22]
Unlike Protestant denominations, however, the Orthodox Church is identified
with "the first Christian experience [or] "that which was from the beginning"
(1 John 1:1)".[23] The Orthodox Church has existed since Pentecost: it has faithfully preserved the Apostolic teachings that transcend "every contingency of
history".[24]

Ushered into being by Jesus Christ himself, the Orthodox Church "claim[s]
to demonstrate the existence of a universal church in history",[25] the church
which is not circumscribed temporally or spatially. Instead, "the experience of
the Church belongs to all times"[26] and to all peoples. The wholeness and fullness of the Church, represented by the concept of catholicity, realize the oneness
in the Spirit of the faithful from all over the world and the union in Christ of the
living and the dead. A. Khomiakov asserts that "future generations who have
not yet begun their earthly journey" are, too, members of the Catholic Church:
"God hears the prayers and knows the faith of those who have not yet been
called out of non-existence to existence".[27]

The supra-historical nature of the Church is revealed in Tradition, which
renders the Orthodox Church an indubitably "necessary pattern of Christian
life together" (Ensign-George):

> The Church alone is the living witness of Tradition; and only from within
> the Church, can tradition be felt and accepted as a certainty. . . . [I]t is no
> outward historical authority, but the eternal, continual voice of God—not

only the voice of the past, but the voice of eternity. . . . To accept and understand tradition we must live within the Church. . . . [L]oyalty to tradition means not only concord with the past, but, in a certain sense, freedom from the past, as from some outward formal criterion. . . . Tradition is the constant abiding of the Spirit and not only the memory of the words. Tradition is a charismatic, not a historical, principle.[28]

From the Orthodox perspective, the absolute character of the Orthodox Church, as exemplified in Tradition, surmounts the purely historic nature of denominations, which only underscores their relativity. Human customs and conventions are surpassed by "[t]he one Holy Tradition, which constitutes the self-identity of the Church through the ages and is the organic and visible expression of the life of the Spirit in the Church". This tradition, according to John Meyendorff, "is not to be confused with the inevitable, often creative and positive, sometimes sinful, and always relative accumulation of human traditions in the historical Church".[29]

Experiencing the Church from within, partaking of her Tradition, one is able to tell the sacred from the contingent, or the catholic from "a simple . . . historical accident".[30]

In his essay on denomination, Ensign-George proceeds to locate denomination at the crossroads of what he calls "the church universal and the local congregation": "[D]enominations exist to mediate between [these] two realities". Denominations are authenticated by their functionality: "[T]hey serve as a means for something else—a means by which congregations live into the affirmation that the church is one".

In the Orthodox ecclesiological vocabulary, there is no "middle term" for ecclesiality. The middle term would counter the very confession of faith in the "one, holy, catholic and apostolic church". The Church is an organic whole historically realized in the Orthodox communion; she is the one, true Church founded by Christ.

There is no disparity in the Orthodox theology between the universal church and local congregations. Local churches manifest the Church fully, that is, the catholicity of local churches is rooted in their irrevocable identity with the ecclesiological whole. Sketching out the shape of Orthodox ecclesiology, one of the leading contemporary Orthodox theologians, George Dragas, maintains:

Orthodox ecclesiology operates with a plurality in unity and unity in plurality. For Orthodoxy there is no "either/or" between the one and the many. No attempt is made, or should be made, to subordinate the many to the one (the Roman Catholic model), nor the one to the many (the Protestant model). It is both canonically and theologically correct to speak of the Church and the churches, and vice versa. . . . From an Orthodox perspective, the Church is both catholic and local, invisible and visible, one and many.[31]

Metropolitan John Zizioulas contends that there is no asymmetry in the relationship between local and universal in Orthodoxy, and that it is the Eucharist that underlies "the *simultaneity* of both local and universal": "There is only one eucharist, which is always offered in the name of the "one, holy, catholic and apostolic Church". The dilemma "local or universal" is transcended in the eucharist".[32] Eucharistic communion vouchsafes the unity of the Church.

The catholicity of local congregations is also fulfilled in the relationship they share with one another: the unity in faith and practice is seen in the same doctrine, scriptures, canons and sacraments. In the report to the Central Committee of the WCC in 1992, Archbishop Aram Keshishian observed:

> The local church is not a self-sufficient reality; local churches are related to each other at every place and at all times. Koinonia implies inter-relatedness and interdependence. A local church maintains its ecclesiality and catholicity in conciliar relationship with other local churches. *Communio ecclesiarum* is the description of the real nature of the church. The universal (catholic) church is not a worldwide organization but a koinonia of local churches truly united.[33]

Both universal and local, the Orthodox Church is never a vehicle or "a means for something else" (Ensign-George) but the end, itself. Dragas argues: "Orthodox ecclesiology is holistic and does not tolerate any arbitrary division between the one and the many. She is not tied to external uniformity or to pluriformity, but she is unity in multiplicity".[34]

Two other characteristics of denomination that Ensign-George discusses in his work are those of interdependency and partiality. Like pieces of a puzzle, denominations, according to the scholar, "necessarily embody only part of the fullness of Christian life and witness". Recognition of their fragmentary nature is essential to the livelihood of denominations.

The categories of interdependency and partiality are likely to strike the Orthodox as an endorsement of the Branch theory. The Orthodox Church does not see herself as yet another part of the family tree or another member of the household. The fullness of the apostolic faith resides in the Orthodox Church; the oneness of the Church rests on the indivisibility of Christ. In 1950, the WCC sought to put to rest the fears of the Orthodox in connection with the Branch theory by publishing the Toronto Statement. The ecumenical document has served as a safeguard against the Council's association with the infamous idea.

To the Orthodox mind, Christian denominations cannot claim to be different expressions of the same faith—there is no room in Orthodox ecclesiology for what Ensign-George calls "part of the fullness". The Final Report of the Special Commission on Orthodox Participation in the WCC, issued in 2002, contrasts the Orthodox ecclesiological proclivity, whereby the Orthodox churches are de facto the "one, holy, catholic and apostolic church", with that of other, Protestant churches which describe themselves as together comprised in the "one, holy, catholic and apostolic church". A more solemn note was struck back in 1961 by the Third Assembly of the WCC, held in New Delhi, India:

> The ecumenical problem, as it is understood in the current ecumenical movement, is primarily a problem of the Protestant world. . . . Accordingly, the problem of Christian unity, or of Christian Reunion, is usually regarded in terms of an interdenominational agreement or Reconciliation. In the Protestant universe of discourse such approach is quite natural. But for the Orthodox it is uncongenial. For the Orthodox the basic ecumenical problem is that of schism. The Orthodox cannot accept the idea of a "parity of denomination" and cannot visualize Christian Reunion just as an interdenominational adjustment. . . . The Orthodox Church is not a confession, one of many, one among the many. For the Orthodox, the Orthodox Church is just the Church.[35]

The subsequent Orthodox gatherings would seemingly paraphrase the above position in declaring that "[t]he Orthodox Church . . . does not accept the idea of the "equality of confessions" and cannot consider Church unity as an interconfessional adjustment".[36] For the Orthodox, the restoration of Christian unity entails a return to the one faith of the one Church of Christ.

The Orthodox insistence on the oneness of their Church, however, has baffled Protestants who, upon observing an assortment of Orthodox organizations, like the Alexandrian, Antiochian, Russian, Greek, or Serbian churches, perceive in these churches a semblance to denominations. The Orthodox explain the puzzling phenomenon by the concept of autocephaly, which they view as a practical one. According to John Zizioulas, "The principle of autocephaly is based on the modern concept of the nation, as it was developed mainly in the [nineteenth] century. According to this principle, the Orthodox Church in each nation is governed by its own synod without interference from any other Church and has its own head".[37] While "administratively independent of one another", autocephalous churches remain "united in faith, sacraments, and canonical discipline"[38]; hence, there can be no intimation of denominationalism in relation to the Orthodox Church.

The Orthodox persistently demur at the suggestion that what divides them and the non-Orthodox is purely adiaphoric. From the Orthodox perspective, it is dogmatic essentials that hinder the way to unity, and many of the Protestant families who are part of the ecumenical scene ignore theological differences that exist between them and the Orthodox Church. According to the late Fr. John Meyendorff, "[A]uthentic Orthodox theology can be neither sectarian nor denominational, but only ecclesial. It presupposes the existence of a catholic church that receives the fullness of divine revelation for the sake of the salvation of all people".[39] The issues of doctrine, as well as practice, had been attended to and settled by the Ecumenical and local councils of the Church. The only way to a doctrinal and thus veritable unity of the Christian faith is through recognizing the substantial differences which exist between Christian families that see themselves as denominations and the Orthodox. This recognition would lead to the long-awaited answer to the Orthodox prayer "for the union of all", as all would turn to the ancient repository of tradition within Orthodoxy. Until then, intercommunion is considered by the Orthodox to be unacceptable.

Ensign-George's further criterion of permeability can be applied to the Orthodox Church only in the sense that she welcomes new converts and keeps her exits unobstructed for those who may decide to leave. However, the Orthodox Church has repeatedly expressed apprehension over other Christian bodies proselytizing Orthodox believers, particularly in the traditionally Orthodox countries following the fall of Communism. The Orthodox called attention to the problem in the 1991 Report of an Inter-Orthodox Consultation of Orthodox WCC Member Churches, "The Orthodox Churches and the World Council of Churches":

> Many Orthodox churches, due to persecution, have been weakened and their weakness is a prey to . . . various forms of proselytism. The latter should be denounced with utmost vigor. In particular, the Orthodox should call their partners in ecumenical dialogue to denounce themselves the unfair action of some of their own "missionaries", thus avoiding a flagrant contradiction between official language among "sister churches" called to a "common witness" and actual practice which amounts to "unchurching" the Orthodox Christians.[40]

The 1992 Message of the Primates of the Most Holy Orthodox Churches echoes this concern:

> [E]very form of proselytism—to be distinguished clearly from evangelization and mission—is absolutely condemned by the Orthodox. Proselytism, practiced in nations already Christian, and in many cases even Orthodox,

sometimes through material enticement and sometimes by various forms of violence, poisons the relations among Christians and destroys the road towards their unity.[41]

Statements such as these show that the Orthodox Church has been anxious about the proselytism of Orthodox adherents for quite some time. Back in 1920, the Ecumenical Patriarchate expressed its misgivings about the practice in the encyclical, *Unto the Churches of Christ Everywhere*.

The Russian Orthodox Church was particularly sensitive to Protestant efforts to proselytize Russians after the dissolution of the USSR in 1991. The Russian Orthodox Church had seen herself as the historical mother Church of the Russian people, and the post-Soviet era served a blow to the Church's hopes for a collective return of the Russian prodigal sons and daughters. When the Soviet experiment failed, Russia was flooded with missionaries representing a diverse spectrum of religious belief, and the Orthodox Church had a hard time accepting and navigating an intensely competitive spiritual environment.

Everything considered, the Orthodox stance on denomination reflects the Orthodox Church's view of herself as the Church founded by Jesus Christ, to which he promised that "the gates of hell will not prevail against her". The Orthodox Church has preserved intact the Apostolic faith of the ancient undivided Church and thus serves as the fullest expression of the original faith of Jesus Christ and the apostles. From the Orthodox perspective, denomination is a Christian family of a more recent origin that needs to accept the Apostolic Tradition as timeless, and the biblical and canonical teachings of the Orthodox Church as claiming universal applicability.

Lamenting the actual dividedness among Christians, Metropolitan Nicholas of Detroit identifies the root of the problem as "our lack of a common unity in God". For the Metropolitan,

> This is not to imply that other Christian denominations may not have a legitimate experience of Christianity through their localized traditions. Instead, this means that the full and catholic experience of Divine Life, which is the true, divine, and apostolic inheritance of the Orthodox Church, is not a common treasure held by all. . . . The Christian message as lived upon the earth is most full, complete and catholic when it is Orthodox.[42]

In the same vein, the representatives of the Greek Orthodox Church in the USA, at the North American Faith and Order Study Conference held in Oberlin, Ohio, in 1957, issued a statement in which they averred: "[The] unity in the Church of Christ is for us a Unity in the Historical Church, in the fullness of

faith, in the fullness of continuous sacramental life. For us, this Unity is embodied in the Orthodox Church".[43] Hence, the fundamental postulates of the
Orthodox faith are absolute and non-negotiable.

The Orthodox perspective on denomination may have perturbed other participants in the ecumenical movement. Without doubt, in the Orthodox
Church,

> [t]here are those who believe that all non-Orthodox are in the patristic
> category of "heretics" . . . and dwell in an undifferentiated state of grace-
> lessness. The canons which forbid "prayer with the heretics", therefore,
> are interpreted as referring not to the Gnostics or Manichaeans, but to
> Roman Catholics and Protestants. . . . Inspired by the Fathers at their most
> polemical and largely forgetting them at their most irenic and inclusive,
> treating the Church's canons in a monolithic and homogenous way, seeing
> them not as living tradition but as a dead letter, some Orthodox do not
> acknowledge grace and salvation outside the canonical borders of the
> Orthodox Church.[44]

The Orthodox who subscribe to this view do not represent the Church at large.
There are many Orthodox faithful who may see other Christian bodies as
"branches which have become separated" from the body of the one true Church
but do not automatically "regard all non-Orthodox Christian confessions as
withered branches".[45] The late Russian Orthodox priest Alexander Men
advised his flock: "Yes, there will be diversity, but it need not turn into antago-
nistic, divisive groupings. . . . When you encounter other forms of Christianity,
I urge you to patience, even if it's difficult. Confrontation is not worthwhile.
Each one must attend to his calling—let God be the judge of all".[46] Metropolitan Philaret of Moscow also expressed a charitable Orthodox sentiment when
he avowed: "I dare not call false any Church which confesses Jesus to be the
Christ".[47]

To appreciate the conceptual non-existence of denomination in the Orthodox ethos and thus the Orthodox position on denomination, one needs to recall
the schism of 1054 and the subsequent fall of Byzantium to the Turks in 1453.
Both events cut off the Orthodox Church from her Western counterparts, and
"for many centuries the Orthodox East was virtually absent from the life of the
West, took no role in it, and, what is equally important, was not considered part
of it".[48] The defining moments of religious history of the West, like the Reformation and the Counter-Reformation, had little if any bearing on the Orthodox
Church. Unaffected by the changes that shook up the West, the Orthodox
Church clung to her treasure chest of tradition. The Orthodox Church saw herself

as the sole guardian of the tradition which at one time was a fountainhead of life claimed by all Christian believers. According to Alexander Schmemann, "This Eastern isolation of the Orthodox church and her very real identity with tradition as formulated and accepted before the Western schism explain those basic presuppositions which conditioned" the story of Orthodox involvement in ecumenical relations.[49]

Some Orthodox scholars believe that the tensions between the East and the West are ever present because "from its very beginning the ecumenical movement was heavily dominated by Western religious and theological problems".[50] The organization of the WCC has been shaped by the idea of denomination, which reflects a particularly "Western [and specifically Protestant] religious situation".[51] As a result, the Orthodox Church has found herself on the periphery of the ecumenical movement both ideologically and numerically.

Ecumenical rapprochement between the East and the West appears at times unattainable. Both parties have had a hard time grasping each other's theological and spiritual problematics. Hopefully, Ensign-George's thoughtful work which clarifies the idea of denomination will foster reciprocally attentive and conscientious efforts at a constructive dialogue between the Orthodox Church and Western Christian families and, thus, in his own words, "will have ecumenical value".

Notes

1 John Meyendorff, *Witness to the World* (Crestwood, NY: St. Vladimir's Seminary Press, 1987), p. 13.
2 Ibid., pp. 42–43.
3 Jeffrey Gros, Eamon McManus, and Ann Riggs, *Introduction to Ecumenism* (New York: Paulist Press, 1998), p. 154.
4 Gennadios Limouris, (comp.), Report on an Inter-Orthodox Consultation, "The Ecumenical Nature of Orthodox Witness," New Valamo, Findland, 24–30 September 1977, in *Orthodox Visions of Ecumenism: Statements, Messages and Reports on the Ecumenical Movement 1902–1992* (Geneva: World Council of Churches, 1994), p. 68.
5 Alexei Khomiakov, *Tserkov" odna* (The Church is One) (Moscow: Dar, 2005), p. 47.
6 Sergei Bulgakov, *Pravoslavie* (The Orthodox Church) (Moscow: Terra, 1991), pp. 391–98.
7 Metropolitan John Zizioulas, "The Self-understanding of the Orthodox and Their Participation in the Ecumenical Movement", in *The Ecumenical Movement, the Churches and the World Council of Churches: An Orthodox Contribution to the Reflection Process on "The Common Understanding and Vision of the WCC"*, (ed.) George Lemopoulos (Geneva: WCC Publications, 1996), p. 37.
8 Ibid.

9 Meyendorff, *Witness to the World*, p. 17.

10 Metropolitan John Zizioulas, "The Self-understanding of the Orthodox and their Participation in the Ecumenical Movement," p. 39.

11 Georges Florovsky, "The Limits of the Church," *The Church Quarterly Review* (1933): 117–18.

12 Ibid., p. 118.

13 Ibid., p. 119.

14 Ibid., p. 126.

15 Ibid., p. 128.

16 Metropolitan John Zizioulas, "The Self-understanding of the Orthodox and their Participation in the Ecumenical Movement," pp. 37–39.

17 Central Committee of the World Council of Churches, "Toronto Statement," July 8–15, 1950, *World Council of Churches website:* www.oikoumene.org/en/resources/documents/central-committee/toronto-1950/toronto-statement.html; accessed 7 April 2009.

18 Limouris, (comp.), Report of an Inter-Orthodox Consultation of Orthodox WCC Member Churches, "The Orthodox Churches and the World Council of Churches," Chambésy, Switzerland, September 12–16, 1991, p. 191.

19 Bishop Hilarion Alfeyev, "Will the Ecumenical Ship Sink?" *In Communion, website of the Orthodox Peace Fellowship,* www.incommunion.org/2006/04/23/will-the-ecumenical-ship-sink; accessed April 7, 2009).

20 Metropolitan John Zizioulas, "The Self-understanding of the Orthodox and Their Participation in the Ecumenical Movement", p. 44.

21 Primates of the Orthodox Churches, "Message of the Primates of the Orthodox Churches," *Ukrainian Orthodox Church of the United States of America website,* October 12, 2008: www.uocofusa.org/news_081012_3.html; accessed April 7, 2009.

22 Robert G. Stephanopoulos, "Denominational Loyalties and Ecumenical Commitment: A Personal View," *Journal of Ecumenical Studies,* 17, 4 (1980): 638.

23 Ion Bria, *The Sense of Ecumenical Tradition: The Ecumenical Witness and Vision of the Orthodox* (Geneva: Word Council of Churches, 1991), p. 62.

24 Vladimir Lossky, "Tradition and Tradtions," in *Eastern Orthodox Theology: A Contemporary Reader,* (ed.) Daniel B. Clendenin (Grand Rapids, MI: Baker Academic, 2003), p. 134.

25 Bria, *The Sense of Ecumenical Tradition*, p. 62.

26 Georges Florovsky, *Bible, Church, Tradition: An Eastern Orthodox View,* Collected Works, vol. 1 (Belmont, MA: Nordland Publishing, 1972), p. 45.

27 Khomiakov, *Tserkov" odna*, pp. 3–4.

28 Florovsky, *Bible, Church, Tradition*, pp. 46–47.

29 John Meyendorff, *Living Tradition: Orthodox Witness in the Contemporary World* (Crestwood, NY: St. Vladimir's Seminary Press, 1978), p. 21.

30 Florovsky, *Bible, Church, Tradition*, p. 50.

31 George Dragas, "Orthodox Ecclesiology in Outline," *The Greek Orthodox Theological Review,* 26 (1981): 185.

32 Metropolitan John Zizioulas, *Being as Communion: Studies in Personhood and the Church,* Contemporary Greek Theologians, no. 4 (Crestwood, NY: St. Vladimir's Seminary Press, 1985), p. 133.

33 Aram Keshishian, "Growing Together toward a Full Koinonia," *The Ecumenical Review* 44, 4 (1992): 495.

34 Dragas, "Orthodox Ecclesiology in Outline," p. 192.
35 Limouris, (comp.), Third Assembly of the World Council of Churches, New Delhi, India, 1961, p. 30.
36 Limouris, (comp.), Decisions of the Third Preconciliar Pan-Orthodox Conference, "The Orthodox Church and the Ecumenical Movement", Chambésy, Switzerland, 28 October–6 November 1986, p. 113.
37 Metropolitan John Zizioulas, *Being as Communion*, p. 253.
38 John Meyendorff, "Doing Theology in an Eastern Orthodox Perspective," in *Eastern Orthodox Theology: A Contemporary Reader*, (ed.) Daniel B. Clendenin (Grand Rapids, MI: Baker Academic, 2003), p. 81, n. 2.
39 Ibid., p. 95.
40 Limouris, (comp.), Report of an Inter-Orthodox Consultation of Orthodox WCC Member Churches, "The Orthodox Churches and the World Council of Churches," Chambésy, Switzerland, 12–16 September 1991, p. 194.
41 Ibid., Message of the Primates of the Most Holy Orthodox Churches, Phanar, 1992, p. 197.
42 Metropolitan Nicholas of Detroit, "On Unity and Unity of Faith," *Orthodox Research Institute website*, www.orthodoxresearchinstitute.org/articles/dogmatics/pissare_unity_of_faith.html; accessed April, 20, 2009.
43 Representatives of the Greek Orthodox Church in USA, "Statement of the Representatives of the Greek Orthodox Church in USA at the North American Faith and Order Study Conference, Oberlin, Ohio," September 3–10, 1957, *Orthodox Research Institute website*, www.orthodoxresearchinstitute.org/articles/ecumenical/gocamerica_faith_order_sept_1957.htm; accessed April 20, 2009.
44 Peter Bouteneff, "Orthodox Ecumenism: A Contradiction in Terms?", 9 July 1997, *In Communion, Website of the Orthodox Peace Fellowship*, 9 July 1997, www.incommunion.org/2004/10/24/bouteneff-on-ecumenicm ; accessed April 21, 2009.
45 Bishop Hilarion Alfeyev, *The Mystery of Faith: An Introduction to the Teaching and Spirituality of the Orthodox Church* (London: Darton, Longman and Todd, 2002), p. 121.
46 Alexander Men, *About Christ and the Church*, (trans.) Fr. Alexis Vinogradov (Torrance, CA: Oakwood Publications, 1996), p. 40.
47 Cited in Bishop Hilarion Alfeyev, *The Mystery of Faith*, 123.
48 Alexander Schmemann, "Moment of Truth for Orthodoxy," in *Eastern Orthodox Theology: A Contemporary Reader*, (ed.) Daniel B. Clendenin (Grand Rapids, MI: Baker Academic, 2003), p. 205.
49 Ibid.
50 Ibid., p. 207.
51 Ibid., p. 209.

Chapter 7

The Denomination in Classical and Global Pentecostal Ecclesiology: A Historical and Theological Contribution

Wolfgang Vondey

Classical Pentecostalism emerged in a complex North American ecclesiastical environment that was itself already reactionary to the European culture of Christendom. A diverse mix of circumstances—immigration, migration, urbanization, fundamentalism, revivalism, the advance of liberal religion and the rise of modern Protestantism—formed the seedbed for an understanding of ecclesiality that is perhaps best described as "post-Christendom", surfacing at the end of and in conscious response to the concept of the church upheld by the established denominations of the colonial period.[1] In this context, following the revivals in Topeka in 1901, and the Azusa Street Mission in 1906, Pentecostalism was immediately designated as a "movement" rather than a "church" or "denomination". More precisely, the concept of "movement" functions as a middle term between church and denomination, stretching the idea of ecclesiality towards both ends while emphasizing the dynamic quality of Pentecostal ecclesiology.[2] From that perspective, the term "movement" has persisted as the most dominant ecclesiological designation of classical Pentecostalism for the first one hundred years of its history and represents the foundational context for evaluating the Pentecostal contributions to a theological account of denominations.

Pentecostalism accounts for perhaps the largest growth of denominations during the twentieth century; it has been responsible for a virtual explosion of small congregations, ecclesial bodies, fellowships and churches.[3] The situation is further complicated by the globalization of Pentecostalism beyond the North American realm and the exposure of the Western concept of denominationalism to the social, cultural and ethnic diversity of the global ecclesiastical landscape.[4] Contemporary Pentecostal literature does not reflect a consistent use of the concept of denominations or even a general acceptance of the term beyond sociopolitical considerations.[5] At this time, the ecclesiological spectrum ranges from outright rejection of denominationalism among the so-called non-denominational or Free churches to clear acceptance of denominational status as an indication of permanent and independent organizational patterns. As Peter Hocken summarizes the situation in the *New International Dictionary of Pentecostal and Charismatic Movements*, the impact of denominationalism "did not . . . produce any distinctively pentecostal view of the church".[6] Much groundwork still needs to be done before a comprehensive, systematic account can be offered of Pentecostal ecclesiology or, perhaps more accurately, ecclesiologies. The present essay emerges from this motivation.

In light of the worldwide variety of Pentecostal communities, it is not possible to offer a generalized theological account of denominations among Pentecostals. Instead, I argue that the motivation for the acceptance or rejection of the denominational label depends on the ecclesiological self-understanding of Pentecostal groups and their identification with the ecclesiality of classical Pentecostalism, that is, with the origins of the movement in North America during the early twentieth century. More precisely, the Pentecostal contribution to an assessment of the ecclesiological quality of denominations arises from a transformation of the classical Pentecostal movement into global Pentecostalism.[7] This essay is therefore as much about classical Pentecostalism as it is concerned with the global dimensions of the movement. Ecclesiologically, at least, these two aspects of Pentecostalism are inseparable. The classical Pentecostal response to the challenges of denominationalism in North America is characterized by an initial rejection of denominational patterns, followed by a reconsideration of traditional, denominational concepts of ecclesiality. The tendency of Pentecostalism to move towards globalization locates a general assessment of contemporary Pentecostal ecclesiology towards the latter end of the spectrum. I conclude with an analysis of the implications of this development for a contemporary ecumenical account of denominations.

I. Classical Pentecostalism:
A Movement Rejecting Denominational Patterns

The notion of "movement" as a designation of classical Pentecostal ecclesiality arose from the concrete experience of what was frequently described as the "stagnation" and "institutionalism" of the so-called old churches.[8] Pentecostal pioneers found the term "church" or "denomination" to be a sectarian designation, since these terms were typically attached to a particular form of ecclesiastical institution to validate its own authority. In contrast, classical Pentecostalism emerged from roots that were already commonly designated as "movements" within the church—most prominently, the Holiness Movement and the Apostolic Faith Movement. Both movements were nourished by the revivalism and popularity of restorationist ideas in the nineteenth century.[9] Similarly, the Pentecostal movement sought the reinstatement of "the old time religion, camp meetings, revivals, missions, street and prison work and Christian Unity everywhere".[10] Most Pentecostals understood their own identity to be in radical opposition to the historical consciousness of the established churches.

> We believe with all our hearts in the "Apostolic Movement" not as a name for a church, but as a religious "reform movement" composed of all clean people who will join in our battle cry and reform slogan of "Back to Christ and the apostles!" . . . But this is only a "reform movement", not a church, not the church, not the churches of God. As many churches as like can belong to this reform movement, as many do; but it is not a church, the church nor the churches; and it is a mistake we ought to get out of to call a Bible congregation of believers set in divine order by any sort of sector nickname.[11]

The repeated distinction of the term "movement" from the designation "church" highlights both the awareness of ecclesiastical categories among Pentecostals and the rejection of established classifications. The dismissal of the term "church" or "denomination" as an identifier of Pentecostal groups was rooted in the conviction that "church" was fundamentally the title of an eschatological, not a doctrinal, community. The term "church" did not function as an equivalent to "local congregation" in history, but rather was embraced as the idea of the whole family of God in its undivided, universal dimensions (although not all Pentecostal pioneers operated with a clear sense of this understanding of the term).[12] From that perspective, classical Pentecostals were convinced that no particular faith community could claim the right to be called "church".[13] The concept of "denominations", on the other hand, was often associated with the established ecclesiastical traditions and indicated a historical designation that carried a visible resistance to ecumenical unity. This conviction was further consolidated by the fact that most Pentecostals found themselves designated as "denominations" or "sects" and thus as "outcasts from the ecclesiastical camps".[14] From the classical Pentecostal perspective, denominationalism and institutionalism were often synonymous patterns of an ecclesiology that proved irreconcilable with the Pentecostal ethos.

> The older denominations have a past which is their own in a peculiar sense; they can trace the beginnings of their church and the course of its history subsequent to its foundation. The time between the beginning and the present has been sufficient to establish precedent, create habit, formulate custom. In this way they have become possessed of a two-fold inheritance,

a two-fold guide of action, a two-fold criterion of doctrine—the New Testament and the church position. The Pentecostal Movement has no such history; it leaps the intervening years crying, "Back to Pentecost!"[15]

As a movement, Pentecostals understood themselves as carriers of the transformation and change brought about by the biblical "Pentecost"—a watchword that referred at once to the historical events recorded in Acts 2, the operation of the Holy Spirit in the apostolic community, and the continuing outpouring of the Spirit in Christian history.[16] The slogan—"Back to Pentecost!"—expressed the desire to revive an event that was suppressed in its unfolding by the habits, customs and structures of the denominational churches.

Classical Pentecostals found any ecclesiastical designation misleading as long as it remained within the boundaries of normative socio-historical authority. Of course, Pentecostals understood themselves as thoroughly placed in history—albeit from an eschatological perspective that questioned the extent of history's jurisdiction.[17] Pentecostal pioneers saw themselves as part, not of a historical organization, but of an eschatological movement in history, and the revival of Pentecost at the beginning of the twentieth century was taken as the eschatological continuation and completion of the historical work of God who "started this movement in AD 33".[18] To designate their ecclesiality from an eschatological perspective, Pentecostals typically indentified the contemporary revival with the day of Pentecost and used the term "Latter Rain Movement" to indicate that "the first Pentecost started the church, the body of Christ, and this, the second Pentecost, *unites* and *perfects* the church into the coming of the Lord".[19] The Pentecostal movement was not the fulfillment of God's work but the work *itself*, not an organization or institution but a tangible "forward moving"[20] expression of the outpouring of the Holy Spirit and the formation of the church as an eschatological community through history and the world.

> In speaking of the present "movement" it is to be noted that this is not a "movement" in the ordinary sense in which the word is used. The chief justification for using the word is that the Blessed Holy Spirit is moving in anew upon men, women, and children mightily. There is no human leader or head and no organization at the back of it.[21]

This resistance to established classifications is characteristic of the early history of Classical Pentecostalism. Pentecostals criticized the "formalism", "institutionalism", "ritualism", "ecclesiasticism" and "denominationalism" of "human organizations".[22] The heart of this criticism was levelled at the existence of the "many different religious organizations each enclosed by its own particular sectarian fence".[23] The origins of Pentecostal ecclesiology were deeply rooted in an ecumenical reading of history rather than in an isolated structural criticism.

Despite the broad appeal to the apostolic faith community, Pentecostals made no serious effort to trace and develop a historical connection with the primitive church.[24] The reason for this neglect lay in the conviction that any bonds of apostolic succession had been severed by the organizational efforts of the Constantinian church to prescribe its faith and praxis in the form of creeds.[25] Pentecostals adamantly proclaimed that they were "not fighting men or churches, but seeking to displace dead forms and creeds or wild fanaticisms with living, practical Christianity".[26] The concerns were as much structural as they were ecumenical. However, at their root stood an ecumenical idea of the church that differed radically from the dominant definitions of ecclesiality.

The main effect of the primitivism of Classical Pentecostals was what Grant Wacker has called an "antistructuralist impulse" that culminated in "a determination to destroy the arbitrary conventions of denominational Christianity in order to replace them with a new order of primal simplicity and purity".[27] Pentecostals illustrated their anti-structuralist impulses by drawing a sharp distinction between the "mechanistic" denominations of Christendom and an "organic" notion of the church.[28] They painted the chief contrast as between the "institutional structures" of the visible churches and the "spiritual dynamic" that animates the whole Christian body.[29]

> The rise or fall of Christianity depends upon where we put the emphasis. It is either upon organization or Spirit-filled men. If upon organization, then Christianity is dominated by stagnation. If upon Spirit-filled men, whose lives are yielded to God's will for the need of the world, then the church grows and the Kingdom expands with accelerated power.[30]

With the invocation of episcopal authority over spiritual decision-making and creedal authority over the use of scripture, the creeds represented for Pentecostals the prime event whereby the church had "*organically* fallen".[31] This "organic" characterization of "church" was based on two biblical images, the Body of Christ and the Bride of Christ. The first served to define the ecumenical depth of the church; the second, its eschatological dimension. Fused by a pneumatological imagination, the images were joined together by a common concern for Christian unity.

> We must have unity of the Spirit. Getting everybody into one church organization would not settle the world's problems, nor the problems that confront religious leaders. Everybody in one church organization would not mean spiritual unity, but would make for spiritual disaster.[32]

It was the pneumatological aspect that distinguished the church as an organism from human organization and denominations. As a human structure, the church was formed by "creeds, doctrines, and ceremonies"[33] that yoked the spiritual freedom and general priesthood of believers and were to be abandoned because they had led to separation. The healing of the divisions was found in the unity of the Spirit (Eph. 4.13), interpreted as the sanctification of the carnal nature of the church (Rev. 19.7–8) and the liberation from the entanglement of organized institutions.[34] The oneness of the church was heralded among Pentecostals as an eschatological reality made possible in history by the outpouring of God's Spirit. This pneumatological perspective stood in sharp contrast to the established forms of denominationalism. In the eschaton, the kingdom of God and the church of God are identical. Until then, however, the name "church" designated "more a movement of the Spirit than a structure wedded to the present age".[35] The title "denomination" simply seemed not applicable to the eschatological vision of early classical Pentecostalism.

From the perspective of a movement-ecclesiology, classical Pentecostalism existed in ecclesial grassroots communities that generated a new, dynamic sense of ecclesiality. The dominant ecclesiology was confronted not "with the expansion of an existing ecclesiastical system . . . but with the emergence of another form of being church".[36] More precisely, Pentecostals understood themselves as a movement that was *becoming* church. A particular community, denomination or even the Pentecostal movement as a whole was considered transitory and expected to be surpassed by the continuing outpouring of the Holy Spirit and the resulting transformation of Christianity.[37] "So all Christendom, made up of many parts, is aiming to become one gigantic, organized movement".[38] As this expectation met reality, the challenge of how this movement could be organized led to a reconsidering of the entire thought world of early Pentecostal ecclesiology.

II. Global Pentecostalism:
A Movement Reconsidering Denominational Structures

At the beginning of the twentieth century, the ecclesiological use of the term "movements" was not very well established. It derived its identity from European political language that associated movements with asymmetry, mobilization and revolution.[39] Established ecclesiological ideas tended to identify the church with the cultural habits and traditions that supported its authority, and to discuss ecclesial movements largely in terms of their cultural dissidence and religious instability.[40] From a socio-historical perspective, "movements" were synonymous with "sects" and existed only on the fringes of the ecclesiastical spectrum. Only as the Pentecostal movement began to expand with unprecedented force during the first decades of the twentieth century, did the question of the structure and organization of a movement rise to the forefront. Pentecostalism was shaping itself into a national movement that reached far beyond the structural organization of the first local communities. Moreover, the worldwide expansion of the charismatic experience fuelled the debates about the ecclesiality of the movement in the global context. Four aspects exerted the most critical influence: the numerical and geographical expansion of Pentecostalism, the occurrence of internal divisions, the Pentecostal movement's increasing ecumenical exposure, and the demands of global missionary activity.

First, the growth of Pentecostalism initially confirmed its self-understanding as a movement. The expansion of the original local communities was seen as mimicking the growth of the apostolic community from Jerusalem, to Judea and Samaria, "and to the ends of the earth" (Acts 1.8). Pentecostalism was seen as the movement of the Spirit that swept *across* the existing denominations and thus *became* the church. On the other hand, Pentecostals also found much resistance to growth, not only from outsiders but from the movement's internal observations, and a lack of organization often seemed to be preventing further expansion.[41] By the second decade of the twentieth century, the movement had become "a composition of several branches of Pentecostal bodies".[42] The "inconsistencies and failures and counterfeits and different grades of experience following along with this movement" demanded the development of organizational structures that would bring coherence and unity. As a result, Pentecostals turned to the visible structures of denominations surrounding them. However, the establishment of this form of organized leadership was initially specifically connected with the Christian assembly, which in the scriptures carries the simple name, "church". An adaptation to the existing forms of ecclesiality therefore supported the use of the title "church" for Pentecostal communities, and "church" or "assembly" became the designation of choice for most local Pentecostal bodies.[43] This ecclesiological choice significantly hampered an unfolding of the eschatological self-understanding of Pentecostalism as a movement towards its global realization of becoming the church. The use of the title "church" for the local assembly competed with the original concept of a "movement" and prevented that concept from becoming part of a more fully developed ecclesiology. The concept of denominations emerged within this tension as a structural concept adopted in contrast to both the reality of the diverse local assemblies and the eschatological vision of the united church.

Second, the movement was plagued by internal fractures, debates, and divisions. Classical Pentecostals divided over disagreements on doctrine, personalities, church politics, and praxis.[44] In response, many Pentecostals noted the need for organizational patterns beyond the local assembly.[45] In the effort to meet the demands of the situation, Pentecostals began to interpret the established concepts of ecclesiality in distinction both to one another and to groups who did not seem to follow the original intentions of the Pentecostal revival.[46] The eschatological orientation of the early movement-ecclesiology was overshadowed by the structural demands of the rapidly expanding Pentecostal communities.[47] Traditional ecclesiology could not hold step with this development. The identification of churches with the stability and survival of the movement nourished an ecclesiology of competition. As a result, and mimicking the established ecclesiological patterns, the title "church" frequently moved from the local assembly to the group of assemblies that associated one another with like doctrine, personalities, politics and spiritual life. Others identified the ecclesiality of this group as a denomination. Internal dissention and schisms hastened the process of institutionalization, including groups who rejected any denominational designation outright.[48] On a conceptual level, the shift of Pentecostal ecclesiality to the realm of denominations complicated the use of the designation "church" and effectively shut the door to a more pronounced eschatological and ecumenical ecclesiology.

The ecumenical exposure of Pentecostalism represents a third influence on the shaping of the ecclesiology of the movement. Recent scholarship has established that the origins of classical Pentecostalism are thoroughly steeped in ecumenical practices.[49] As a movement, Pentecostalism was almost universally regarded as the fulfillment of Jesus" prayer for Christian unity (John17.21).[50] The designations of Pentecostal bodies as churches or denominations, however, could not sustain the same ecumenical impulse. Rather, the adoption of the traditional ecclesiological classifications inevitably led to confrontation internally as well as with other churches and denominations. Since Pentecostals were adamant that they did not "desire to tear down churches but to make new churches out of old ones",[51] the understanding of Pentecostal ecclesiality had to be altered to allow for the existence of multiple churches and denominations. This decision, however, further consolidated a sense of competition and an exclusivist attitude towards other non-Pentecostal communities.[52] Largely in response to a widespread rejection by the established ecclesial traditions, Pentecostalism reverted to a "spiritual" ecumenism, and as a result, its self-understanding as a movement became ecclesiastically invisible. The application of the concept of denominations signaled questions about the adoption of an ecclesiology that was irreconcilable with the sense of ecclesiality that had originated with the original grass-roots communities.

Finally, Classical Pentecostals understood themselves to be fundamentally a missionary movement of the Holy Spirit. Their publications were filled with accounts of men and women who had left their homes to preach the gospel in other cultures.[53] The understanding of the nature of Pentecostalism as a "movement" was largely synonymous with the idea of the church's mission.[54] However, as the movement expanded, the missionary workers suffered most visibly from the disorganization and divisions among early Pentecostals. As Allan Anderson observes, "Many of them were independent, without financial or organizational backing, and they related only loosely to fledgling Pentecostal congregations in their home country. After all, the Spirit had set them free from human ecclesiastical institutions".[55] The initial, and spontaneous, confidence that Pentecostals had "the simple but effective Scriptural Plan for evangelizing the world"[56] eventually made room for the somber realization that the absence of plans and support structures severely hampered the growth and effectiveness of the Pentecostal movement. The establishment of missionary structures therefore represented the primary catalyst for the institutionalization and denominationalization of classical Pentecostalism. Designations such as "church" and "denomination" promised growth, stability and survival, and dramatically reshaped the missional ecclesiology of early Pentecostals. Designated as such, Pentecostal denominations were seen not as the realization but as the anticipation of the kingdom of God in the world. In turn, missionary activity became an ecclesial rather than eschatological endeavor. The movement no longer journeyed *towards* its full realization as the church of God; the church was now located *within* the Pentecostal movement or, more accurately, *among* the Pentecostal denominations.[57] This perspective not only juxtaposed ecclesiology and eschatology, it also had a profound impact on the cultural self-understanding of an ever-expanding Pentecostal movement.

Despite the worldwide growth and exposure of Pentecostalism, established ecclesiological categories have been unable to define the ecclesiality of a "movement" from either a grass-roots or a global perspective. The change of self-designation from "movement" to "church" or "denomination", and the failure to provide a sustained definition of the ecclesiality of these terms, supported the interpretation of Pentecostalism as a movement in terms of a simple sect–church development—characteristic of a variety of religious communities and not distinctive of Pentecostalism.[58] If Pentecostalism is a movement, the question arises whether it is "useful or valid to talk about ecclesiology at all".[59] By adopting the established denominational patterns, Pentecostal ecclesiology has sidestepped a debate on the impact of modernism, modernity and cultural formation, supporting the separation of the ecclesiastical realm from the arena of politics, economics and the secular, and strengthening the autonomy of culture.[60] As a result, the organic ecclesiality of Pentecostalism, its pneumatological basis and eschatological orientation, remained largely undeveloped.

III. Implications of Pentecostal Ecclesiality for a
Denominational Ecclesiology

The Pentecostal story is unique among the ecclesiastical patterns of the twenti-eth century and perhaps better fits a narrative account than any generalized, analytical forms of ecclesiology.[61] From the latter perspective, the least we can say is that the emergence of worldwide Pentecostalism has dramatically changed the way denominations are perceived within the movement. The widespread acceptance of denominational language among Pentecostals suggests that the concept does fulfill a particular ecclesiological purpose and is not likely to be removed in the near future. On the other hand, the negative impact of the con-cept on the formal development of a genuine Pentecostal ecclesiology suggests that a theological account of denominations from a Pentecostal perspective faces a number of significant boundaries. These limitations are intimately con-nected with the Pentecostal self-understanding as a movement, which marks the principal characteristic of Pentecostal ecclesiality. From that perspective, the immediate task is much less the conceptual development of a theory of denomi-nations than the integration of the praxis of denominationalism into the various existing ecclesiologies. A number of recommendations for such an endeavor can be extracted from the Pentecostal experience.

On a primary level, the concept of denominations is a *structural* designation. In this sense, it applies to the institutional elements of the church, to use a con-cept of Avery Dulles, and denominations "must ultimately be justified by their capacity to express or strengthen the Church as a community of life, witness, and service, a community that reconciles and unites men in the grace of Christ".[62] The emergence of global Pentecostalism has located this capacity in the corre-spondence of denominational structures to the various socio-cultural contexts of the churches worldwide. Classical Pentecostalism upheld the idea that the indigenous church is a self-governing, self-supporting and self-propagating entity that proclaims an unchanging gospel to all cultures and contexts.[63] The worldwide expansion of Pentecostalism has turned the focus instead to the con-textualization of ecclesiality on the grass-roots level and to an experience of being church that seeks to be relevant and meaningful in a particular context while being fundamentally shaped by its culture. A theological account of denominations must therefore emphasize the importance of a multicultural ecclesiology that seeks its identity not in the church as an abstract and figurative religious system but in the living reality of personal, social, economic and politi-cal relations.

Global Pentecostalism does not propose one particular denominational struc-ture but suggests that ecclesiality is experienced most concretely in a diversity of ecclesial rhythms in which church and culture meet in a mutual movement that shapes the denomination within that particular context. As structural entities connected with the life rhythm of the churches, the ecclesiality of denominations should therefore be defined not only at the institutional level but also in the liturgical realm. Otherwise, denominations risk isolation from local communities and cultures. The tendency to define denominations primarily on a doctrinal level contributes to this isolation and makes denominations appear as no more than bureaucratic shells that need to be filled with the faith and praxis of the churches.

On a secondary level, and as a consequence of the former, the concept of denominations is a *historical* descriptor. This aspect offers an important contribution to the integration of the denominational praxis in the contemporary ecclesiological landscape. In a sense, denominations are the history books of the churches, offering color and depth to the story of the faithful in the diverse situations of global Christianity. On the other hand, the primarily historical orientation of denominational life stands in contrast to the eschatological orientation of the body of Christ. While the Christian community is thoroughly placed in history, the nature and mission of the church is always directed towards the kingdom of God and therefore supersedes the extent of history's jurisdiction on any one particular denomination.[64] The context of history has to be complemented by an eschatological ecclesiology. Perhaps an oversimplification, Pentecostals understand the denominations in this sense as the concretization of the eschatological church in history. This perspective is based on two presuppositions: (1) that denominations are of a transitory, or better, liminal character; and (2) that denominations can function only in particular ecumenical contexts.

1. Transitoriness is primarily a historical or temporal attribute. Denominations are transitory because they represent the churches in history but not the church in eternity. However, this distinction is misleading unless we deny any form of transformation to the denominations and simply hold that they will pass away at the consummation of the kingdom of God. This perspective further consolidates an abstract, disconnected institutional view of denominations, which are seen as mere categories and not reflective of the faith and praxis of the local assemblies. Liminality, on the other hand, can be applied to emphasize not only the transient but also the transformative nature of denominations.[65] Pentecostals have emphasized that denominations can exhibit a liminal character in their critical function towards the established ecclesial culture and its ecclesiastical structures.[66] The individual identifies with the denomination that represents the historical anti-structure acted out in the local assembly.[67] At the same time as the local community

emulates the denominational pattern, the denomination itself tends towards the realization of its own structure in the eschatological church. Denominations therefore stand in tension between both the local assembly and the whole church as the catalysts that pull the historicity of the former into the eschatological realization of the latter.

2. The concept of denominations can function only in particular ecumenical contexts because no single denomination represents the fullness of either the diversity of local assemblies or the eschatological fulfillment of the one church. Put differently, a denomination does not exist in the singular. The denominational landscape is not the result of an expansion of one particular trans-historical origin of the church but of the birth of new communities from within different ecclesial contexts and as a result of particular socio-cultural and historical phenomena. The diversity of local assemblies is thus the soil for denominations, the building of a living church from a multiplicity of grass-roots communities.[68] The challenge of this relationship is that the ecclesial character of the denominations can only be recovered in the ecumenical contexts of the local assemblies that reflect the dynamic of a group or individual rather than the culture of the denomination. From the perspective of these base ecclesiologies, the church might be called "a mosaic within a mosaic", a "bricolage under construction", or an "immense laboratory".[69] Denominations are a partial, visible manifestation of this development.

The movement-ecclesiology proposed by global Pentecostalism locates the ecclesiality of denominations in their liminal and ecumenical character. The immediate focus of these groups must be a movement of the church into the social life and culture of the individual and the family. The goal is not, to use the words of Catholic ecumenist Heribert Mühlen, a new movement in the Church but the Church in movement.[70] This notion of movement is neither synonymous with denominations nor opposed to their reality but points to a transformation of the existing reality. The denominations can thus act as catalysts of the one church in the world and correct any ecclesiocentric perspective of the Christian life (and of contemporary ecclesiology). In turn, this correction might allow Pentecostals to develop their own form(s) of ecclesiology. The result is likely not a systematic, analytical perspective, since this would contradict the structural and historical nature of denominationalism among Pentecostals. Nonetheless, if the reality of denominations can be reconciled with the coherence, unity and mission of the Pentecostal movement worldwide, then Pentecostals might be in a unique position to contribute to the formulation of a number of viable ecclesiologies in the future.

Notes

1 Cf. Robert T. Handy, *A History of the Churches in the United States and Canada* (Oxford: Clarendon, 1976), p. 136–311.

2 Cf. Wolfgang Vondey, "Point de vue pentecôstiste (Dossier à propos du document Nature et Mission de L'"Église)" *Unité des Chrétiens* 149 (January 2008): 23–26; idem, "Pentecostal Perspectives on The Nature and Mission of the Church: Challenges and Opportunities for Ecumenical Transformation", in *"The Nature and Mission of the Church:" Ecclesial Reality and Ecumenical Horizons for the Twenty-First Century*, (eds) Paul M. Collins and Michael A. Fahey, *Ecclesiological Investigations*, 1 (New York: Continuum, 2008): 55–68; idem, "A Pentecostal Perspective on the Nature and Mission of the Church". *Ecumenical Trends*, 35, no. 8 (2006): 1–5.

3 See Vinson Synan, *The Holiness–Pentecostal Movement: Charismatic Movements in the Twentieth Century* (Grand Rapids, MI: Eerdmans, 1997); Frank S. Mead et al. (eds), *Handbook of Denominations in the United States*, 12th edn (Nashville, TN: Abingdon, 2005), chapters 10 and 18; Everett LeRoy Moore, "Handbook of Pentecostal Denominations in the United States", (Master of Arts thesis, Pasadena College, 1954).

4 See, for example, Amos Yong, *The Spirit Poured Out on All Flesh: Pentecostalism and the Possibility of Global Theology* (Grand Rapids, MI: Baker Academic, 2005), pp. 17–30; Wolfgang Vondey, "Pentecostalism and the Possibility of Global Theology: Implications of the Theology of Amos Yong", *Pneuma: Journal of the Society for Pentecostal Studies*, 28, no.2 (2006): 289–312.

5 There is no reference to denominations in standard Pentecostal encyclopedias or dictionaries. The contemporary literature on Pentecostal ecclesiology is small and has not engaged the concept in any substantial fashion. The application of the term "denomination" is debated within a number of churches yet not among the different groups. For an introduction to Pentecostal ecclesiology, see Veli-Matti Kärkkäinen, *An Introduction to Ecclesiology: Ecumenical, Historical & Global Perspectives* (Downers Grove, IL: InterVarsity Press, 2002), pp. 68–78; Simon Chan, "Mother Church: Toward a Pentecostal Ecclesiology", *Pneuma: Journal of the Society for Pentecostal Studies*, 22, no. 2 (2002): 177–208. For a Free Church account see Miroslav Volf, *After Our Likeness: The Church as the Image of the Trinity* (Grand Rapids, MI: Eerdmans, 1998).

6 Peter D. Hocken, "Church, Theology of The", *New International Dictionary of Pentecostal and Charismatic Movements*, (eds) Stanley M. Burgess and Eduard M. Van Der Maas, revised edn (Grand Rapids, MI: Zondervan, 2002), pp. 544–51 (546).

7 For a broad development of this development, see Wolfgang Vondey, *Beyond Pentecostalism: The Crisis of Global Christianity and the Renewal of the Theological Agenda*, Pentecostal Manifestos 3 (Grand Rapids, MI: Eerdmans, 2010).

8 See, for example, *Word and Witness*, 8, no. 6 (20 August 1912): 2; S. D. Kinne, "The Assembly", *The Bridegroom's Messenger*, 1, no. 22 (15 September 1908): 2.

9 Cf. Jay Riley Case, "And Ever the Twain Shall Meet: The Holiness Missionary Movement and the Birth of World Pentecostalism, 1870–1920", *Religion and American Culture*, 16, no. 2 (2006): 125–59; Edith Blumhofer, "Restoration as Revival: Early American Pentecostalism", in *Modern Christian Revivals*, (eds) Edith L. Blumhofer and Randall A. Balmer (Urbana, IL, IL: University of Illinois Press, 1993), pp. 145–61; Grant Wacker, "Playing for Keeps: The Primitivist Impulse in Early

Pentecostalism", in *The American Quest for the Primitive Church*, (ed.) Richard T. Hughes (Urbana, IL: University of Illinois Press, 1988), pp. 196–219.

10 *The Apostolic Faith*, 1, no.1 (September 1906): 2.

11 *Word and Witness*, 8, no. 6 (20 August 1912): 2.

12 For a broader treatment of the ecclesiology of Pentecostals in an ecumenical context, see the essays in Wolfgang Vondey (ed.), *Pentecostalism and Christian Unity: Ecumenical Documents and Critical Assessments* (Eugene, OR: Pickwick, 2010), pp. 3–98.

13 See "One Church", *The Apostolic Faith*, 1, no. 2 (October 1906): 4; A. J. Tomlinson, "The Lord's Church", *The Bridegroom's Messenger*, 2, no. 33 (1 May 1909): 4.

14 Cf. Stanley H. Frodsham, "The Last Commission", *The Weekly Evangel*, 156 (9 September 1916): 6.

15 B. F. Lawrence, "Apostolic Faith Restored, Article I", *The Weekly Evangel*, 121 (1 January 1916): 4.

16 See "Transformed by the Holy Ghost", *The Apostolic Faith*, 1, no. 6 (February–March 1907): 5.

17 See Richard T. Hughes (ed.), *The American Quest for the Primitive Church* (Urbana, IL: University of Chicago Press, 1988), p. 5; Edith L. Blumhofer, "The Christian Catholic Church and the Apostolic Faith: A Study in the 1906 Pentecostal Revival", Paper presented at the Annual Meeting of the Society for Pentecostal Studies, Pasadena, CA, 1982.

18 "Fires Are Being Kindled by the Holy Ghost throughout the World", *The Apostolic Faith*, 2, no. 13 (May 1908): 1. See Wacker, "Playing for Keeps", pp. 199–207.

19 D. Wesley Myland, *The Latter Rain Covenant and Pentecostal Power* (Chicago: Evangel Publishing House, 1910), p. 101. Cf. Donald W. Dayton, *Theological Roots of Pentecostalism* (Peabody, MA: Hendrickson, 1987), pp. 26–28.

20 See Arthur T. Pierson, *Forward Movements of the Last Half Century* (New York: Funk & Wagnalls Co., 1900).

21 B. F. Lawrence, "The Works of God, Article VII", *The Weekly Evangel*, 142 (3 June 1916): 4. See also "Bible Pentecost", *The Apostolic Faith*, 1, no. 3 (October 1906): 1.

22 See W. F. Carothers, "Position of the Old "Movement"," *The Weekly Evangel*, 127 (19 February 1916): 5.

23 Leila M. Conway, "United We Stand, Divided We Fall", *The Weekly Evangel*, no. 185 (14 April 1917): 5.

24 Cf. Lawrence, "Apostolic Faith Restored I", p. 4.

25 Cf. Dale M. Coulter, "The Development of Ecclesiology in the Church of God (Cleveland, TN): A Forgotten Contribution?" *Pneuma: The Journal of the Society for Pentecostal Studies*, 29, no. 1 (2007): 59–85. The early ecclesiology of the Church of God seems to anticipate in a more accelerated fashion the general development among Pentecostals at the beginning of the twentieth century.

26 *The Apostolic Faith*, 1, no.3 (November 1906): 2.

27 Wacker, "Playing for Keeps", pp. 209–10.

28 See "Christ and His Body", *The Pentecostal Evangel*, no.567 (11 October 1924): 5. Cf. Walter J. Hollenweger, *The Pentecostals: The Charismatic Movement in the Churches* (Minneapolis, MN: Augsburg, 1973), pp. 424–29.

29 See R. G. Spurling, *The Lost Link* (Turtletown, TN: n.d., 1920), pp. 12–16; Fred Lohmann, "Ye Shall Receive Power", *The Pentecostal Evangel*, nos. 450–51 (24 June 1922): 2.

30 William M. Faux, "Man Power", *The Pentecostal Evangel*, no. 549 (7 June 1924): 10. See also W. S. Norwood, "The Need of Spiritual Organization", *The Christian Evangel*, 2, no. 13 (28 March 1914): 5–6.

31 Spurling, *The Lost Link*, 8. My emphasis. A contemporary "organic" approach to Pentecostalism can be found in Wolfgang Vondey, "Christian Amnesia: Who in the World Are Pentecostals?" *Asian Journal of Pentecostal Studies*, 4.1 (January 2001): 21–39.

32 Jonathan E. Perkins, "The Quartet that Raised the Roof", *The Pentecostal Evangel*, no. 555 (19 July 1924): 4.

33 "Letter from Bro. Seymour", *The Bridegroom's Messenger*, 1, no. 5 (1 January 1908): 2. See also A. J. Tomlinson, "Oneness", *The Bridegroom's Messenger*, 2, no. 37 (14 May 1909): 2.

34 See Tomlinson, "The Lord's Church", p. 4; A. J. Tomlinson, "Unity of the Faith", *The Bridegroom's Messenger*, 1, no. 11 (1 April 1908): 2; E. A. Saxton, "Organization", *The Bridegroom's Messenger*, 5, no. 103 (1 February 1912): 1. A biblical order of government is often contrasted with the established institutional forms of organization.

35 Steven J. Land, *Pentecostal Spirituality: A Passion for the Kingdom*, JPT Supplement 1 (Sheffield, UK: Sheffield Academic Press, 1993), p.178.

36 Leonardo Boff, *Ecclesiogenesis: The Base Communities Reinvent the Church*, (trans.) Robert R. Barr (Maryknoll, NY: Orbis, 1986), p. 2. The literature on connections between Pentecostalism and Latin American base communities is large. For a brief introduction, see Adoniram Gaxiola, "Poverty as a Meeting and Parting Place: Similarities and Contrast in the Experiences of Latin American Pentecostalism and Ecclesial Base Communities", *Pneuma: The Journal of the Society for Pentecostal Studies*, 13, no. 2 (1991): 167–74.

37 Carothers, "Position of the Old Movement", p. 5. The diverse ways in which this ecclesiology functioned in early North American Pentecostalism remains an important subject of future research.

38 A. S. Copley, "The Seven Dispensational Parables", *The Pentecost*, 1, no. 7 (June 1909): 7.

39 Alberto Melloni, "Movements: On the Significance of Words", in *"Movements" in the Church*, (ed.) Alberto Melloni (London: SCM Press, 2003), pp.7–26.

40 David Lehmann, "Dissidence and Conformism in Religious Movements: What Difference Separates the Catholic Charismatic Renewal and Pentecostal Churches?" in Melloni, *"Movements" in the Church*, pp. 122–38.

41 David G. Roebuck, "Restorationism and a Vision for World Harvest: A Brief History of the Church of God (Cleveland, TN)", *Cyberjournal for Pentecostal-Charismatic Research*, 5 (February 1999), available at http://pctii.org/cyberj/cyberj5/roebuck. html, accessed 10 July 2008.

42 "We Are One", *The Pentecostal Holiness Advocate*, 1, no. 3 (17 May 1917): 8.

43 The name "Church of God" is among the most popular. Cf. Vinson Synan, *The Holiness–Pentecostal Movement in the United States* (Grand Rapids, MI: Eerdmans, 1971), pp.77–93.

44 Cf. Robert Mapes Anderson, *Vision of the Disinherited: The Making of American Pentecostalism* (New York: Oxford University Press, 1979), pp.192–94; Land, *Pentecostal Spirituality*, pp. 178–79.

45 See B. F. Lawrence, "The Works of God, Article IV", *The Weekly Evangel*, 139 (13 May 1916): 5.

46 See J. H. King, "From the General Superintendent", *The Pentecostal Holiness Advocate* (6 September 1917): 10.

47 Cf. D. William Faupel, *The Everlasting Gospel: The Significance of Eschatology in the Development of Pentecostal Thought*, JPT Supplement 10 (Sheffield, UK: Sheffield Academic Press, 1996), pp.77–114.

48 See Anderson, *Vision of the Disinherited*, p. 194.

49 See Veli-Matti Kärkkäinen, " "Anonymous Ecumenists?" Pentecostals and the Struggle for Christian Identity", *Journal of Ecumenical Studies*, 37, no. 1 (2000): 13–27; Jeffrey Gros, "Pentecostal Engagement in the Wider Christian Community", *MidStream*, 38, no. 4 (1999): 26–47; Cecil M. Robeck, Jr., "Pentecostals and the Apostolic Faith: Implications for Ecumenism", *Pneuma: The Journal of the Society for Pentecostal Studies*, 9, no. 1 (1987): 61–84.

50 Cf. Cecil M. Robeck, Jr., "Name and Glory: The Ecumenical Challenge", Paper presented at the Annual Meeting of the Society for Pentecostal Studies, Cleveland, TN (March 1983), pp. 12–19.

51 *The Apostolic Faith*, 1, no.1 (September 1906): 4.

52 Cf. Kärkkäinen, "Anonymous Ecumenists", pp. 15–18.

53 See, for example, *The Apostolic Faith*, 2, no. 13 (May 1908): 1–4.

54 Cf. Allan Anderson, *Spreading Fires: The Missionary Nature of Early Pentecostalism* (London: SCM Press, 2007); Michael Bergunder and Jörg Haustein (eds), *Migration und Identität: Pfingstlich-charismatische Migrationsgemeindedn in Deutschland* (Frankfurt: Lembeck, 2006), pp. 155–69.

55 Allan Anderson, "Spreading Fires: The Globalization of Pentecostalism in the Twentieth Century", *International Bulletin of Missionary Research*, 31, no. 1 (2007): 10.

56 *Word and Work*, 29, no. 4 (April 1907): 117.

57 E. A. Saxton, "Increasing Missionary Activity", *The Bridegroom's Messenger*, 3, no. 69 (1 September 1910): 1; *The Pentecostal Evangel*, no.580 (17 January 1925): 3.

58 See Luther P. Gerlach, "Pentecostalism: Revolution or Counter–Revolution", in *Religious Movements in Contemporary America*, (eds) Irving I. Zaretsky and Mark P. Leone (Princeton, NJ: Princeton University Press, 1974), pp. 669–99; Bryan R.Wilson, "Role Conflict and Status Contradiction of the Pentecostal Minister", *American Journal of Sociology*, 64 (1959): 494–504.

59 Paul D. Lee, "Pneumatological Ecclesiology in the Roman Catholic—Pentecostal Dialogue: A Catholic Reading of the Third Quinquennium (1985–1989)", Ph.D. dissertation, Pontificia Studiorum Universitas a S. Thoma Aq. in Urbe, 1994, p. 15.

60 See Susie C. Stanley, "Wesleyan/Holiness Churches: Innocent Bystanders in the Fundamentalist/Modernist Controversy", in *Re-forming the Center: American Protestantism, 1900 to the Present*, (eds) Douglas Jacobsen and William Vance Trollinger, Jr. (Grand Rapids, MI: Eerdmans, 1998), pp. 172–93.

61 Cf. Roger Haight, *Christian Community in History*, vol. 2, *Comparative Ecclesiology* (New York: Continuum, 2005), pp. 453–54.

62 Avery Dulles, *Models of the Church*, expanded edn (New York: Doubleday, 2002), pp. 37–38.

63 See, for example, the influential works by Melvin L. Hodges, *The Indigenous Church* (Springfield, MO: Gospel Publishing House, 1976); *A Theology of the Church and Its Mission: A Pentecostal Perspective* (Springfield, MO: Gospel Publishing House, 1977); *The Indigenous Church and the Missionary: A Sequel to the Indigenous Church* (Springfield, MO: Gospel Publishing House, 1978).

64 See Vondey, "Pentecostal Perspectives on "The Nature and Mission of the Church"," p. 4.

65 The concept was originally developed in the context of ritual studies by Victor Turner, *The Ritual Process: Structure and Anti-Structure* (Chicago: Aldine, 1969).

66 For an application to Pentecostalism, see Daniel E. Albrecht, *Rites in the Spirit: A Ritual Approach to Pentecostal/Charismatic Spirituality*, JPT Supplement 17 (Sheffield, UK: Sheffield Academic Press, 1999); Bobby C. Alexander, *Victor Turner Revisited: Ritual as Social Change*, AAR Academy Series 74 (Atlanta, GA: Scholars Press, 1991).

67 Bobby C. Alexander, "Pentecostal Ritual Reconsidered: Anti-Structural Dimensions of Possession", *Journal of Ritual Studies*, 3, no. 1 (1989): 109–28; Jon Michael Spencer, "Isochronisms of Antistructure in the Black Holiness-Pentecostal Testimony Service", *Journal of Black Sacred Music*, 2 (Fall 1988): 1–18; John Wilson and Harvey K. Clow, "Themes of Power and Control in a Pentecostal Assembly", *Journal for the Scientific Study of Religion*, 20, no. 3 (1981): 241–50.

68 See the connections made earlier with Boff, *Ecclesiogenesis*, pp. 1–9 [see note 36].

69 Cf. Jean-Pierre Bastian, *Le protestantisme en Amérique Latine: Une approche socio-historique*, Histoire et société 27 (Geneva: Labor et Fides, 1994), pp. 257–70; Manuel J. Gaxiola–Gaxiola, "Latin American Pentecostalism: A Mosaic within a Mosaic", *Pneuma: The Journal of the Society for Pentecostal Studies*, 13, no. 2 (1991): 107–29.

70 Heribert Mühlen, "Kirche in Bewegung—keine neue Bewegung in der Kirche", *Erneuerung in Kirche und Gesellschaft*, 2 (1977): 22–25. See Wolfgang Vondey, *Heribert Mühlen: His Theology and Praxis. A New Profile of the Church* (Lanham, MD: University of America Press, 2004), p. 157.

Chapter 8

DENOMINATION BEYOND THE NORTH ATLANTIC ECCLESIAL WORLD

ANN K. RIGGS

Final-examination questions in African church history arrived at the end of a recent term at Friends Theological College in Western Kenya. Exams for one course of study offered at our small Quaker theological college are set at the ecumenical St. Paul's University, Limuru, and distributed to us and the nine other colleges across Kenya and into Uganda and Sudan that are affiliated with the shared program. One question began: "When did your denomination become independent of the missionary society?"

A Kenyan colleague pointed to the query and remarked that Kenyan Friends (Quakers) are not yet an independent denomination. I, a North American missionary in Kenya, recalled that the General Board of Friends United Meeting (FUM), the transnational ecclesial body to which both my Kenyan colleague and I belong, had determined some months before that it does not understand FUM to be a denomination.[1] Rather, the General Board of FUM names—"denominates"—itself as an association of yearly meetings, that is, an association of numerically smaller and geographically less-extensive bodies. These yearly meetings claim to be heirs of a single, but variegated, Quaker doctrinal heritage and partner with one another in a shared history of ministries and missions. By this, the General Board meant to indicate that the intertwined elements of doctrine, church order and ethics, what Friends call "faith and practice", are the proper concern of the yearly meetings. Yearly meetings might choose to disassociate themselves from one another based on differences in doctrine, church order and ethics. But the yearly meetings have no authority over one another in these matters, either in articulating teachings or in carrying out church order and life.[2] Although my thought was more connected with the current ecumenical discussion of denomination, the examination question and my colleague's response to it may offer more insight into the ecclesiological and broader theological import of "denomination".

As the framer of the examination query rightly understood, a historical connection with the realities referred to by the term "denomination" was and continues to be determinative of the history and present life of many Christian communities in areas that formerly were civil and ecclesial colonies, however the Christian bodies involved may describe themselves. Consideration of these historical realities sheds theological light on the meaning of denomination in North America and elsewhere and directs our attention to multiple philosophical–theological dimensions and social–scientific actualities of effective, independent "agency" in relation to "denomination".

In this essay, I will reflect upon agency in relation to denomination, moving through a consideration of the beginnings of the Friends Mission and the Friends Church in Kenya, the independence of the Kenyan Friends Church from the missions, and concluding reflections on effective, independent "agency" in connection with "denomination". In considering the beginnings of the Friends Mission in Kenya, I will focus particularly on agency directed outward, towards secular government and the wider society. In considering the emerging independence of Kenyan Friends, I will focus on inward ecclesial matters of doctrine, order and ethics, both articulated and lived.

My reflections will be oriented towards an ecumenical theological understanding of "denomination". The term "agency" is used in the fields of religious studies and theology in relation to two approaches: first, sociology and social science; and second, philosophy and philosophical theology. In Eastern Africa and among Friends, one ecclesial location beyond the North Atlantic world, an observable longing for a "denomination" of their own on the part of some Kenyan Friends suggests that an adequate theological understanding of denomination requires a simultaneous consideration of it in relation to both philosophical– theological and social–scientific understandings of "agency".

The Beginnings and Development of the
Friends Mission and the Friends Church in Kenya

Establishment of the Mission

As with many churches in Eastern Africa, the beginnings of the Quaker mission to establish a "self-supporting, self-propagating native church"[3] in Kenya are tied to the British Empire. The impulse towards an African mission was rooted in personal and communal Friends' faith experiences in the late nineteenth and early twentieth centuries in the midwestern region of the United States.[4] But the establishment of the mission compound at Kaimosi in 1902 required the purchase of 850 acres of land from the colonial administration, and on-going relationship with the colonial offices and colonial realities.[5]

In 1904, a *Mzung*, (a person of European descent) who was visiting the mission was killed in a conflict between the Nandi, a local tribe hostile to European/Euro-American presence, and the colonial police. In subsequent months colonial armed forces occupied the mission. Transfer of a mission site in nearby Vihiga that Friends had purchased from the Church of England required government approval. When the Quaker mission sought to convey equipment for a saw mill being constructed at Kaimosi, government officials loaned government workers to Friends to build a public road from the closest railway station to the mission.[6] More than a century later, portions of that road continue to serve as one of the major transportation routes in Western Kenya. In later years, an early Kaimosi missionary wrote to the Commissioner for Local Government Lands and Settlement of the area: "I taught the first Lumbwa to plow. Today they are self-supporting, selling thousands of tons of maize. Gov't is collecting many thousands of Pounds annually in taxes, none of which could have been collected had the Lumbwa remained in the state in which I found them".[7] At the same time, it was the District Commissioner, rather than other missionaries in the area, who provided early Quaker translators with the foundational resources to translate the Bible into Luragoli, a local vernacular.[8] Missions analyst Ron Stansell speculates that the colonial government's prohibition of a new Friends mission station in Malava, north of Kaimosi, between 1915 and 1919 may have allowed a more culturally sensitive form of evangelization to have emerged during that period.[9]

Mission and church in later ecumenical and secular relationships

In later years, relations between the missions and the colonial government were often carried out ecumenically. By the early 1950s, provision for education in Kenya was developing through a missions–government partnership. A Catholic bishop, the Christian Council of Kenya (CCK) (in which Friends participated), and government officials conferred to enhance needed services. Fred Reeve, a Quaker missionary educator from 1954–1963, describes their meetings as "usually conducted in a most affable manner, both government and missions recognizing that each would be ineffective without the other".[10] The missions and related churches provided buildings and general management, and maintained academic standards. The government provided monthly aid to the schools for teachers' salaries and other modest financial support to schools of sufficient size and elaboration to qualify. Student tuition fees covered other school expenses.[11] The CCK had sufficient status and capacity as a collaborator to effectively challenge and transform colonial educational policy to greatly expand the opportunities for less-gifted students.[12]

While many aspects of Kenyan education have changed over subsequent decades, the religious–secular partnership continues to the present day. The CCK has developed into the National Council of Churches of Kenya (NCCK).[13] Whereas the former body was an organization of Protestant missions, the current body is a council of independent Protestant and Orthodox churches. NCCK, along with the Anglican Church of Kenya, the Presbyterian Church of East Africa, the Methodist Church of Kenya and the Reformed Church of East Africa operate the Diploma in Theology program at St. Paul's in which the examination question, "When did your denomination become independent of the missionary society?" was posed.[14]

Through the NCCK, in addition to other ecumenical activities, member churches continue to speak to the Kenyan government. On 8 September 2010 the National Council of Churches of Kenya Coast Regional Committee released a characteristic press statement titled, "Embrace Justice and Equity",[15] in which the committee articulates its mandate for addressing the government and all Kenyan society in biblical terms:

> **Our Role in the Society**
>
> In our reflections, we considered the words recorded in Jeremiah 29:5–7, from which we learn that as Christians, we have a mandate to seek and pray for the prosperity of our nation. Our prayers are also offered for our counties, constituencies and villages, for we know that when they prosper, we too shall prosper. Our primary guide in this is Deuteronomy 16:20 *"Follow justice and justice alone, so that you may live and possess the land the Lord your God is giving you"*.
>
> Holding this commitment to the wellbeing of our region in particular and the nation in general, we wish to share the following message.[16]

Other bodies such as the Catholic bishops" Kenya Episcopal Conference,[17] Organization of African Instituted Churches,[18] individual churches,[19] or bodies within or related to churches[20] may likewise address government and society on issues of Christian social concern.

In the colonial context both missions and emerging churches were clearly dependent on an implied notion of "denomination". It is because British colonial officials recognized specific groups as carrying different, but legitimate, Christian "names" that they were given access to land and other resources to carry out the desired missions.

In the present context Kenyan churches, Christian bodies and ecumenical entities seek to continue speaking to and with government and society. In light of our consideration of the term "denomination" beyond the North Atlantic context, there are intriguing differences in the usage of the term among these bodies. The NCCK describes itself as made up of member "Churches and Christian bodies".[21] The Organization of African Instituted Churches (OAIC) describes itself as "an association of African Independent, Instituted or African founded Churches (AICs)" that "brings together over 1000 denominations with total membership over 15 million across the [African] continent".[22] Certainly, the absence of the term "denomination" in the NCCK constitution reflects the presence within the council of Orthodox Churches, who reject the application of the term to themselves. Nevertheless, the appearance of the term within OAIC usage, the examination question regarding the processes of becoming independent of originating mission societies, and the response to the term by my African colleague prompt the suggestion that within the East African context "denomination" has, through some historical process, come to be associated with "independence".

In 1963, Kenya became an independent nation state. Friend Thomas Lung'aho was then chairman of the CCK. He addressed the people of the new nation:

> The Christian Council of Kenya, in the name of all of its churches and missions and other Christian organizations within its membership, takes this opportunity of sending its greetings to all the people of Kenya on the occasion of their independence. . . . As Christians we have a deep concern for the establishing of basic human rights, the administration of justice, the security of the home and family and for all that concerns the life more abundant. We rejoice in the provision made in our constitution for these basic human rights". [23]

Many Kenyan Friends today would strongly affirm the importance of clear provision by the secular government for human rights, including the right of religious freedom for all religious actors. At the same time, some are highly distrustful of secular governmental processes, no doubt due at least in part to the terrifying violence that followed the 2007 elections and the government's struggle to maintain safety and orderly public life. The new constitution, affirmed in August 2010 in a general referendum, was widely opposed by Christian leaders through ecumenical organizations and by individual churches and church leaders. In addition to general questions about the quality of the new constitution and the wisdom of various specific structural provisions, church leaders feared that the legalization of abortion to save the life of the mother could lead to more indiscriminate use of the procedure. Many considered that a provision for broadening the availability of courts providing judgments under Sharia law for Muslim citizens living outside the ancient Muslim settlement area along the Indian Ocean coast gave special favors to the Muslim community that were not offered to other religious communities.

Clearly, the easy recognition and working relationship between the missions and the colonial government had already been replaced by a more secular social approach by the time Kenya had gained national independence. It may be that the wistful desire to be a denomination is in some cases more connected to a memory of connectivity between the missions and the colonial administration than it is with any status of effective agency on the part of the Christian churches that could be realized in the current, more secular context.

The Ecclesial Independence of Kenyan Friends

The creation of East Africa Yearly Meeting, 1946

The original intention of the Friends Africa Industrial Mission (later Friends Africa Mission) was that all its diverse activities in evangelism, medical services, education, translation and industry be ordered towards the development of a "self-supporting, self-propagating native church".[24] The mission was thus located within a well-established nineteenth-century tradition of theory and policy for African missions. There was wide agreement among Protestant, Catholic European and North American missions that the aim was to build up the churches, and not only the salvation of individuals. "Africa must be converted by Africans" was a widely used missionary axiom. In the 1840s, the Holy Ghost Fathers oriented their efforts towards the "training of an African clergy and the establishment of a hierarchy, running dioceses of the universal church".[25] In the subsequent decade Anglican Henry Venn, Secretary of the Church Missionary Society, developed a mission policy aimed at developing a native ministry with a native episcopate in a self-supporting, self-governing, self-extending church.[26]

The Friends' mission was designed to quickly prepare and employ African evangelists.[27] Promising young converts were informally trained for independent outreach ministries by accompanying missionaries on visits to villages that were distant from the mission compounds. The mission's earliest schools were intended in particular to provide for the educational needs of the evangelists and emerging native church leaders.[28] Translation and publication of a Luragoli-language version of the Bible was a collaborative effort between missionaries Deborah Rees, Emory Rees, and Jefferson Ford and local Friends Ahonya, Amagune, and Joeli Litu.[29] It became a core ministry resource.

During the mid-1920s, as early missionaries began to retire after long African service, they felt that African leaders were prepared for greater responsibilities in the Friends Church. Friends Theological College is the product of hopes that first began to be formed at that time for an institution for ministerial education.[30] In 1931, the Friends Africa Mission asked the Mission Board in the United States for information on a process for the development of an African yearly meeting. The requests were reiterated several years later, prior to the meetings in 1935 and 1940 of North American Quakers in the Five Years Meeting (predecessor to Friends United Meeting). Finally, in 1945, the Mission Board brought to the 1945 Five Years Meeting a recommendation that a yearly meeting be established in Kenya. Four North American Friends were appointed to be present on the occasion, 17–18 November 1946, of whom two were in the event unable to participate due to family needs.

After a Sabbath Day of worship and spiritual preparation the formal creation of the new yearly meeting was carried out on 18 November. Levinus Painter read an opening "minute" (i.e. a formal ecclesial action):

> As an appointed representative of the Five Years Meeting of Friends in America it becomes my privilege to declare East Africa Yearly meeting of Friends assembled in its first annual session. You are authorized to organize a yearly meeting, to act as a corporate Christian body, to set up departments of religious work, to establish your own Christian ministry and to carry on evangelistic, educational and missionary service as a yearly meeting. You will continue with renewed energy the training religious and educational leaders. For some years you may feel the need of understanding assistance from Friends in America. But increasingly you will depend upon your own resources, always humbly seeking divine guidance. . . . We pray God's richest blessing upon you. May you grow in grace and in the knowledge of our Lord and Savior, Jesus Christ.[31]

The meeting continued with the designation and seating of six yearly meeting officers, one each from six different sub-tribes. A book of "discipline" (i.e. church order), prepared by a group of North Americans, was presented, treated as a draft, and revised. A final draft was accepted by the assembly and enacted.[32]

The yearly meeting and the mission worked together at times and at others parallel to one another from 1946 to 1963. In October 1963, weeks before the independence of Kenya colony, administrative responsibilities of the mission were transferred to the yearly meeting. The following February, the property of the mission was transferred to East Africa Yearly Meeting (EAYM). A missionary of the time reflected that "East Africa Yearly Meeting has become an adult member in the world family of Friends, still in need of opportunity to consult with other members of the family, yet at the same time exhibiting a healthy measure of independence".[33] From time to time in the subsequent decades EAYM–Kaimosi and other former mission sites requested assistance from FUM and missionaries with specific expertise were sent in response. As an example, the yearly meeting asked assistance in the administration and on-going development of the theological college in the mid-1990s. Since that time the principal (or president in US usage) of the college has been a North American and a stream of volunteer faculty members and consultants have contributed to operating and building the college.

From a single East Africa Yearly Meeting to eighteen East African Yearly Meetings

From the inception of East Africa Yearly Meeting (now often referred to within Kenya as EAYM–Kaimosi or Kaimosi Yearly Meeting) sub-tribal awareness was an evident matter of unease. There had been friction among some of the sub-tribal groups within the new yearly meeting for such a long time that it had come to be considered traditional. Others were perhaps more simply culturally and physically distant from one another. As the Friends community in Kenya has continued to expand the diversity has grown. African Church Historian John Baur has noted that the Luhya tribe, to which still the overwhelming majority of Kenyan Friends belong, and the nearby Luo tribe, both traditionally organized in sub-tribal units, have the highest frequency of independent African churches in Eastern Africa.[34]

Kenyan Friends profess to have no doctrinal differences among themselves. It must be taken at face value that Kenyan Friends have no doctrinal differences that they perceive to be a barrier to unity among themselves. Many of the yearly meetings in Eastern Africa make use of the common body of doctrine, church order, and ethics found in Friends United Meeting in East Africa, *Christian Faith and Practice in the Friends Church*, 2002. Others prepare and utilize their own *Faith and Practice* articulations, as do the FUM yearly meetings in the United States.

Attentive observation and listening do reveal substantive theological diversity rooted at least in part in variations in theological perspectives among the original missionaries. Kenyan Friends, as Friends elsewhere, place emphasis in both doctrine and spirituality on personal and social holiness. Friends' widely familiar work in race relations and gender equality, and Quaker status as one of the Historic Peace Churches are all expressions of Quaker understandings of holiness.

The group of three missionaries who first arrived at Kaimosi had met one another in the circles of the Cleveland Bible Institute. However, the theological perspectives of the three men appear to have differed in nuance from one another and in some cases more strongly from the theological perspective of Five Years Meeting (later the FUM) and missionaries who arrived in subsequent years.[35] Arthur Chilson's theology and spirituality appear to have been best characterized as a Holiness form of charismatic/pentecostal Quakerism. He professed faith in a definitive second work of grace—sanctification by the in-filling of the Holy Spirit. But while the three branches of the Pentecostal African Church of the Holy Spirit claim Chilson as their founder, there appears to be no evidence that he held Pentecostal doctrinal views.[36]

In the 1920s, Chilson, his wife and children lived at the new mission station at Malava. In 2010, the Holiness doctrine of sanctification by the in-filling of the Holy Spirit is still a distinctive doctrine of Malava Yearly Meeting. And charismatic/pentecostal spirituality is more common and widely approved among Friends in Malave Yearly Meeting than in other areas within the Kenyan Friends community.[37]

On a variety of commonly recognized indicators and evaluation systems Kenyan society appears to be one of the most corrupt in the world.[38] Administration in churches and church-related institutions and ministries involves a constant struggle to protect the organization from damage from widespread corruption. Opportunities to participate are frequently offered, and the temptations must be great for those without ready access to the luxuries of Western resources. Some separations among the Kenyan yearly meetings may well be rooted in differences concerning Christian ethics, that is, in tolerance for corruption within meeting leadership and administration.

Aspirations for greater unity among Kenyan Friends

Whether the continuing fragmentation of Kenyan yearly meetings is to be connected more with cultural and sub-tribal social impulses or theological differences in spirituality, doctrine and ethics is not readily obvious.[39] In any case, there is a simultaneous centripetal force in Kenyan Quakerism. Ministries of Friends United Meeting, including Friends Theological College, nurture cohesion among the yearly meetings and support opportunities for collaboration. Friends Church Kenya, a national organization of the yearly meetings in Kenya, focuses its attention on needs and activities which ought rightly to be carried out by Kenyan Friends for themselves, without extensive undergirding by the international Quaker community. The context of these unity-seeking ecclesial impulses is one location in which an aspiration to be a denomination arises.

Denomination and Agency

How, then, might the Kenyan Yearly Meetings become a denomination? What would need to happen to effect such development?

There are three ecclesial forms Kenyan Friends might utilize. Kenyan Friends might become once again a single yearly meeting. In Friends' understanding such a body would have agency to articulate doctrine and church order and act within secular society—act ecclesially and legally—on its own behalf as seemed faithful and wise. It could choose to define itself as a denomination, could relate to other Christian bodies self-identifying as denominations, and could address secular society and government with that self-given name.

Or the many Kenyan yearly meetings could join together to create a body to which each agrees to subordinate itself in some matters of faith and practice and/or in some matters of civil social life. Five Years Meeting (and Friends United Meeting in its years) was such a form of super-ordinate meeting: a hierarchy of meetings as might be contrasted with a hierarchy of persons.

Or some or all Kenyan yearly meetings might determine that a particular yearly meeting is itself a "denomination".

Each path towards "denomination" requires appropriate agency to be effected. A brief consideration of the terminology of agency as it is used in social science and in philosophical theology will be helpful.

"Agency" in social science usage

In sociology and other social sciences the term "agency" is used to refer to capacity for free action available to individuals within a social context. Agency is contrasted with "structure(s)" which delimit the space of action for individuals. In Western social analysis, structures that impinge upon human freedom have for several decades often been discussed in terms of gender, race, and class.

Thoughtful analysts in the West have come to see this as a limited and culturally bounded list of structural terms. In many social contexts religion creates agency-limiting social structural constraints both overt and covert. By law one cannot be King or Queen of England if one is Catholic or married to a Catholic (overt structural limits). In the United States, one may be elected governor of Louisiana if one is South Asian, but it is unlikely that Governor Jindal could have been elected if he had remained Hindu rather than becoming a Catholic Christian (covert structural limits).

In early twentieth-century Western Kenya colonial structures limited individual freedoms in ways that might impinge on ecclesial activities, with North America missionaries having certain freedoms (agency) that might not be available to indigenous church leaders. In the early twenty-first century North American missionaries might have fewer freedoms (agency) than indigenous church leaders, either overtly or covertly.

Some such freedoms (agency) might be matters of law, while others might lie within more elusive social processes. The formation of a denomination requires certain forms of agency: individuals must have the social freedom to carry out necessary social activities. We have seen, above, in reference to the Organization of African Instituted Churches that the legal freedoms and agency of the post-colonial era have expressed themselves in the creation of a large number of African instituted denominations.

Yet, for many ecclesial bodies, the sociological agency of individuals comprises only one form of needed agency. Let us return to the decision of the Friends Untied Meeting General Board that FUM is not a denomination. The Board determined that General Board meant to indicate that doctrine, church order, and ethics, what Friends call "faith and practice", are the proper concern of the yearly meetings. In this understanding, for the ecclesial body to be a denomination, the body would need to be able to determine doctrine, church order, and ethics and carry out or oversee the carrying out of all necessary ecclesial actions: they would need to have ecclesial agency with regard to doctrine, church order, and ethics.

Is this a matter of agency in the sociological sense? In the case of the Religious Society of Friends it is not. Among Friends, a "meeting for church affairs" or a "meeting for worship with attention to business" is not a collection of individuals, each enjoying greater or lesser degrees of sociologically defined agency, in action on any matters to which they wish to address themselves.

"Agency" in philosophical–theological usage

In philosophy and philosophical theology an agent, an entity with agency, may or may not be an individual human person. For instance, in Marxist philosophical perspective human "agency" is the collective agency of human beings acting in concert. In philosophy and philosophical theology even non-existent persons or entities may be ascribed agency. It is possible in this usage to speak of the agency of the Holy Spirit or of a demon in taking possession of a human being (demonic possession), even if one does not personally believe in the Holy Spirit or in demons.

To speak of the agency of the Holy Spirit and demonic possession points towards conceptual and philosophical notions of power and authority in relation to agency. In some civil and ecclesiastical thought the terms power and authority are understood as relating to differing dimensions of agency.

Reference to the ordination rites of the Episcopal Church may offer a helpful example. In the Preface to the Ordination Rites we learn that "No persons are allowed to exercise the office of bishop, priest, or deacon in this Church unless" they are ordained "by solemn prayer and the laying on of episcopal hands".[40] During the service of the ordination of a priest the bishop lays hands on the head of the ordinand and at the same time prays: "Therefore, Father, through Jesus Christ your Son, give your Holy Spirit to N.; fill [him or her] with grace and power, and make [him or her] a priest in your Church . . . ." After additional intervening prayers and actions, the bishop gives a Bible to the newly ordained and speaks to her or him: "Receive this Bible as a sign of the authority given you to preach the Word of God and to administer his holy Sacraments. Do not forget the trust committed to you as a priest of the Church of God".[41] Note that the power referenced comes from the Holy Spirit; it is not humanly delegated. This consecration of the ordinand follows a dialogue of willingness and commitment, called the "Examination".[42] The ordinand is asked repeatedly to commitment herself or himself to the responsibilities of the priesthood, by answering "I do" or "I will" to such questions as "Will you endeavor so to minister the Word of God and the sacraments of the New Covenant, the reconciling love of Christ may be known and received?" Yet, it is not the ordinand's commitment that gives power and authority. "May the Lord who has given you the will to do these things give you the grace and power to perform them" prays the bishop.[43] Ordination to the priesthood is understood by the believers of this church to be "theandric"—involving both human and divine agency.

In classical Friends' understanding a "meeting for church affairs" is likewise theandric. Further, the human dimension of the "meeting" as it involves itself in solemn decision making is corporate rather than individual. The language of a seventeenth-century admonition is still normative in many yearly meetings and speaks of a shared aspiration among twenty-first century Friends:

> in the holy Spirit of truth and righteousness, all things [are] to be carried on; by hearing, and determining every matter coming before you, in love, coolness, gentleness and dear unity;—I say, as one only party, all for the truth of Christ, and for the carrying on of the work of the lord, and assisting one another in whatsoever ability God hath given; and to determine things by a general mutual concord, in assenting together as one man [person] in the spirit of truth and equity, and by authority thereof.[44]

Philosophical/theological usage is an important resource for ecumenical discussion of agency in connection with "denomination". To be a "denomination", a body requires not only the authority necessary to make certain ecclesial decisions and carry out certain ecclesial actions; it needs also the power to do so, whatever the source of such is understood to be.

Agency and denomination in the post-colonial era

In post-colonial Africa, power and authority are for obvious reasons highly charged matters. As we noted above denomination is the term with which the member bodies of the Organization of African Instituted Churches refer to themselves. Both that fact and the examination question from the ecumenical university St Paul's, Limuru with which we initiated our discussion that began, "When did your denomination become independent of the missionary society?", point towards an important dimension of agency in relation to "denomination". In post-colonial Africa to be a denomination is to declare both sociological and philosophical–theological ecclesial agency relative to others.

In the contemporary North Atlantic ecumenical milieu it is not uncommon in some ecclesial locations to use the term "denomination" as a way to acknowledge that other ecclesial bodies may also possess ecclesial validity. In other ecclesial locations one frequently hears that denominations are becoming less and less significant. Perhaps humanly political dimensions of the denomination construct, so overt in Eastern Africa, may be at work in other regions of the world, as well, in more covert or nuanced ways. Might the self-designation of denomination at times be used by those who believe themselves to be culturally dominant as a form of gracious concession to others, a kind of noblesse oblige? Might a decline of the importance of denomination(s) among some suggest that the group feels less need to claim this form of social prestige?

* * *

In this essay we have reviewed the establishment of a Friends mission in colonial East Africa, the ecclesial independence of East Africa Yearly Meeting, and the subsequent establishment of multiple yearly meetings in Eastern Africa, within the context of the political independence of Kenya as a nation state. We have observed the importance of denomination within the history of colonialism in East Africa and its significance as a vehicle for laying claim to social and ecclesial validity in the post-colonial context.

We have noted the implied Quaker understanding of denomination as a body with the ecclesial agency needed to articulate and carry out all necessary tasks of the intertwined elements of doctrine, church order, and ethics. We have observed one Quaker body, Friends United Meeting, reject denomination as a designation of itself, locating ecclesial agency elsewhere within the ecclesial body. We have remarked on the aspiration of some African Friends for social status and ecclesial agency associated by some with denomination.

We have explored the fact that apprehension of the self-understood agency of a particular "denomination" or other ecclesial body may require both sociological and philosophical–theological insights. Within a particular ecclesial self-understanding the agency of churchly bodies may be believed to be communal, theandric, or both, rather than based solely or primarily in the personal sociologically defined agency of the individuals within that body.

For the author, the tri-dimensional intersection of sociologically defined agency, other forms of ecclesial agency, and use of the term "denomination" and the particular history of Friends in Eastern Africa point towards matters within the ecumenical study of the church for further study: What is the import for ecclesiology more broadly of the fact that diverse cultural and social contexts impact the apprehension and development of key ecclesiological concepts and elements, as the current significance of denomination in Africa has clearly been shaped by changing contexts of the colonial and post-colonial periods? In the present study there have been intimations that in ecclesial self-denomination, self-naming the Christian church and the Gospel do not so much enter into existing African culture as shape and transform African cultural experience. What implications or lessons might this have for all as we seek to relate in Christian fellowship beyond the North Atlantic ecclesial world?

Notes

1   "We are an international association of Friends Meetings and Churches, organized for evangelism, global partnership, leadership development and communications. Our purpose is 'to energize and equip Friends through the power of the Holy Spirit to gather people into fellowships where Jesus Christ is known, loved and obeyed as Teacher and Lord'." Friends United Meeting homepage, www.fum.org/about/index.html.

2   Friends United Meeting General Board, Unpublished Minutes, September 2009, Richmond, IN.

3   Walter R. Hotchkiss, *Sketches From the Dark Continent* (Cleveland, OH: The Friends Bible Institute and Training School, 1901), p. 147, quoted in Ron Stansell, *Missions by the Spirit; Learning from Quaker Examples* (Newberg, OR: Barclay Press, 2009), p. 27.

4   Christina H. Jones, *American Friends in World Missions* (Elgin, IL: Brethren Publishing House for the American Friends Board of Missions, Richmond, IN, 1946) pp. 183–208 (186–188); Levinus King Painter, *The Hill of Vision; The Story of the Quaker Movement in East Africa 1902–1965* (Nairobi, Kenya: The English Press, 1966) pp. 18–21; Burnette C. Fish and Gerald W. Fish, *The Place of Songs; A History of the World Gospel Mission and the Africa Gospel Church in Kenya* (Nakuru, Kenya: World Gospel Mission, and Kericho, Kenya: Africa Gospel Church, 1989) pp. 22–36 (22–23); Stansell, pp. 13–63 (15–19).

5 Fish and Fish, p. 24; an additional 150 acres were acquired by leasehold, see Painter, p. 23.
6 Painter, pp. 29–30.
7 Fish, p. 31.
8 Painter, p. 43. The more widely used Swahili is itself a foreign language in the area emanating from the coastal regions inland.
9 Stansell, pp. 54–4.
10 Fred Reeve, "Education for a New Day", in Painter, pp. 116–30 (118).
11 Reeve, pp. 116–30.
12 Reeve, p. 119.
13 www.ncck.org; accessed 12 September 2010.
14 www.stpaulslimuru.ac.ke/index.php?Cat_Id=history; accessed 12 September 2010
15 www.ncck.org/index.php?option=com_content&view=article&id=186:coastregion al&catid=43:news&Itemid=29; accessed 12 September 2010.
16 Ibid.
17 www.kec.or.ke; accessed 12 September 2010.
18 www.oaic.org; accessed 12 September 2010; see especially the "Stand Up Campaign for a Just Community" at www.oaic.org/images/stories/pdf/oaic%20just%20communi- ties-mdg%20workshop%202010.pdf, and the "Concept Paper for Just Communi- ties" at www.oaic.org/images/stories/pdf/just%20communities%20concept%20 paper%20.pdf.
19 E.g. "Pastoral Letter From Friends Church (Quakers), Kenya", 8 January 2008, www.kffriends.org/Kenya-Friends.htm; accessed 12 September 2010.
20 E.g. the Jesuit Hakimani Center, Nairobi, www.jesuithakimani.org; accessed 12 Sep- tember 2010 and the American Friends Service Committee Africa Regional Office, Nairobi, http://afsc.org/region/africa; accessed 12 September 2010.
21 National Council of Churches of Kenya, "Constitution and By-Laws; Ammended in August 2008", at www.ncck.org/index.php?option=com_content&view=category& layout=blog&id=93&Itemid=109; accessed 12 September 2010.
22 Stand Up Campaign for a Just Community, www.oaic.org/images/stories/pdf/ oaic%20just%20communities-mdg%20workshop%202010.pdf.
23 *Harambee na Makanisa*, CCK Uhuru Souvenir, 1963, quoted in Painter, pp. 99f.
24 Walter R. Hotchkiss, *Sketches From the Dark Continent*, p. 147, quoted in Ron Stansell, *Missions by the Spirit; Learning from Quaker Examples*, p. 27.
25 John Baur, *2000 Years of Christianity in Africa; An African Church History*, 2nd revised. edn, (Nairobi, Kenya: Paulines Publications Africa, 1998) p. 108.
26 Ibid.
27 Hotchkiss, p. 153, quoted in Fish, p. 25.
28 Jones, pp. 199–205; Painter, pp. 50–63.
29 Jones, pp. 199–201; Painter, pp. 43–9.
30 Painter, pp. 65, 70, pp. 111–15.
31 Reprinted in Painter, pp. 68–9.
32 Ibid., pp. 68–9.
33 Harold Smuck, observations published in Painter, pp. 132–34 (134).
34 Baur, p. 495.
35 Stansell, pp. 13–63 (40f., 62). Cf. "Sin and Salvation", "Spiritual Maturity", and "Justification and Sanctification", Appendix A: *Richmond Declaration of Faith*, in Friends United Meeting in East Africa, *Christian Faith and Practice in the Friends Church* (Kaimosi?: Friends United Meeting in East Africa, 2002) pp. 1, 3f., 31f.

36 Stansell, pp. 16, 33, 39–41, 59–63, drawing on Edna H. Chilson, *Ambassador of the King* (Wichita, KS: Edna H. Chilson, 1943), Arthur Chislon, unpublished personal diary, 1902–1904, in the possession of Anne Choate Fuqua, Witicha, KS; Edna Chilson, unpublished personal diary, 1814–1920, in possession of Anne Choate Fuqua, Witicha, KS; Ane Marie Bak Rasmussen, *A History of the Quaker Movement in Africa* (London: British Academic Press, 1995).

37 Francis Kutima, Malava Yearly Meeting pastor, personal interview with the author, 13 September 2010 and personal observation.

38 E.g., analyses and reports by Transparency International, www.transparency.org/publications/gcr; Global Integrity Institute, http://commons.globalintegrity.org/2008/09/users-guide-to-measuring-corruption.html; United Nations Development Program partner organizations Open Society Institute, www.afrimap.org; and International Bar Association Human Rights Institute and International Legal Assistance Consortium Kenya Report, www.afrimap.org/english/images/documents/IBA-HRI-kenya_report_feb_2010.pdf.

39 For an account of some of the earlier separations and attempts to restore a single yearly meeting in Eastern Africa, see Harold Smuck, *Friends in East Africa* (Richmond, IN: Friends United Press, 1987).

40 *The Book of Common Prayer and Administration of the Sacraments and Other Rites and Ceremonies of the Church, Together with the Psalter or Psalms of David, According to the Use of The Episcopal Church* (New York: The Seabury Press, 1979) p. 510.

41 Ibid. pp. 533f.

42 Ibid. pp. 531f.

43 Ibid. pp. 532.

44 London Yearly Meeting, Christian Faith and Practice in the Experience of the Religious Society of Friends (London, London Yearly Meeting, 1966), Extract 354.

Chapter 9

PRESBYTERIANISM AND DENOMINATION

AMY PLANTINGA PAUW

Introduction

There is a non-exclusive impulse at the heart of denomination: to claim a denominational identity is to see one's own body as a part of the universal church but not as the whole church. Presbyterianism has been a paradigm form of denomination in its readiness to recognize the legitimacy of other Christian communities. It shares this trait with other members of the family of Reformed churches. As Eberhard Busch pointed out, at the center of being Reformed is a paradoxical openness to relativizing one's own denominational identity: to be strong in one's Reformed identity is to affirm one's denominational weakness.[1] While Presbyterians have certainly not overcome all temptations to arrogance and self-righteousness, a degree of humility is built into their denominational self-understanding. As Busch summed up this fundamental conviction of Reformed ecclesiology, "One does not need to belong to the Reformed faith in order to be a member of the church of Jesus Christ".[2]

Presbyterians have lived into this self-relativizing form of church gradually and unevenly across their history, and they continue to work out its full implications in their contemporary ecumenical relations. Presbyterianism first existed in non-denominational form. Denominationalism assumes the legitimacy of at least some degree of ecclesial plurality in polity and theology, and the earliest Presbyterians by and large neither desired nor anticipated that within a given civil government there would be a plurality of religious adherence. At the end of the seventeenth century, Presbyterianism emerged from the violent tumult of the Scottish Reformation as the foundation for the theology and polity of the national Church of Scotland, a function that continues in a substantially modified form to this day. The antecedents of Presbyterianism as a denomination lie in the failure in that same century to develop a national Presbyterian church in England. After protracted struggles over church order, English Presbyterians, alongside Congregationalists, Baptists and, eventually, Quakers, became a loyal but dissenting Christian body in relation to the established Church of England.

Presbyterianism was never the established church anywhere in colonial North America, instead growing from the bottom up amid a variety of other forms of Protestantism. In this pluralistic context, Presbyterians in the colonies *functioned* for decades as a denomination. However, their denominational self-understanding came to full expression only at the founding of the Presbyterian Church of the United States of America in 1789, in American revisions to the *Westminster Confession*, the confessional standard for much of Presbyterianism. Whereas the original 1647 document gave the civil magistrate the power "to call Synods, to be present at them, and to provide that whatsoever is transacted in them, be according to the minde of God", the revised section reads as follows:

> Yet, as nursing fathers, it is the duty of civil magistrates to protect the church of our common Lord, without giving the preference to any denomination of Christians above the rest, in such a manner that all ecclesiastical persons whatever shall enjoy the full, free, and unquestioned liberty of discharging every part of their sacred functions, without violence or danger. And, as Jesus Christ hath appointed a regular government and discipline in his church, no law of any commonwealth should interfere with, let, or hinder, the due exercise thereof, among the voluntary members of any denomination of Christians, according to their own profession and belief.[3]

As this revision shows, eighteenth-century Presbyterian citizens of the new republic saw themselves as a denominated, or named, Christian body sharing social space with other Christian bodies. They conceded the authenticity of other churches even as they claimed their own.[4] It was not in fact true that these early Presbyterians granted this authenticity to "all ecclesiastical persons whatever". The revisers of the *Westminster Confession* had in mind a rather limited array of Protestant bodies, and significant expansion of Presbyterian ecumenical sensibilities would not occur until the twentieth century.

A self-critical, evolving theological identity

In contemporary Presbyterianism, the self-relativizing impulse of denomination continues to evolve. Since their Reformation beginnings, Presbyterians have almost always accepted baptisms performed by other Christian churches, rejecting the need for new members to be re-baptized. Early eucharistic practices, however, maintained an uneasy balance between broad invitation on the one hand and table-fencing designed to protect doctrinal and disciplinary order on the other. The movement in contemporary Presbyterianism is towards inviting all baptized Christians to share in Presbyterian eucharistic celebrations, regardless of their church affiliation. The full recognition of clergy from other Christian bodies is arguably the most challenging implication of a denominational self-understanding. Here, Presbyterians have made some progress with other Reformed denominations, with mission partnerships often leading the way. Clearly, more work in this area remains. But Presbyterianism's trajectory seems clear: from its beginnings as a movement of Reformed Protestantism that was not especially amenable to Christian plurality, Presbyterianism has for the most part acquired a thoroughly denominational self-understanding wherever it has taken root around the world.

The non-exclusive impulse of denomination fits well with a deep ecumenical receptivity. Presbyterians recognize that their particular emphases and traditions are to be complemented and enriched by those of other Christian communities. The ecumenical orientation for Presbyterians is provided by the Pauline metaphor of the body of Christ. The metaphor does not set up a rigid hierarchy of functions and relations among Christians, nor does it simply establish a principle of cooperation among originally independent members. Rather, the metaphor indicates that the members of the Christ's body mutually constitute each other: each member brings gifts needed for the well-being of the whole. This is the sense in which Presbyterians affirm Barry Ensign-George's assertion that denomination represents a "partial" manifestation of church. According to Presbyterian understandings of the church universal, no member of Christ's body can say to another, "I have no need of you" (1 Cor. 12.21).

Another mark of Presbyterianism's embrace of denominational identity is its self-critical willingness to re-examine and reform its own theological teachings. The Reformed communion of churches to which Presbyterians belong has allowed for considerable diversity in its confessional standards. There is no authoritative list of authentic Reformed confessions; they have been written by many authors over the centuries and continue to be created at an impressive rate across the global church. Confessions are seen as subordinate standards, never equal in authority to the Bible, and always in principle open to additions and revisions. As the Bernese Synod of 1532 insisted: "If something would be brought forward to us from our pastors or others, which leads us closer to Christ and which is, according to the Word of God, more conducive to general friendship and Christian love than the opinion recorded now, we are happy to accept it and do not want to block the way of the Holy Spirit".[5] Presbyterians have fought repeated battles over the appropriateness of strict subscription to the *Westminster Confession* and *Catechisms*, and these remain the sole confessional standards for many Presbyterian bodies. Yet some, such as the Presbyterian Church of New Zealand and the PC(USA), exhibit the classically Reformed sensibility of the Bernese Synod by supplementing the *Westminster* standards with other confessional statements from both the sixteenth and twentieth centuries. These collections of confessional standards are understood to be imperfect and unfinished. For example, the PC(USA) is currently considering modifying its *Book of Confessions* by replacing its current English translation of the 1563 *Heidelberg Catechism* and adopting the 1986 *Belhar Confession* from South Africa. Presbyterian and other Reformed churches which adhere to a single or a fixed number of confessions have generally been willing to emend them as continuing faithfulness in changing circumstances seems to require, as the 1789 North American revisions of the *Westminster Confession* illustrate. One hope for the recent formation of the World Communion of Reformed Churches is the deepening of Reformed identity through shared reflection on its multiple confessional resources. This self-critical and evolving approach to their own confessional tradition makes it easier for Presbyterians to embrace one of the hallmarks of denomination: recognizing the legitimacy of confessional heritages other than one's own.

Polity and Denomination

Differences in polity generally prove more intransigent than doctrinal differences in ecumenical relations. Yet it is arguably a prerequisite for denominational self-understanding to recognize that particular ways of ordering of Christian communal life are always means to a greater end. Here, too, Presbyterianism has been a paradigm form of denomination in its self-relativizing perspective on diverse ways of ordering church life. The perennial Christian strategy, as Lutheran ethicist Larry Rasmussen has noted, is to gather the folks, break the bread, and tell the stories.[6] But every Christian community has to figure out how people gather and who gets to break the bread and tell the stories. That is, every Christian group has polity, that is to say, *political*, questions to address. They need to decide how power is to be distributed in their life together, to the end of establishing an enduring, cooperative form of communal life that both assures the sustenance of the church's vital ministries and is in some way transparent to their convictions about God. According to classic Presbyterian sensibilities (though their rhetoric and practice have sometimes belied this), no one form of polity is a good in itself, but derives its authority and legitimacy from its faithfulness of scriptural teaching and from how it serves the worship, edification, and mission of the church.

Though they have stubbornly championed their own form of church order on both scriptural and pragmatic grounds, Presbyterians have generally recognized that God has given the church no single mandate regarding polity. Communal

Christian negotiations around polity are never carried out in isolation from other forms of political life, and are therefore always to some degree contingent and provisional. Over the centuries, Christians have appropriated and adapted various models of human organization that were available in the larger society: the household, the empire, the nation state and the corporation, to name a few. Each of these models has implications for how Christian communities relate to the larger social order. The struggle over appropriate ways of ordering Christian community is apparent from New Testament times onward. It is an ongoing struggle, even in traditions whose basic polity has remained unchanged for centuries, since changes in the social order, both large and small, often prompt renewed attention to church polity. In North America, for example, past and present changes in the social status of African Americans, women, and gay and lesbian persons have provided contexts for Presbyterianism to reconsider the appropriate role of these groups in church leadership as it attempts to live in faithfulness to Jesus Christ.

Acknowledging the historical embeddedness of different polities, including its own, Presbyterianism has insisted that government of the church is an area which, in the words of the *Westminster Confession*, is appropriately "ordered by the light of nature and Christian prudence, according to the general rules of the Word, which are always to be observed".[7] That is, while Scripture must provide general guidance, considerable room is left for human reason and communal wisdom in deciding the appropriate form of ecclesial polity. Within the Reformed family of churches congregationalist, presbyterian and episcopal structures have all been embraced. As the North American Presbyterian *Confession of 1967* insists, "The institutions of the people of God change and vary as their mission requires in different times and places. The unity of the church is compatible with a wide variety of forms".[8] Tradition and precedent can never have the last word in Presbyterian understandings of polity.

Stemming in part from their rather well-developed sense of the dangers of ecclesial tyranny, Presbyterians have developed a connectional polity in which responsibility for governance and discipline is provided by pastors and elders gathered in conciliar bodies, starting with the local session in each congregation and extending to presbytery, then synod, and finally General Assembly levels. The biblical passage that has most resonance for Presbyterian church polity is not the promise in Matthew 16.18 that Peter is the rock on which Jesus will build the church, but the account in Acts 15 of the Council of Jerusalem, in which apostles and elders met, and after "much debate" (Acts 15.7) found a common way forward. Presbyterian polity seems designed to encourage argument. Presbyterians, in fact, have a rather positive theological perspective on argument: since the church is composed of fallible people, a structure that permits argument is the best medium for allowing the truth to emerge. As Heinrich

Bullinger, a sixteenth-century Reformed pastor averred, "It pleases God to use the dissensions that arise in the Church to the glory of his name, to illustrate the truth, and in order that those who are in the right might be manifest".[9] Presbyterians have been wary of concentration of power in the church, whether in the form of absolute congregational autonomy or a hierarchical episcopate. However, they do not see polity differences among Christian communities as barriers to full mutual ecclesial recognition. As the PC(USA) *Book of Order* insists, the Presbyterian "form of government is established in the light of Scripture to give order to this church but is not regarded as essential to the existence of the Church of Jesus Christ nor to be required of all Christians".[10]

This functionalist, provisional understanding of polity informs Presbyterian approaches to the Catholic and Orthodox communions. While Presbyterians can appreciate the contribution of the historic episcopate to the unity and stability of the church across the centuries and in the present, they concur with the assertion of the ecumenical document *Baptism, Eucharist and Ministry*:

> [I]t is increasingly recognized that a continuity in apostolic faith, worship, and mission has been preserved in churches which have not retained the form of historic episcopate. This recognition finds additional support in the fact that the reality and function of Episcopal ministry have been preserved in many of these churches, with or without the title "bishop".[11]

Presbyterian rejection of bishops has been on functional, rather than dogmatic, grounds: bishops are not necessary to the continuity of the apostolic faith of the church, and their presence can encourage abusive uses of power in the church. Though their unhappy historical experiences have sometimes led to vehement denunciations of the episcopate, especially in its Roman Catholic form,[12] Presbyterians are not in principle opposed to it. Any argument for introducing bishops into the Presbyterian polity, however, would need to be made on scriptural and functionalist grounds and in a way that did not exclude a central role for conciliar forms of Christian discernment.[13] In the meantime, the Presbyterian view of the historic episcopate is well-expressed once again by *Baptism, Eucharist and Ministry*: Presbyterians "appreciate the episcopal succession as a sign, though not a guarantee, of the continuity and unity of the Church".[14] In refusing to regard their own church order as normative and immutable, Presbyterians embrace the status denomination.

However, this stance puts Presbyterians at odds with some of their most important ecumenical partners. The unwillingness to regard polity as adiaphora contributes to the refusal by some Christian communities to accept the designation *denomination* altogether. Disagreements about the status of ecclesial polity thus introduce an awkward asymmetry in ecumenical relationships.

Confessing the sin of the denominational church

It is perhaps yet another marker of their status as a paradigm denomination that Presbyterians would not reject outright the charge that they are ecclesially defective. It has been one of the special tasks and privileges of Presbyterianism to insist on the peccability of the church, that is, the church's proneness to sin. Presbyterians have been the standard bearers for that conviction, and sometimes dramatic illustrations of it as well. The perception of scandalous failings in the established church significantly shaped Reformed doctrines of the church from the beginning. God has entrusted the church with the "power of the keys" (Matt. 16.19), but churches can so abuse this trust that in them, according to John Calvin, "Christ lies hidden, half buried, the gospel overthrown, piety scattered, the worship of God nearly wiped out".[15] Though *peccable* is not among the adjectives Ensign-George uses to describe denomination, it seems consonant with a denominational self-understanding. From a Presbyterian perspective, no Christian community or tradition ever instantiates a full and non-defective form of church. The church of Jesus Christ lives by confession of its sins and assurance of God's pardoning grace. It is only in mutual acknowledgement of their failures and shortcomings that different Christian communities can find true reconciliation and communion.

Christian communions that reject a denominational self-understanding will have to find their own way to this ecclesial penitence. In the meantime, the shortcomings of denomination are clear enough and should be confessed. Both in their origins and in their concrete manifestations, denominational churches are evidence that the body of Christ on earth is a broken and diseased body, mirroring the ills and divisions of the larger human society. Acknowledgement of ecclesial peccability funds a heartfelt repentance for the way the reality of denomination has wounded the life and mission of the church. The two cardinal sins of denomination have been nationalist idolatry and divisiveness. Examining these in turn will demonstrate that, even in its sins, Presbyterianism once more proves to be a paradigm form of denomination.

There is a lacuna in Ensign-George's approach to denomination, in that he abstracts the phenomenon from one of its principal functions: "to define the relation of religious movement to the social order".[16] One of the striking features of denomination since its inception is its observance of national boundaries. Presbyterianism as a tradition embraces a denominational self-understanding, but it is not strictly speaking a denomination. Rather, the Presbyterian Church of Pakistan is a denomination, as is the Presbyterian Church of Ghana. These two churches share a common theology and polity, but they are distinct denominations precisely because of their respective national affiliations. *Denomination* has typically signaled, among other things, an alignment between Christian identity and a particular national identity. This is true even when the national government is overtly hostile to Christianity, as in the case of the Presbyterian Church of Pakistan. It is true even when certain member congregations of the denomination are located outside its national boundaries, as is the case with Presbyterian Church of Ghana congregations in North America. Though nationalism is not intrinsic to the concept *denomination*, denominational identity has almost always made its home within national boundaries. The conciliar structure of Presbyterian denominational polity works quite well to link Christians at local, regional and national levels. But there its ecclesial horizon ends. Transnational relationships occur widely *among* denominations within the larger Presbyterian tradition, through various structures and to varying degrees, but there is no provision for these relationships to occur *within* a given denomination. Thus it is an overstatement to claim, as Ensign-George does, that "denominations exist to mediate between two realities: the church universal and the local congregation". Larger denominational traditions have some claim to this mediatorial role, but denomination as a rule serves to mediate only between the church national and the local congregation. Martin Cressey asserts that the national boundedness of Presbyterianism "is not a product of any lack of concern for the universality of the church. It arises from the difficulty, first in terms of means of communication and later in terms of the multicultural, multiracial nature of the worldwide church, of real meeting beyond the horizons of nations and particular peoples".[17] While the logistical, cultural and linguistic difficulties of transnational communion among Christians are undeniable, the fact that the phenomenon *denomination* has typically restricted itself to a national identity in its very self-definition must be seen as an enormous weakness. While in itself the restricted ecclesial horizon of denomination is not in itself a sin, it has repeatedly opened the door to the sin of nationalist idolatry.

Despite its keen recognition of the pervasive human tendencies to idolatry, Presbyterianism has been a paradigm of the liability of denomination to worship at the altar of the nation. Many factors come into play, including its roots in the magisterial Protestant Reformation's notion of "imperial cities",[18] its transformative social tendencies, and its emphasis on education, which appeals to persons of higher socio-economic status. The struggles of the Orthodox Church with ethnophyletism and the difficulties of nationally established churches in other countries reveal that the liabilities of Christian identity bounded by the nation state do not belong to denominational Protestants alone. In fact, one might have hoped that denomination, with its presumption of a plurality of legitimate religious expressions within one political jurisdiction, might have provided a framework in which Christian bodies could avoid subservience to state authority and develop a less nationally circumscribed Christian identity. Although some denominational churches in some periods have undoubtedly succeeded more than others on this score, the overall tendency of denomination has been to merge national identity and Christian identity, and Presbyterians have been prominent offenders.

The perennial temptation of denomination to shrink its horizons to national dimensions is at the root of H. Richard Niebuhr's scathing 1929 critique of American Protestant denominations, in which he condemns

> the failure of the churches to transcend the social conditions which fashion them into caste–organizations, to sublimate their loyalties to standards and institutions only remotely relevant if not contrary to the Christian ideal, to resist the temptation of making their own self-preservation and extension the primary object of their endeavor.[19]

Even today, one can qualify but hardly deny the unhappy reality to which Niebuhr pointed: denomination in North America often replicates the cultural, economic and racial divisions of the nation, and remains both preoccupied with its own preservation, and consciously or not, beholden to national interests. North American Presbyterians had long been at the forefront of efforts to establish "a Christian America", and they measured their strength and success as a church principally in terms of their influence on larger American culture. Faced now with a decline in both numbers and social prominence, some North American Presbyterians are issuing reactionary calls to "rebuild the Presbyterian establishment" by once again conforming its leadership demographics to the profile of American politics and business in a bid to restore the church's national influence.[20]

The sin of nationalist idolatry is not confined to national borders. Niebuhr was perhaps less conscious than we are today of the role of denomination in furthering national interests and mores on a global level. An example from the Uniting Presbyterian Church in Southern Africa illustrates this problematic role. Nineteenth-century Scottish missionaries to South Africa insisted that female Christian converts adopt the formal black clothing then worn by women in Scotland. While alien to African culture (and climate), these church "uniforms" eventually became a sign of Christian self-understanding and dignity for African Presbyterian women. Uniforms may seem like a trivial example of national imperialism, but this imposition of European cultural mores has had tragic racial consequences. In the wake of the dismantling of apartheid in South Africa, there was a desire to unite Presbyterian churches that had been divided along racial lines. Ironically, contemporary white South African women, sometimes themselves of Scottish descent, refused to accept the adopted cultural mores of their black fellow Presbyterians regarding church uniforms for women. The conflict over whether wearing uniforms is an "essential" of the faith has led to bitter conflicts and even threatens to derail the reconciliation of black and white Presbyterian in South Africa.[21] When denomination assumes a national affiliation, its international mission and relief efforts risk becoming dangerously intertwined with its political interests and cultural mores, often with unforeseen and lasting consequences.

Another cardinal sin of denomination is divisiveness. In addition to dividing along national boundaries, denomination has readily divided to accommodate members' convictions and affinities of every sort. Many denominational traditions had their start in splitting from other, more established denominations, such as Methodism from Anglicanism, or the Disciples of Christ tradition from Presbyterianism. But the fissiparous character of denomination comes also from divisions *within* a single denominational tradition. Whenever a serious disagreement arises among persons within the same denomination, the specter of institutional divorce looms. Faced with conflicts about theology, polity and cultural engagement, Protestants have repeatedly opted to form small, homogeneous groups of the like-minded, preferring to settle the truth about a controverted issue in the church by breaking fellowship with all who disagree.

The fissiparous character of Protestantism manifested itself long before the advent of denomination. The hope among sixteenth-century reformers that a wholly biblical theology, purged of dangerous speculative and devotional accretions, would unite the church was dashed early on by divisions over the practice of baptism, and Protestants have gone on to fulfill the gloomiest Roman Catholic predictions about the tendency of their movement to divide the church. The incentives provided by the structure of denomination in Protestantism have only exacerbated this propensity to choose division more often than reconciliation. In the contemporary period, the almost inexhaustible accommodations of religious preference within denominational Christianity mirror the consumerist patterns of the larger capitalist culture. Church becomes a highly differentiated commodity in which each denomination serves a tiny market niche. The Canadian social philosopher Charles Taylor has described with great incisiveness the culture of authenticity and expressive individualism that arose in the modern West but is now pervasive in many places worldwide. According to Taylor, one effect of this culture has been a fragmentation of religious identity: "We are now living in a spiritual super-nova, a kind of galloping pluralism on the spiritual plane". The role of the divisiveness of denominational Protestantism in this accelerated religious fragmentation deserves examination.[22]

With regard to denominational divisiveness, Presbyterianism has once again been a paradigm sinner. In South Korea alone, there are approximately one hundred different Presbyterian denominations. Among all the Christian traditions, Presbyterians and other Reformed Christians have been among the quickest to split and the slowest to reconcile, raising serious questions about the tradition's ecclesial density. Presbyterians" fissiparous tendencies have perhaps been related to a radical decentralization of power in their decision-making structures, and to their refusal to tie the integrity of the sacraments to episcopal authority. Perhaps the theological emphasis on the invisible church has contributed to a devaluing of the unity of the visible church. Whatever the reasons for Presbyterians" divisiveness, their inability to live as one body with those theologically and culturally closest to them undermines their expressed commitment to ecumenical solidarity and cooperation.

The gifts of denomination

Wherever denomination manifests itself, there is sin, but sin is not the whole story. Appreciating the gifts of denomination begins with an appreciation of the internal diversity of the Christian tradition. Denomination both acknowledges this diversity and carries out important theological work within the larger Christian ecology. According to Dale Irvin, Christianity has had a rhizomatic development, "agglomerating and stabilizing at times around common experiences or locations, but then branching off and spreading rapidly at other times, in several directions at once. It is a decentered, or multicentered, system flowing across multiple material and subjective fields".[23] The natural result of this development has been a plethora of strong, distinctive theological and liturgical traditions. In any given ecclesial context, some traditions are given official expression and others are neglected or submerged, ready to be drawn on as new circumstances demand. Against this backdrop, denomination can be seen, not as a betrayal of some "golden age" of Christian theological and structural unity, but as a contemporary inheritor of a faith that has always been complex and multicentered.

The visible church will always be pluriform because it needs to express the universal gospel in every human vernacular. Denomination instantiates the need for a thorough-going indigenization of the Christian faith into "every nation, from all tribes and peoples and languages" (Rev. 7.9). The way in which denomination provides a place to incarnate particular styles of Christian belief and practice, and even particular cultural mores, can often be seen as positive, or at least benign, a matter of the gospel taking on flesh in a specific culture. These parochialisms can sometimes turn malignant, as the issue over women's uniforms in South African Presbyterianism shows. However, denomination recognizes that authentic Christianity is always spoken with a distinctive accent. As the ecumenical document *The Nature and Mission of the Church* declares, "Each local church must be the place where two things are simultaneously guaranteed: the safeguarding of unity and the flourishing of a legitimate diversity".[24]

The divisiveness of denomination is to be lamented, but its encouragement of a legitimate cultural, theological and liturgical diversity in the local church should be celebrated.

Denominational responsibilities for training ministerial leadership reflect the theological judgment that those best suited to provide leadership to a given community are people who are rooted in its soil, indigenous to its language and culture. Churches which embrace a denominational self-understanding have generally permitted, even encouraged, clerical marriage, and this practice, too, has solidified the cultural and social bonds between the clergy and the laity. This is not to sanction the denominational tendency to form congregations that are racially, politically, and economically homogeneous, but it is to recognize the importance of ministers who are steeped enough in a particular culture that they can effectively communicate the gospel within it. It has been one of the gifts of denomination to stress the link between ordained office and the life of the local Christian community.

Individually and collectively, denominations do important theological work. Paradoxically, given denominational divisiveness, denomination is a unifying and conserving force in Christianity, nurturing and carrying forward distinctive theological traditions. According to James Nieman, denominations create multi-stranded identity narratives that are strong and flexible enough to recall denominational mistakes and failures, preserve marginalized or forgotten voices, and situate themselves within a larger ecumenical ecology.[25] This role is especially significant against the backdrop of the contemporary Protestant trajectory towards non-denominational expressions of church that draw freely on a variety of theological traditions without claiming allegiance to any one in particular. These non-denominational churches are living off the theological capital of more established Christian traditions, including those of denominational Protestantism. However, it is not clear how the distinctive resources of Wesleyanism, for example, will remain available without the efforts of Methodist denominations. Despite their manifest imperfections, the earthen vessels of denomination have been used to conserve precious theological ointment.

In the words of a recent PC(USA) confessional statement, "In life and in death, we belong to God".[26] God, not church, is the ultimate locus of belonging for Presbyterians, and the ultimate source of Christian identity. The God to whom Presbyterians belong is disturbingly free to confound human expectations and dismantle human constructs in God's ongoing action to consummate and redeem creation. The church of Jesus Christ is called to share in God's freedom by sitting lightly to the current configurations of this world, including the current configurations of the church. Christians are citizens of another commonwealth, in which the existing territorial and cultural boundaries of human existence do not apply.

It is obvious that denomination has an extremely precarious place in this larger theological understanding. Denomination is a provisional structure of Christian existence that has taken diverse forms across space and time. It is currently experiencing many strains and fissures, and may evolve in new ways or even disappear altogether.[27] For denominational churches, this radical contingency is part of their identity. The Christian church existed before the phenomenon of denomination and will certainly survive its demise, whenever and however that comes. For a Christian body to embrace a denominational self-understanding is thus to embrace a deep sense of its provisional place in God's greater intentions for the church. Yet that is not to say that God is not free to use it. In its humble work of gathering and connecting the followers of Jesus Christ, denomination points beyond its own limitations and failures to give us a glimpse of God's promised future.

Notes

1 Eberhard Busch, "Reformed Strength in Its Denominational Weakness", in Wallace Alston and Michael Welker (eds), *Reformed Theology: Identity and Ecumenicity*, (Grand Rapids, MI: Wm. B. Eerdmans, 2003), pp. 20–33.
2 Busch, "Reformed Strength in Its Denominational Weakness", p. 21.
3 *The Constitution of the Presbyterian Church (U.S.A.)*, Part I, *Book of Confessions* (Louisville, KY: Office of the General Assembly, Presbyterian Church (U.S.A), 1991), 6.129. Most of the illustrations of Presbyterianism in this essay will come from my own denomination, the Presbyterian Church of the United States of America, or the PC(USA). I will also attempt to reflect the realities of Presbyterianism worldwide, recognizing that the PC(USA) is not always representative of Presbyterianism in general.
4 Russell E. Richey, "Denominations and Denominationalism: An American Morphology", in Robert Bruce Mullin and Russell E. Richey (eds), *Reimagining Denominationalism: Interpretive Essays* (Oxford: Oxford University Press, 1994), p. 76.
5 G.W. Locher (ed.), *Der Berner Synodus von 1532*, vol. 1 (Neukirchen-Vluyn: Newkirchener Verlage, 1984), p. 26.
6 Larry Rasmussen, "Shaping Communities", in Dorothy C. Bass (ed.), *Practicing our Faith* (San Francisco: Jossey-Bass, 1997), p. 119.
7 Presbyterian Church (U.S.A.), *Book of Confessions*, 6.006
8 Presbyterian Church (U.S.A.), *Book of Confessions*, 9.34
9 Presbyterian Church (U.S.A.), *Book of Confessions*, 5.133
10 *The Constitution of the Presbyterian Church (U.S.A.)*, Part II, *Book of Order* (Louisville, KY: Office of the General Assembly, Presbyterian Church (U.S.A.), 2005–2007), Form of Government, G-4.0304.
11 *Baptism, Eucharist, and Ministry*, Faith and Order Paper no. 111 (Geneva: World Council of Churches, 1982) Ministry, paragraph 37.
12 See, for example, the Reformed critique of the papacy in the *Second Helvetic Confession* (1566), in Presbyterian Church (U.S.A.), *Book of Confessions*, 5.131–132.

13 See George Hunsinger, *The Eucharist and Ecumenism: Let Us Keep the Feast* (Cambridge: Cambridge University Press, 2008), where Hunsinger urges the acceptance of bishops in the Reformed tradition "for the sake of ecumenical unity and rectification", p. 207.

14 *Baptism, Eucharist, and Ministry*, Ministry, paragraph 38.

15 John Calvin, *Institutes of the Christian Religion*, (ed.) John T. McNeill, (trans.) Ford Lewis Battles (Philadelphia, Westminster Press, 1960), 4.2.12.

16 Richey, "Denominations and Denominationalism", p. 77.

17 Martin Cressey, "On Being a Conciliar Church: The Ecclesiology of Presbyterian Order", *Ecumenical Review* , 51, no. 4 (October 1999): 361–62.

18 See Bernd Moeller, *Imperial Cities and the Reformation: Three Essays* (1962; repr. edn Grand Rapids, MI: Baker Book Group, 1982)

19 H. Richard Niebuhr, *The Social Sources of Denominationalism* (New York: Henry Holt and Company, 1929; repr. edn, Hamden, CT: The Shoe String Press, 1954), p. 21. In a preface to the 1954 edition, Niebuhr states that he "continues to believe in the essential soundness" of his central thesis.

20 William J. Weston, "Rebuilding the Presbyterian Establishment", Office of Theology and Worship, Occasional Paper Series No. 3 (Louisville, KY: Presbyterian Church (U.S.A.), 2008).

21 I am grateful to Clifton Kirkpatrick for this example.

22 Charles Taylor, *A Secular Age* (Cambridge, MA: The Belknap Press of Harvard University Press, 2007), p. 300. Taylor himself sees North American denominationalism, which had its heyday in the nineteenth century, as a kind of preparation for what he calls the Age of Authenticity, p. 529.

23 Dale Irvin, *Christian Histories, Christian Traditioning: Rendering Accounts* (Maryknoll, NY: Orbis Books, 1998), p. 47.

24 *The Nature and Mission of the Church: A Stage on the Way to a Common Statement*, Faith and Order Paper no. 198 (Geneva: World Council of Churches, 2005), p. 36.

25 James R. Nieman, "The Theological Work of Denominations", in David A. Roozen and James R. Nieman (eds), *Church, Identity, and Change: Theology and Denominational Structures in Unsettled Times* (Grand Rapids, MI, Wm B. Eerdmans Publishing, 2005), pp. 625–53.

26 "A Brief Statement of Faith", in Presbyterian Church (U.S.A.), *Book of Confessions*, 10.1.

27 Russell Richey has provided a typology of various forms that North American denominations have taken over their history in "Denominations and Denominationalism", pp. 74–98.

Chapter 10

IS THERE A FUTURE FOR DENOMINATIONALISM?
REFLECTIONS FROM THE PERSPECTIVE OF
ROMAN CATHOLIC ECCLESIOLOGY AND FROM THE
PERSPECTIVE OF THE FUTURE OF THE ECUMENICAL MOVEMENT

PETER DE MEY (K. U. LEUVEN)

That it is possible to publish a collective volume on denomination containing no article on the Roman Catholic Church points up this Church's uneasy relationship with denominationalism. According to Catholic historiography, we find ourselves in a time when Catholicism is no longer the exception to, or an example of, perfect assimilation to the denominational pattern of church life, but is a Church with a number of distinctive characteristics in relation to that pattern.

When the current challenges for denominations in the United States are described, these challenges mirror the topics of the day in Roman Catholic ecclesiology: the confrontation with de-traditionalization and pluralization, independent congregations and independent denominations. In this essay I consider these parallel challenges. I will also attend to the evolution in post-conciliar magisterial teaching on the Episcopal conferences, evaluating those conferences as a potential counterpart to the denomination.

In the final section of this essay, I consider the relationship of the denomination to the future of the ecumenical movement. If one believes that the model of church unity to be pursued is a fellowship or communion of churches, then there is a very important role for the denominations; if one believes that the model to be pursued consists of organic unity, then the sacrifices for the denominations will be bigger.

1. The Catholic Church in the United States a denomination?

American theologian H. Richard Niebuhr, in his 1929 book *The Social Sources of Denominationalism*, drew on the notion of denomination after realizing that the church–sect distinction which the German theologian and philosopher

Ernst Troeltsch had developed in *The Social Teachings of the Christian Churches* (1912) was only with difficultly applicable to the religious situation in the United States. The Constitution of the United States in its First Amendment defends the separation of church and state: no single religion could impose itself as the state religion – as the Church of England had done in England. But the state also guarantees religious freedom for all churches. As a result, these churches – and originally this pertained only to the three colonial churches: Congregational, Presbyterian and Anglican – "would turn into 'denominations', formally equal under the Constitution and competing in a relatively free, pluralistic, and voluntaristic religious market".[1] According to José Casanova, Catholic and Jewish immigrants organized themselves in the same way, as denominations, so that "America became the 'Judeo–Christian' nation, and Protestant, Catholic, and Jew became the three denominations of the American civil religion".[2] According to this author, American denominationalism even succeeded in providing space for new generations of Islamic, Hindu and Buddhist immigrants.

Still we have to be careful to identify American Catholicism completely as a denomination. Frank Adloff offers interesting reflections on this in his essay "Katholizismus in den USA – Kirche, öffentliche Religion oder Denomination?"[3] The Catholic Church in the United States can in his opinion not entirely be considered a denomination in that it sees itself as part of the universal Catholic Church governed by the Pope. This does not mean that the Catholic Church in the United States has not tried to organize itself nationally. The attempt was especially realized through the establishment of an Episcopal conference in 1917, which with its 1919 *Bishop's Program of Social Reconstruction* immediately tried to exercise some influence in the public debate. During the Second Vatican Council, John Courtney Murray was able to incorporate the position of American Catholicism as a public religion in the Decree on Religious Freedom. But he did not identify American Catholicism with a denomination: "The Catholic may not, as others do, merge his religious and his patriotic faith, or submerge one in the other. The simplest solution is not for him. He must reckon with his own tradition of thought, which is wider and deeper than any that America has elaborated; He must also reckon with his own history, which is longer than the brief centuries that America has lived".[4] Even if the Episcopal conference in the United States was able to exercise its public role after the Council – with, for example relevant contributions on matters of social justice, such as the 1986 pastoral letter *Economic Justice for All* – the author also indicates a number of important challenges for American Catholicism. In the years since the 1960s a greater amount of individualism and pluralism can be felt among the Catholic laity, which oftentimes considers the teaching of the American bishops alienating.

Sociologist David Carlin, reflecting on "The Denomination Called Catholic", is convinced that, even if the Roman Catholic Church doesn't correspond to the characteristics of the church and of the sect as defined by Weber and Troeltsch, she successfully abstained from being identified as a denomination until the 1960s, given that her insistence that she is the one true church proved hardly reconcilable with the high level of tolerance within the Protestant churches. As a result of the "liberal reform proposals" of the Second Vatican Council, however, the Catholic Church became much more akin to "the liberal or mainline Protestant churches" and simply became "the biggest of America's many denominations".[5] Carlin even adds that "the price for 'going mainline' has been numerical decline"; for, "being broadly tolerant of other religions makes it difficult to be enthusiastic for their own".[6] The author finds reasons for hope in "the prior knowledge of Protestant denominationalism,[7] the influx of anti-denominational converts, the un-denominational internationalism of Catholicism, and the conservative structure of the Catholic hierarchy". The conclusion of the author's reflection is painfully clear, even if the author doesn't have the immediate solution at hand:

> If American Catholicism is to save itself, it must deliberately reject denominationalism. But it cannot do this unless it can find some other path to follow, and in the United States it can become neither a local sect nor a national American church. Finding some fourth way of being a religious organization will be a challenge of enormous proportions. Yet unless this challenge is met, the future of American Catholicism will be a relentless erosion of Christian content and a steady decline in membership.[8]

The editor of the collective work *American Denominational History: Perspectives on the Past, Prospects for the Future* chose, boldly, to open the volume with a contribution on "Catholic Distinctiveness and the Challenge of American Denominationalism" by Amy Koehlinger.[9] Koehlinger admits on the first page of her article that "including Catholicism under the rubric of denominationalism is somewhat novel for scholars of US Catholic history".[10] Previous generations of historians tended to remain altogether silent about the role of Catholicism in American culture, whereas Catholic historians – certainly prior to Vatican II – preferred to speak about Catholicism as the one true Church and not as a denomination. Koehlinger sketches three paradigms of the historiography of US Catholicism and how American Catholics look at denominationalism. The first paradigm – mainly operative from the 1940s till Vatican II – looked at Catholics as "a numerical minority who were fundamentally different from their Protestant neighbors".[11] Studies focused on the oddities of specific Roman Catholic devotions or convictions. Koehlinger gives the telling example that, in overviews on American religious history Catholics are often treated, together with Muslims and Jews, during the "others week".[12] A second paradigm is called "Americanism and Assimilation". Here, the Catholic differences are minimized, and one praises the level of assimilation into American culture of "American Catholicism", as distinct from "Roman Catholicism".[13] Attention was focused on aspects of the conciliar teaching which matched points of emphasis in American culture, such as the Council's endorsement of collegiality. After the Council attention often focused on the growing dissatisfaction of progressive Catholics with Roman Catholicism.

Current historiography of Catholicism in the United States, while not entirely ignoring either elements of assimilation or exceptional elements in American Catholicism, emphasizes the "distinctiveness" of aspects of the Catholic tradition compared to other religious traditions,[14] and recognizes that this distinctiveness is the inspiration for a particular relationship with American culture. Aspects of this distinctiveness are "documented" in such series as *American Catholic Identities: A Documentary History* (published by Orbis Books). Particularities of (American) Roman Catholicism which historians have recently identified are "Transnational Catholic identity"; "the parish as a central institution of Catholic experience"; "celibacy and monasticism in congregations of vowed religious"; "Catholic sexuality, particularly the prohibition against contraception"; "sacramentalism and Catholic devotional practices"; "anti-Catholicism"; and "Latino presence, perspectives, and traditions".[15]

The conclusion of the article makes it clear that paying attention to the distinctiveness of the American Catholic tradition isn't exactly the same as studying Catholicism as a denomination:

> As the dialectic of Catholic exceptionalism and Americanist assimilation in the historiography of American Catholicism continues to resolve itself into renewed consideration of those elements of religious experience that are distinctive to Catholics, religious historians in this field enter new terrain of history that is more self-consciously attentive to the ways that religious traditions function not just as denominations, but more so as the ground of human experience, cultural meaning, and social engagement.[16]

2. What can Roman Catholic ecclesiology learn from the current challenges in Protestant denominations?

The 2005 Eerdmans volume *Church, Identity, and Change. Theology and Denominational Structures in Unsettled Times* gives, especially in the concluding chapters written by the editors, a good overview not only of the challenges which all American Protestant denominational systems experience in our times but also of the theological significance of denominations. [17]

David Roozen makes it clear that national denominational structures have to engage "with postmodernity",[18] with "the emerging and evolving de-traditionalization and pluralization within the broader society",[19] and with the challenges of "expressive individualism, congregational localism, increasingly diverse and divisive constituencies, and the fragmentation of grand narratives",[20] terms which also frequently occur in recent reflections on the Roman Catholic Church in Europe and elsewhere.[21]

The impact of postmodern culture particularly affects the relation between the diverse local congregations and national denominational staff. Not only is the staff at national level decreasing, but local congregations often prefer the ministry resources offered by other churches "to those produced by their national denominational structure". Whether local congregations feel some affinity with their denomination seems largely to depend upon whether the local clergy is still willing to "link local life to the denomination's narratives".[22]

This point is developed further in the concluding piece by co-editor James R. Nieman, "The Theological Work of Denominations".[23] One should realize, Nieman believes, that "most adherents in denominations are formed in their theological identity primarily through congregations", more precisely "through regular contact with fellow members and clergy".[24] Oftentimes, "the national level seems an impediment to identity formation, distant from the lives and concerns of ordinary believers".[25] The most important theological function of the denomination is to contribute to the construction of the theological identity of individual believers and congregations. But the congregations have a constructive role to play as well. As Nieman puts it, "it is no more satisfactory for the national (or judicatory) level to be seen as a resource supplier for congregations than for congregations to be seen as branch offices for a denominational brand name".[26] The ideal situation seems to be that the denomination is able to offer a variety of "multistranded"[27] "theological identity narratives".[28] These narratives should not be the expression "of self-reliant theological isolation"[29] but should be construed "in relationship with other groups". The editors of this volume therefore no longer seem to be able to repeat Niebuhr's criticism that the existence of denominations is a counter witness to Christian unity, but they consider "structural differentiation, denominational or otherwise" as "invaluable whenever it results in diversity of witness to the source of the gift of unity".[30]

For Craig Van Gelder, the United States has become "a mission field".[31] The successful period of the "denominational, organizational church" lies behind us. Shailer Mathews's 1912 *Scientific Management in the Churches* initiated the influence of modern bureaucracy on church organization, an influence that lasted until 1970, when "the continued downsizing of national agencies and church-wide staff" started. Since then, according to Van Gelder, we find ourselves in a "period of transition". A "fresh understanding of ecclesiology from a missiological perspective, which has come to be known as the missional church" has begun to replace "a functional approach to ecclesiology". The focus is no longer on what churches have to do, but on what they are, on their missionary nature.[32] The emphasis is no longer on the level of the denomination, but on congregational mission.[33]

A final challenge pertains to potential tensions between the denomination and the Church at large. The decision of both the House of Deputies and the House of Bishops of the Episcopal Church USA (ECUSA) in 2003 to give their consent to the election of Gene Robinson to the see of New Hampshire, led to an unprecedented worldwide crisis threatening the unity of the Anglican Communion. Of course, the crisis has also had ecumenical consequences. Inspired by the Common Declaration on the Doctrine of Justification (1999) between Lutherans and Roman Catholics, a commission of mainly Anglican and Roman Catholic bishops had been installed in 2001 to pave the way towards a similar declaration as sign of the profound reception of the results of 40 years of dialogue between both churches. In 2007, this International Anglican Roman Catholic Commission on Unity and Mission was only able to present the "working paper" *Growing Together in Unity and Mission*. Luckily, a new round of Anglican–Roman Catholic international dialogue has recently been announced, with a particular focus on the discernment (in common) of right ethical thinking.

In a 2006 article with the clear title "The End of a Church and the Triumph of Denominationalism: On How to Think About What Is Happening in the Episcopal Church"[34] Philip Turner situates the Robinson case amid other examples of Episcopalian attunement "to the latest movements of liberal culture",[35] including the regular invitation of "non-baptized people to share in the Holy Eucharist".[36] The freedom of the denomination sometimes confronts the concern for unity of the entire Church.

> It is entirely likely that the bishops of the Global South will say to ECUSA that membership in the Anglican Communion requires conformity to the faith and practice of a worldwide fellowship of churches – even if that conformity runs against the grain of the culture in which Christians happen to find themselves. ECUSA will then have to decide if it wants to remain in its denominational niche or if it wants to affirm its identity as a church that is part of a worldwide communion of churches.[37]

The alternative, however, is not, as another author in the same volume insists, to give up being a distinct Episcopal, Lutheran or Roman Catholic Church in the

U.S.A.[38] "There is a divine vocation for Catholicism in America: but one bound up with the passage of Jesus Christ through the Cross".[39] "The struggle for American Catholicism is the struggle of the world's redemption: but it must be a struggle – that is, it must embrace even the American repudiation of its truth within the form of our parochial denominations – if truly it redeems".[40]

The Episcopal Conferences as the
Roman Catholic Church's Counterpart of the Denomination

The main reason the Roman Catholic Church is absent from a lot of studies on denominationalism is that its two most powerful levels of organization are the diocese and, even more importantly, the universal Church. When *Lumen Gentium*, the Dogmatic Constitution on the Church, makes reference to the college of bishops, it has in most cases the universal college of bishops in mind, which only exceptionally convenes in a council. Section 23 of *Lumen Gentium* pays substantial attention, though, to the relationship of communion among the local churches and even seems to define "the one unique catholic church" as existing "in and from these (*in quibus et ex quibus*) particular churches". The existence of a "variety of local churches" in the Catholic Church, enjoying "their own discipline, their own liturgical usage and their own theological and spiritual patrimony" is not only welcomed as an expression of "the catholicity of the undivided church" but is also seen as the work of the "divine providence". The paragraph ends with an explicit acclamation of the Episcopal conferences: "In a similar way Episcopal conferences can today make a manifold and fruitful contribution of the spirit of collegiality".

In the *Herder Theologischer Kommentar zum Zweiten Vatikanischen Konzils* the Tübingen ecclesiologist Peter Hünermann disapproves of the fact that the episcopal conferences are seen not as a limited and temporal expression of collegiality, but merely as an expression of a collegial affection (*collegialis affectus*).[41]

According to Archbishop Quinn, in his famous book on *The Reform of the Papacy*, the fact that the exposition on episcopal conferences did receive its place in the Council's teaching on collegiality is more important than the attempt to restrict its authority. For him, the reference to the "divine Providence" in a passage dealing with decision making at the intermediary level[42], shows that the Council Fathers found this level really important, perhaps more important than their contemporary successors who continue to make this distinction between "affective" and "effective collegiality". "The Second Vatican Council, then, does not reflect the idea that there are only two divinely based expressions of the episcopal office, the relationship of the individual bishop to the Pope and the formal united and collegial action of the bishops of the world in an ecumenical council. In addition to these, there is the providential development of episcopal conferences, which are not mere administrative conveniences but a reflection of the communion of the local churches in a region or country and a manifestation of the diversity and catholicity of the Church".[43]

Since the publication of the 1992 *Letter to the Bishops of the Catholic Church on Some Aspects of the Church Understood as Communion*, the magisterium of the Catholic Church seems to have moved away from developing an ecclesiology which considers the universal church as a communion of churches. The Congregation for the Doctrine of the Faith (CDF) even found it important to complement the teaching of *Lumen Gentium* 23 on the relationship between the local and the universal Church:

> Hence the formula of the Second Vatican Council: *The Church in and formed out of the Churches (Ecclesia in et ex Ecclesiis)*, is inseparable from this other formula: *The Churches in and formed out of the Church (Ecclesia in et ex Ecclesiis)*.[44]

In 1999 Walter Kasper, then still bishop of Rottenburg-Stuttgart, formulated a sharp criticism on the teaching of *Communionis Notio*, which formed the start of the so-called Ratzinger–Kasper debate.[45]

In 1998 Pope John Paul II promulgated *Apostolos Suos*, a papal document which denies that the episcopal conference enjoys the same authority as the college of bishops or the individual bishop. Paragraph 9 reads:

> The supreme power which the body of Bishops possesses over the whole Church cannot be exercised by them except collegially, either in a solemn way when they gather together in ecumenical Council, or spread throughout the world, provided that the Roman Pontiff calls them to act collegially or at least freely accepts their joint action.

The following paragraph contains the implications for regional gatherings of bishops:

> Equivalent collegial actions cannot be carried out at the level of individual particular Churches or of gatherings of such Churches called together by their respective Bishops.[46]

In paragraphs 19 and 20 the document deems it necessary to delineate the authority of the episcopal conference from the authority of the diocesan bishop:

The authority of the Episcopal Conference and its field of action are in strict relation to the authority and action of the diocesan Bishop and the Bishops equivalent to them in law. (. . .) Bishops, whether individually or united in Conference, cannot autonomously limit their own sacred power in favour of the Episcopal Conference.

According to the French Dominican ecclesiologist Hervé Legrand, the existence of this post-conciliar document has made the beautiful Section 23 of *Lumen Gentium* ineffective:

> LG 23, in its conclusion, expressed the hope that the episcopal conferences would play an analogous role to the patriarchates of the ancient Church, namely to promote a legitimate and laudable pluriformity in their communion. This hope has never been realised, because this institution has never overcome the canonical status of a modest organism of practical cooperation between the bishops of the same nation.[47]

In some countries there also exist purely advisory bodies in which representatives of the clergy; religious, lay pastors; and laity regularly discuss important topics with the bishops,[48] but it cannot be said of the Roman Catholic Church that "the ultimate worldly authority for all American Protestant denominational systems is their national assemblies, all of which act through some form of participatory democracy".[49]

3. The denomination and the future of the ecumenical movement

Almost 20 years ago the then American Lutheran theologian Michael Root was wondering whether the "reality of the denominations" had some effect on the apparent stagnation of the ecumenical movement.[50] The existence of a great variety of Christian churches has become a most familiar reality in American culture, so that Christians easily participate in the liturgical life of other denominations, or even shift denominations, and no longer seem to desire that the scandal of denominational divisions be overcome. Root observes a tension between the ideal of unity as it is lived within the (mainly Protestant) denominations – a unity which is "more pragmatic, institutional, and bureaucratic"[51] and which "seeks only friendly cooperation between the churches"[52] – and the ideal of visible unity or full communion between the churches as it is explored in the multilateral dialogue of Faith and Order and in the many bilateral dialogues.

The author is aware that, "visible unity, at least in some conceptions, is compatible with the continued existence of distinct denominations or traditions".[53]

He refers in his article to the 1973 Leuenberg Agreement between the majority of Lutheran and Reformed churches of continental Europe. The denomination plays a crucial role in this so-called model of Church fellowship or communion between churches.[54] The *Declaration of Meissen* between the Evangelical Church in Germany (EKD) and the Church of England (1988) is an example of a form of limited Church fellowship, also termed "interim eucharistic sharing". Eucharistic hospitality is possible, but it does not yet include full interchangeability of ministries because of a remaining dissensus on episcopacy. Full Church communion has, since the approval of the Porvoo Declaration (1992), been realized between the Anglican Churches on the British Isles and most Lutheran Churches in Scandinavia and the Baltic countries (except Denmark and Estland). Agreements of the same type are the Declaration of Waterloo (1997) which establishes full Church communion between the Anglican Church in Canada and the Evangelical Lutheran Church in Canada. In the U.S.A. a similar Concordat of Agreement exists since 1997 between the Evangelical Lutheran Church of America (ELCA) and the Protestant Episcopal Church (now The Episcopal Church), but Church fellowship became final only in 2001.

Root knows from his ecumenical work that the forms of communion which result from such agreements cannot be called "churches" – as neither can the world confessional bodies nor even the denominations themselves. In his opinion, however, "in considering the ecclesial status of the denomination, the predicate "church" need not to be applied in an all-or-nothing fashion" and therefore he believes that denominations and other forms of communion possess an "ecclesial density".[55] Root is aware that most Protestant churches are of the opinion that the denomination or national church is "the sole body capable of making binding decisions, e.g., to enter into a relation of full communion with another church".[56] Less authority is ascribed to the world confessional bodies,[57] even if the organization of the international ecumenical dialogues is their responsibility. In view of making ecumenical progress, Root therefore pleads that the denomination or national church should be understood "as a strictly provisional institution".[58] It is a reality, however, which, on the other hand, has to be taken seriously, also by ecumenists. He therefore also favors ecclesiology being "attuned to both the *theological* and the *social* reality of the churches",[59] and the latter requires attention to the levels of both the congregation and the denomination.

Ten years later the same Michael Root is one of the sixteen signatories of the so-called *Princeton Proposal for Christian Unity*,[60] which was the result of three years of informal ecumenical dialogue facilitated by the Center for Catholic and Evangelical Theology. The authors of the *Princeton Proposal*,[61] several of whom are members of international ecumenical commissions on behalf of their churches, claim to have found an answer to the impasse of the ecumenical movement. The answer is already hinted at in the main title of the document, *In One*

Body through the Cross, words borrowed from Eph. 2.16. The letter to the Ephesians states that the salvation brought about by the cross consists in the reconciliation of Jews and Gentiles in one body. According to the authors of the Princeton Proposal, the ultimate goal of the ecumenical movement consists in the unity of all churches in one body. This unity is in first instance a gift, the fruit of the salvific death of Christ Jesus, but it will also "require of our churches disciplines of self-sacrifice". (§ 1) Time and again the authors repeat that the human efforts asked for consist in the sacrifice of the divisive elements in the churches' denominational identity. The existence of divisions between churches is, in their opinion, a sinful reality.

In an attempt to describe Christian unity, it is distinguished from being a sentimental form of togetherness but also from being "a general principle of social harmony or communal cohesion" (§ 25)[62] If we continue to cultivate "the distinct identities of our churches' (§ 32), our proclamation of the gospel of the crucified Lord runs into danger. "In the cross of Christ, the personal and corporate suffering entailed in giving up aspects of our denominational heritages becomes the grace of fellowship with the Son, who brings us to the Father in the power of the Spirit". (§ 56) In the concluding section, "One Body through the Cross" (§§ 70–72), it is repeated that the way towards unity will be a "penitential" and "ascetical" process for the churches[63] which will imply the loss of their sometimes rich denominational traditions. That this can never be an exclusively human task, makes the drafters hope that the goal will once be realized: "Any true steps toward unity will be a manifestation of new life in Christ, as he reconciles us in one body through the cross" (§ 72).

The authors wish to rehabilitate the view on Christian unity that was expressed during the third assembly of the WCC in New Delhi (1961). According to this statement, which occupies a central place in the Princeton Proposal, this unity

> is being made visible as all in each place who are baptized into Jesus Christ and confess him as Lord and Savior are brought by the Holy Spirit into one fully committed fellowship, holding the one apostolic faith, preaching the one Gospel, breaking the one bread, joining in common prayer, and having a corporate life reaching out in witness and service to all and who at the same time are united with the whole Christian fellowship in all places and all ages, in such wise that ministry and members are accepted by all, and that all can act and speak together as occasion requires for the tasks to which God calls his people. (§ 15)

Surely, the Princeton Proposal is not playing out the model of "organic union" (*Kirchenunion*) against the one of "church fellowship" (*Kirchengemeinschaft*).[64]

Still, given the historical connection between the New Delhi formula of unity and the model of organic unity, it can be asked whether the Princeton Proposal does not contain an implicit plea for organic unity.[65] The introduction to the chapter on "The unity of the Church" in a recent anthology on the ecumenical movement, indicates that New Delhi's vision of Christian unity "is often called" the model of "organic unity".[66] Having been first articulated at the WCC's third assembly in New Delhi in 1961, the vision has been further refined in Uppsala (1968) and especially in Nairobi (1975). At New Delhi the implications of the quest for unity for the denominations had been indicated in a beautiful but abstract way: "The achievement of unity will involve nothing less than a death and rebirth of many forms of church life as we have known them. We believe that nothing less costly can finally suffice".[67] The report of the section "What Unity Requires" of the Nairobi world assembly explains how an organic union of churches is able to realize that "fully committed fellowship" which was mentioned in the New Delhi Statement: "Organic union of separate denominations to form one body does mean a kind of death which threatens the denominational identity of its members, but it is dying in order to receive a fuller life. That is literally the 'crux of the matter' ."[68]

Georg Hintzen gives a good description of the differences between the model of "church fellowship" and the model of "organic union". Full ecclesial communion between churches implies (1) the mutual recognition of the other churches as churches in which the one Church of Jesus Christ becomes visible in this world; (2) the mutual recognition of ministries and the interchangeability of the ordained ministers; (3) the common sharing of the liturgy and sacraments; (4) cooperation at all levels of ecclesial life. Contrary to the model of organic union, however, (1) the churches maintain their own name and confessional identity and (2) their own hierarchical structures; (3) no uniform ministry is needed, but the mutual recognition of the existing ministries is sufficient; (4) the creation of new institutions of cooperation is unnecessary; (5) the creation of new proclamations of faith is equally unnecessary.[69]

Conclusion

By way of conclusion I prefer, as did many of my co-authors in this book, to look back at the criteriology of the denomination developed by Barry Ensign-George. By focusing on intermediary levels in the Roman Catholic Church – and especially on the episcopal conferences within the (national) church provinces – one observes that most characteristics elaborated by Ensign-George can be applied to them as well. As a result, the question of whether the Roman Catholic Church can correctly be identified as a denomination can still be bracketed.

The level of the episcopal conference is, according to the official Roman Catholic ecclesiology, indeed (1) "contingent", "not a necessary pattern of Christian life together". It has become even more contingent since the 1998 document *Apostolos Suos*. Episcopal conferences are indeed (2) "intermediary". They "exist to mediate between two realities: the church universal and the local congregation". In Roman Catholic ecclesiological discourse we would prefer to speak about the local level, so that one can in first instance think about the diocese. (3) The well-being of the conference should depend "on the existence of other denominations for the fullness of Christian life and witness to be embodied in the world". The conference thus should be "interdependent". This also applies to episcopal conferences in the Roman Catholic Church because it is their task to promote ecumenism in their country. The (4) "partiality" of the denomination and of the church provinces in the Roman Catholic Church indicates "that no denomination is ever the full embodiment of the church universal in this time". Barry Ensign-George finally expects denominations to be (5) "permeable", to be open to influences from outside and to not "make total, ultimate claims on its own members". Much depends upon the style of the archbishop in the Roman Catholic Church.

It is indeed possible to also repeat an important conclusion of Ensign-George's: "denomination is potentially one of God's good gifts to the church".

Notes

1 J. Casanova, "Immigration and the New Religious Pluralism: A European Union/United States Comparison", Thomas Banchoff (ed.), *Democracy and the New Religious Pluralism* (Oxford: Oxford University Press, 2007), pp. 59–83 (68).

2 Cf. also Will Herberg, *Protestant, Catholic, Jew: An Essay in American Religious Sociology* (New York: Doubleday, 1955).

3 Frank Adloff, ‚Katholizismus in den USA–Kirche, öffentliche Religion oder Denomination?", Hans G. Kippenberg (ed.), *Die verrechtlichte Religion: der Öffentlichkeitsstatus von Religionsgemeinschaften* (Tübingen: Mohr, 2005), pp. 227–47.

4 John Courtney Murray, *We Hold These Truths: Catholic Reflections on the American Proposition* (Kansas City, MO: Sheed & Ward, 1960), p. XI, as found in Adloff, p. 243.

5 David R. Carlin, "The Denomination Called Catholic", *First Things* (November 1997): 18–21 (19).

6 Ibid., p. 20.

7 Ibid.: "Since liberal Protestants have already tried the experiment, there is no need for Catholics to repeat it. If Catholics are neither fools nor anti-Christians, they will avoid carrying their religion's current denominational tendency through to the bitter end".

8 Ibid., p. 21.

9 Amy Koehlinger, "Catholic Distinctiveness and the Challenge of American Denominationalism", Keith Harper (ed.), *American Denominational History: Perspectives*

on the Past, Prospects for the Future (Tuscaloosa, AL: University of Alabama Press, 2008), pp. 7–30.

10 Ibid., p. 7.

11 Ibid., p. 12.

12 Ibid., p. 14.

13 Ibid., p. 15.

14 In contemporary fundamental theology one sometimes uses the notion of particularity. Cf. Lieven Boeve, "Theological Truth, Particularity and Incarnation: Engaging Religious Plurality and Radical Hermeneutics", Mathijs Lamberigts, Lieven Boeve, and Terrence Merrigan (eds), *Orthodoxy, Process and Product* (Leuven: Peeters, 2009), pp. 323–48.

15 *American Denominational History*, pp. 20–25. The article further mentions "four additional fruitful areas of Catholic distinctiveness for which scholarly literature is just beginning to emerge: 'Children and childhood in Catholicism'; 'Catholic bodies'; 'Catholic arts and literature'; 'African American Catholic experience'. (. . .) Finally, a few areas of Catholic distinctiveness remain largely untouched by recent scholarhip. Hopefully, future students in Catholic Studies will turn their attention to the following: (1) issues of religious power in the authority wielded by the Roman magisterium and its effect on American structures and practices; (2) the pervasive violence in American Catholicism; (3) the singular and unprecedented transformation caused by the Second Vatican Council, particularly how the Council was interpreted, received, and implemented in the American context; and (4) the experience of African American Catholics" (Ibid., pp. 24–5).

16 Ibid., p. 26.

17 David A. Roozen & James R. Nieman (eds), *Church, Identity, and Change. Theology and Denominational Structures in Unsettled Times* (Grand Rapids, MI: Eerdmans, 2005). None of the articles in the volume pays specific attention to the Roman Catholic Church in the United States.

18 David A. Roozen, "National Denominational Structures' Engagement with Postmodernity: An Integrative Summary from an Organizational Perspective", Ibid., pp. 588–624 (588).

19 Ibid., p. 589.

20 Ibid., p. 623.

21 See e.g. Peter De Mey, "The Church from a European Perspective", Gerard Mannion, and Lewis S. Mudge (eds), *The Routledge Companion to the Christian Church* (New York and London: Routledge, 2008), pp. 364–84 (365–66) and Lieven Boeve, "Religion after Detraditionalization: Christian Faith in a Post-secular Europe", Michael Hoelzl and Graham Ward (eds), *The New Visibility of Religion: Studies in Religion and Cultural Hermeneutics* (London: Continuum, 2008), pp. 187–209.

22 Ibid., p. 618.

23 James R. Nieman, "The Theological Work of Denominations", *Church, Identity, and Change*, 625–53.

24 Ibid., p. 639.

25 Ibid.

26 Ibid., p. 641.

27 Ibid., p. 640.

28 Ibid., p. 651.

29 Ibid.

30 Ibid., p. 653.
31 Craig Van Gelder, "Rethinking Denominations and Denominationalism in Light of a Missional Ecclesiology", *Word & World*, 25 (2005:1): 23–33. See for a critique on the denominations from a Presbyterian Church perspective, Edwin Chr. Van Driel, "Church and Covenant: Theological Resources for Divided Denominations", *Theology Today*, 65 (2009): 449–61.
32 According to Van Gelder, important sources of inspiration for this missionary ecclesiology are the "more substantive understanding of ecclesiology in light of the missionary nature of the church" offered by Vatican II's missionary decree *Ad Gentes* (1965) and the ecumenical reflection on the *missio Dei* offered by the Commission on World Mission and Evangelism (Ibid., p. 32).
33 The growing success of "mega-churches" constitutes a specific challenge for the future of the denominations. See e.g. Ryan Wilson, "The New Ecclesiology: Mega-Church, Denominational Church, and No Church", *Review and Expositor*, 107 (2010): 61–72.
34 Philip Turner, "The End of a Church and the Triumph of Denominationalism: On How to Think About What Is Happening in the Episcopal Church", Ephraim Radner, and Philip Turner (eds), *The Fate of Communion: The Agony of Anglicanism and the Future of a Global Church* (Grand Rapids, MI: Eerdmans, 2006), pp. 15–24.
35 Ibid., p. 16.
36 Ibid., p. 23.
37 Ibid., p. 24.
38 Ephraim Radner, "Children of Cain: The Oxymoron of American Catholicism", *The Fate of Communion*, 25–56.
39 Ibid., p. 28.
40 Ibid., p. 56.
41 Peter Hünermann, *Theologischer Kommentar zur dogmatischen Konstitution über die Kirche Lumen Gentium* (Herders Theologischer Kommentar zum Zweiten Vatikanischen Konzil, 2) (Freiburg: Herder, 2004), 263–582, p. 432: "Der abschließende Satz über die Bischofskonferenzen verrät etwas von den Hoffnungen und Perspektiven, die sich für die Kommission und die Konzilsväter mit den Ausführungen über die Kollegialität des Bischofsamtes verbunden haben. Wenn im Zusammenhang mit den Bischofskonferenzen nun lediglich von dem "collegialis affectus", der kollegialen Gesinnung, die Rede ist und darauf verzichtet wird, in den Bischofskonferenzen einen – selbstverständlich begrenzten und endlichen – Ausdruck der Kollegialität an sich zu sehen, so zeigt sich darin und in der anschließenden nachkonziliaren Diskussion die Schwierigkeit, dem wesentlichen Gedanken der Kollegialität des Dienstes in der Kirche in einer umfassenden Weise Raum zu geben".
42 Of course, pleading for a strengthening of intermediary forms of decision-making within the Roman Catholic Church, as seems to be the current task for canon lawyers and ecclesiologists, is not limited to the episcopal conferences, but also includes continental structures of cooperation of bishops. Cf. Myriam Wijlens, "The Intermediate Level in the Roman Catholic Church: An Organisational or Ecclesiological Category?" Leo Koffeman & Henk Witte (eds), *Of All Times and of All Places: Protestants and Catholics on the Church Local and Universal* (Zoetermeer: Meinema, 2001), pp. 95–130 and "Cooperation of Bishops on a Supranational or Continental Level: A New Institution on the Intermediate Level?" Alberto Melloni & Sandra

Scatena (eds), *Synod and Synodality: Theology, History, Canon Law and Ecumenism in New Contact* (Münster: LIT, 2004), pp. 33–60.

43 John R. Quinn, *The Reform of the Papacy: The Costly Call to Christian Unity* (New York: Crossroad, 1999), p. 105.

44 The CDF could rely for the latter formula on an important Christmas address – without doubt thoroughly checked by the same CDF – to the Roman Curia which Pope John Paul II had pronounced in 1990.

45 Within the framework of this contribution it is impossible to treat this debate in further detail. See for a number of important studies of this debate: Kilian McDonnell, "The Ratzinger/Kasper Debate: The Universal Church and the Local Churches", *Theological Studies* 63 (2002): 227–50; Medard Kehl, "Der Disput der Kardinäle. Zum Verhältnis von Universalkirche und Ortskirchen", *Stimmen der Zeit* 128 (2003): 219–32 and Paul McPartlan, "The Local Church and the Universal Church: Zizioulas and the Ratzinger-Kasper Debate", *International Journal for the Study of the Christian Church* 4 (2004): 21–33.

46 Pope John Paul II, "Apostolic Letter issued "Motu Proprio" on the Theological and Juridical Nature of Episcopal Conferences", *Origins* 28 (1998–1999): 152–158. Compare also the preceding *Draft Statement on Episcopal Conferences* from the Congregation for the bishops, *Origins* 17 (1987–1988): 108–12. This draft gave occasion to important theological reflections on this issue, such as Hervé Legrand, Julio Manzanares & Antonio Garcia y Garcia (eds), *Les conférences épiscopales. Théologie, statut canonique, avenir* (Paris: Cerf, 1988), and Thomas J. Reese (ed.), *Episcopal Conferences: Historical, Canonical and Theological Studies* (Washington D.C.: Georgetown University Press, 1989). See also François Guillemette, *Théologie des conférences épiscopales: Une herméneutique de Vatican II* (Montréal : Médiaspaul, 1994).

47 Hervé Legrand, "Églises locales, Églises régionales et Église entière. Éclaircissements sur quelques débats au sein de l' Église catholique depuis Vatican II", Michel Deneken (ed.), *L'Église à venir. Mélanges Hoffman* (Paris: Cerf, 1999), pp. 277–308 (286) : "*Lumen Gentium* 23, en sa finale, avait exprimé l'espoir de voir les conférences épiscopales jouer un rôle analogue à celui des patriarcats de l' Église ancienne pour assurer une légitime et heureuse pluriformité dans la communion. Ce vœu ne s'est jamais réalisé, parce que l'institution n'a jamais dépassé le statut canonique d'un modeste organe de coopération pratique entre les évêques d'une même nation".

48 Peter De Mey, "Is Small Always Synodal? The Episcopal Conference in Belgium and the Netherlands", Alberto Melloni, and Sandra Scatena (eds), *Synod and Synodality: Theology, History, Canon Law and Ecumenism in New Contact* (Münster: LIT, 2004), pp. 435–60.

49 David A. Roozen, "National Denominational Structures' Engagement with Postmodernity", p. 590.

50 Michael Root, "The Unity of the Church and the Reality of the Denominations", *Modern Theology* 9 (1993): 385–401. This article is also mentioned in the article by Barry Ensign-George in this volume.

51 Ibid., p. 394.

52 Ibid., p. 393.

53 Ibid., p. 389.

54 The communion between the Reformed and Lutheran churches in Europe was first expressed as the Leuenberg Church Fellowship, but has since then been "re-baptized" as the Community of Protestant Churches in Europe.

55 Ibid., p. 397.

56 Ibid., p. 398.

57 Cf. also Setri Nyomi, "Christian World Communions in Africa: Their Impact in Overcoming Denominationalism", *The Ecumenical Review* 53 (2001): 333–40.

58 Ibid. Root especially thinks about the dialogue with the Roman Catholic Church: "How does one imagine the divide between any of the Protestant confessions and Rome ever being overcome if one side can only make a binding decision to thirty or a hundred national or regional denominations".

59 Ibid., p. 395.

60 Carl E. Braaten, and Robert J. Jenson (eds), *In One Body through the Cross: The Princeton Proposal for Christian Unity* (Grand Rapids, MI: Eerdmans, 2003). Some reactions to this proposal: Mark E. Chapman, "The Princeton Proposal: Realism and Hope for Renewal of Ecumenism", *Ecumenical Trends,* 32 (2003): 161–66; Ann K. Riggs, "In One Body through the Cross", *The Ecumenical Review,* 55 (2003): 168–72; Peter De Mey, "A Call to Conversion: An Analysis of 'The Princeton Proposal for Christian Unity'," *Ecumenical Trends,* 3 (2005): 49–58.

61 William Abraham, Mark Achtemeier, Brian Daley, John H. Erickson, Vigen Guroian, George Lindbeck, Lois Malcolm, Bruce McCormack, R.R. Reno, Michael Root, William G. Rusch, Geoffrey Wainwright, Susan K. Wood, Telford Work, J. Robert Wright and David Yeago.

62 Ibid.: "When the teaching or behavior of other Christians is so captive to wordly powers that the gospel is falsified, true unity demands rejection of such behavior, not accommodation. (. . .) Many confessional and denominational families now contain within themselves far more serious divions than those that once divided them from other Christian communities; this calls into question their claims that historic divisions are maintained solely for the sake of truth".

63 One is reminded here of the statement of the 1991 statement of the Groupe des Dombes, *For the Conversion of the Churches* (Geneva: WCC, 1991).

64 Only in one of the background papers to the *Princeton Proposal* is the link made between the New Delhi formula of unity and the model of organic unity. See Brian E. Daley, "Rebuilding the Structure of Love: The Quest for Visible Unity among the Churches", Carl E. Braaten, and Robert Jenson (eds), *The Ecumenical Future: Background Papers for "In One Body through the Cross: The Princeton Proposal for Christian Unity"* (Grand Rapids, MI: Eerdmans, 2004), p. 103: "To make real progress towards a more organic and comprehensive unity – towards the 'fully committed fellowship' or *koinonia* held up by the New Delhi statement as the goal of ecumenism – we clearly will need, as individuals and as historic communities, to undergo the process of conversion and illumination that will allow us to loosen our hold on the power and self-satisfaction that our entrenched positions afford us, in order to be created anew".

65 Another opinion on the validity of organic unity as an alternative to denominationalism is found in Sam Portaro, "Whence Pluralism, Whither Denominationalism,?" *Cross Currents,* (Spring/Summer 2000): 203–10 (206): "Modern ecumenism that seeks the organic unity of Christianity is yet another response to the pluralism of Christian denominational communities. The notion of an organically united Christianity seeks the reunion of the many denominated bodies into one body representing true catholicity – that is, a unity embracing the diversity. But organic unity is itself an unlikely (and unworthy) goal, based as it is in an imperial notion of institutional centrality".

66 Michael Kinnamon, and Brian E. Cope (eds), *The Ecumenical Movement: An Anthology of Key Texts and Voices* (Geneva: WCC, 1997), p. 80.
67 World Council of Churches, *New Delhi Speaks* (London: SCM Press, 1962), p. 56, quoted in section 16 of the *Princeton Proposal*.
68 WCC, *New Delhi Speaks*, p. 112.
69 Georg Hintzen, and Wolfgang Thönissen, *Kirchengemeinschaft möglich? Einheitsverständnis und Einheitskonzepte in der Diskussion* (Paderborn, Germany: Bonifatius, 2001), pp. 36–37.

Chapter 11

AFTERWORD: DENOMINATION IN GLOBAL PERSPECTIVE

KIRSTEEN KIM

Different ways of being church arise in different regions of the world in different historical periods. The five main streams of contemporary world Christianity—the Roman Catholic Church, the Orthodox Churches, Protestant denominations, the Evangelical, and Pentecostal churches and movements—bear the imprint of the contexts in which they began.[1] As the various contributions to this volume make clear, "denomination" is a contextual term, used for self-designation in different ways, mainly by certain Protestant church families. Several chapters draw attention to the fact that the present system of denominations is the result of historical and cultural factors. As Wolfgang Vondey puts it, "denominations are the history books of churches". In this concluding reflection, I will first build on these historical and cultural perspectives by adding a geographical point of view. Second, I will engage the discussion found in several chapters about the link between denomination and ecumenism. And third, I will to return to the issue raised by Barry Ensign-George at the start of this volume and ask whether the term "denomination", which is recognizably the product of a particular era and place, nevertheless also carries theological import.

Geography: Denomination as not Universal but Particular

The Protestant system of denominations is closely related to the Reformation and to the rise of modernity and of the nation state. It is an English term which does not translate well into German, for example (Thiessen). It is particularly linked to the history of the United States (as pointed out by De Mey, Richey and Thiessen in this volume). It was in the United States that the Christian pluralism which led to denominational identities was formed. To simplify: the Reformation and the subsequent "Wars of Religion" led to the break-up of the hegemony of the Catholic Church in large parts of northern and western Europe—and later in parts of Southern Europe, too. Instead, by the Peace of Westphalia, rulers each defined national churches to which those within the territory of each of the new nation states were expected to adhere. The Wars of Religion and the constraints on religious freedom in Europe were a push factor in the exodus of adherents of these different churches across the Atlantic. There, freed from the structures of the old world, a situation of religious pluralism was created in which different denominations of Christianity were tolerated in the interests of federal unity. Over time, religious toleration increased in Europe too, and in the more plural European states, such as England, even the established church has begun to take on denominational characteristics and to regard itself as one church among many (Avis). In colonial contexts a plurality of denominations resulting from different missionary initiatives was often recognized by government, as Riggs shows in the case of Kenya.

Unlike the churches of Europe from which they were descended, denominations in the United States asserted their independence from the Church of England, from the British government, and later, from the new federal government, which agreed not to legislate on matters of religion and to allow religious freedom. "Denomination" thus became associated with "independence" or independent agency. Ann Riggs points out that the link between denomination and independence is also strong in the post-colonial context of Kenya. In this case Kenyan denominational independence is from the colonial churches by which they were founded. Thus, belonging to a denomination is "voluntaristic and willed"—to quote Russell Richey—not enforced. Although detachment from the state arguably contributes to the privatization of religion (Avis), John Howard Yoder showed that, in the case of the Mennonites, separation from the state need not mean lack of involvement in civil society.[2] On a global scale in recent years, there are many churches which have never been established yet have been involved in independence movements, democratization, humanitarian initiatives, and the creation of civil society.

By the seventeenth century, Europe was divided into many nation states with fixed geographical boundaries, within which different rulers held sway. The church of each nation state was forced to organize itself by national structures. Groups like the Anabaptists, who wandered across Europe and refused to recognize the jurisdiction of the local monarch, were heavily persecuted. The Catholic Church, as a global body, was also a threat to local rulers, and it necessarily restructured itself in some respects within the nation states of Europe, and also in the United States. However, as Peter De Mey points out, theologically the US Catholic Church has never regarded itself as a denomination, one among equals, but as part of the universal Catholic Church.

Transnational churches, whether they are the Catholic Church or Anabaptists, are always a threat to national governments. Governments have sometimes forced churches to unite within a nation so that they can more easily control them (for example in Japan in 1941 and in China in the 1950s), and churches have opted to unite in order to witness more effectively to nations and governments (e.g. Church of South India, 1947). Having national church structures may be an advantage in the age of the nation state, but it also has the major disadvantage that Christians may no longer see themselves as belonging to a world or universal church or feel joined to other Christians around the world—as Amy Plantinga Pauw points out. Not surprisingly, when the integrity of nation states is being challenged by globalizing forces in late or postmodernity, churches closely bound up with national structures are also weakened.

Vondey notes that Evangelical and Pentecostal churches often define themselves as "non-denominational". It is not surprising that Evangelical and Pentecostal churches, which developed in the United States among persons increasingly detached from their European origins, or who migrated to the United States from other continents, do not recognize the necessity of the distinctions between the historic churches which emerged out of Europe. Pentecostals particularly have preferred the word "movement" to "denomination" because it allows them to transcend historical and doctrinal considerations, which they regard as stifling older churches, and because the word "movement" emphasizes the eschatological and dynamic character of Christianity (Vondey). Evangelicals and Pentecostals consider their churches to be independent of other churches and of governments. These forms of church are not geographically limited, and are generally suspicious of, or even antithetical towards, states. At one extreme, Evangelical rejection, or at least neglect, of national structures is shown by an emphasis on the local congregation. At the other extreme, neo-Pentecostal churches also defy the national structures of denominations by deliberately styling themselves as "international" or "world" (e.g. Kingsway International Christian Centre, London; Church of God International, Benin; Living Faith World Outreach, Nigeria; Universal Church of the Kingdom of God, Brazil). Emerging in the late twentieth century, and following the example of the US American evangelists and mega-church pastors who exercise "international ministries", the pastors of large urban churches in Asia, Africa and Latin America regard the whole world as their mission field and travel extensively.

In its greatest geographical expansion, at least since the first centuries, churches have been spread around the world under systems of globalization emanating from Europe—beginning with the Spanish and Portuguese, then the Dutch, French, British, and now US American. In this process European and North American churches have been exported across the world. The Catholic Church remains one church and Protestant churches are still bound together in global families of churches of each denomination, sometimes understanding themselves as world communions. However, many of the families or communions are only very loosely connected by a common historical origin, and are under severe strain as colonial ties weaken and national churches evolve to meet the needs of their differing contexts. They may well break down in the next few decades. One reason is that the identities of churches of the same denomination diverge over time in different cultural contexts. In the worldwide Anglican Communion, for example, the stance of national churches toward practicing homosexuals has been strongly affected by consideration of the effect this will have on their witness in particular societies, which differ widely in their attitudes to sexuality. Added to this, in any context new issues emerge which may cause further splits in denominations; for example, Presbyterianism in Korea is splintered into a hundred or so groups. On the other hand, local cultural, religious or political factors may lead to unity across what in Europe are intractable barriers. An example of this is the Church of South India, which is a union of episcopal and non-episcopal churches. Another example is Korean Presbyterians and Methodists which, despite the fissiparous nature of Korean Presbyterianism, share a common origin in a holiness-style revival at the turn of the twentieth century and, until very recently, shared the same Bible translation and hymnbook.

A second reason that global church families or world communions may break down is that in different contexts denominational differences play out in new ways. For instance, in some parts of the world—such as India, where Christians are facing the common threat of militant Hinduism, or *Hindutva*—mainline Protestants and Catholics enjoy a relatively close relationship; in others—such as South Korea, where there is religious freedom—they have almost nothing to do with one another. Another way of illustrating the difference that context can make on denominational identity is shown by migration movements between Korea and Britain. On the one hand, in Korea the Anglican Church is a relatively small denomination and is Anglo–Catholic in theology and worship. Korean Anglicans who move to England find the broad church very strange, and the Korean bishops are worried that they will lose what they see as their Anglican identity. Korean Presbyterians, on the other hand, are used to feeling part of the mainstream in Korea. But if they move to England, they find that the United Reformed Church is relatively small and somewhat marginal to national life, and they may feel more at home in the Church of England instead, despite differences in worship style. Reasons of geography, of geo-political region and local culture therefore may lead to the shedding of some of the inherited denominational identities and the formation of new alliances of national churches around the world.

For these reasons of geography, denominational relations are increasingly confused. The global structures which relate churches founded in the colonial period by the same mission boards, or by agencies of the same denomination increasingly bring together churches that are strangers to one another.

Ecumenism: Not only Interdenominational Unity but from the Whole Inhabited Earth

The emergence of the concept of denomination within the plural religious context of the United States shows that it is a response to the awareness of the existence of other churches. It is an accommodating response rather than an assertive one. As Pauw puts it, denomination is a self-relativizing concept: "to claim a denominational identity is to see one's own body as a part of the universal church, but not as the whole church". On the one hand, denomination may be regarded as a legitimate reflection of human diversity or as a proper result of practices of inculturation or contextualization in different parts of the world. For Christians whose church polity follows business models, a plurality of churches and denominations in competition with each other may even be regarded as a matter for celebration because, to use an analogy from supply-side economics, it promotes church growth. On the other hand, others may regard the separation of churches into denominations as one of the worst reflections of human depravity. Clearly, the kind of denominationalism by which Christians show animosity towards one another and do not eat or share together should be condemned (1 Corinthians). Nevertheless, there is an extreme sort of ecumenism which makes people feel guilty about simply existing in varied traditions and having different practices. This kind of ecumenism can result in patronizing and even imperialist attitudes by a church which sees itself as having a rightful precedence in a particular context. There is sometimes an attitude of self-sufficiency, as described by Paul Avis in the case of Anglicans, who do not see the need for other denominations or other forms of Christian expression. In my research on the ministry of the Church of England to the large Korean community in Kingston Borough, London, I found that some Church of England clergy questioned why Koreans would choose to form their own churches, arguing that they should join the existing (Anglican) ones. They could not accept the legitimacy of distinctively Korean Christianity, although the fact that there are Anglican churches in Seoul did not appear to trouble them at all.

In a situation of world Christianity, discussion of religious freedom and Christian plurality should be extended beyond the denominations which arose in the West to include those emerging in other parts of the world. Many newer churches are the result of a separation from another congregation, and so they may appear schismatic. However, this perception may be misguided, as in the case of many African Initiated Churches. These are often described disparagingly as having "broken away" from mission churches, whereas the reality may be that they were forced out by unreasonable expectations of the mission leaders.[3] Those in the older denominations are often understandably alarmed by the growth of new movements which take away their members and threaten their authority. However, if these new churches wish to identify as Christian they will, as they mature, have to connect with the Christian tradition. For example, early Pentecostal church leaders have often been highly critical of the older churches, but now that Pentecostalism is a hundred or so years old many classical Pentecostals value mainstream theological education and ecumenical links. The Pentecostal-charismatic movement is producing many fine theologians who are rooting their tradition among the others, as the adoption of the terminology of denomination suggests (Vondey). In recent years Pentecostal leaders have increasingly participated in activities sponsored by the World Council of Churches, such as the Global Christian Forum and the Edinburgh 2010 project. However, they do so on their own terms, and not because they recognize that other churches have some intrinsic legitimacy which they themselves do not possess.

Several authors perceived a connection between denominations and ecumenism (Thiessen, Avis, Riggs, Richey) in the sense that today "ecumenism" generally refers to a way to overcome denominational or ecclesial differences to work towards greater unity. This is true, but it should be noted that the original meaning of the word "ecumenical" does not relate to denominations but "the whole inhabited earth", and therefore to geography or ethnicity. The ecumenical councils of the first few centuries brought together Christians, not from different denominations, but from different parts of the world and different people groups. Since the colonial era, when European denominations dominated churches worldwide, European Protestants have tended to think primarily in terms of denominational unity, which mainly has to do with solving the historic schisms of Europe, and the World Council of Churches reflects this heritage. This limitation is brought out particularly by Elena Vishnevskaya, writing from an Orthodox perspective. The Orthodox regard themselves as guardians of a truth given to them from the beginning and not as a denomination or a collection of denominations. Nor do they see themselves in terms of the images often used to describe the ecumenical movement: as a branch of an ecumenical tree, or as a member of a family of churches. They regard themselves as the one church, separated into autocephalous churches only by matters which are nonessential to right doctrine. As Vishnevskaya explains, Orthodox membership in the World Council is not an affirmation of the concept of denomination but only reflects a willingness to accept the existence of some claim to ecclesiality beyond the Orthodox Church.

From outside Europe also, preoccupation with Christian unity as overcoming the separation into denominations is difficult to understand today, first because the European controversies which occasioned the differences that are now enshrined in denominations fade even further from memory, and second because European churches no longer wield world power. It is not a foregone conclusion that unity of, say, Anglicans and Lutherans in Europe will lead to unity between those groups in Tanzania. Furthermore, new issues and controversies have arisen in different parts of the world which may be more significant. The World Council of Churches arose out of efforts at the World Missionary Conference in Edinburgh in 1910 to bring the Protestant denominations of Europe into closer cooperation around the world, a move which in the early part of the twentieth century was an important step towards world peace. Now the Council increasingly recognizes the need to work beyond the constituencies of the historic denominations of Europe and the former mission churches if it is to bring together world Christianity. Ecumenical movements should be international as well as inter-ecclesial, and should cross ethnic boundaries—not just denominational ones. Consideration needs to be given not only to global movements such as Evangelicalism and Pentecostalism but also to regional and national movements, such as the house churches of China, African Initiated Churches, indigenous movements in India, and so on. At the country level, national councils of churches or "churches together" movements face new challenges to find ways of including ethnic or migrant churches and other new movements. Some of these may carry the same denominational label ("Methodist", "Episcopal", "Reformed", etc.) as an existing member, although they may express it in a significantly different way. Their different ethnic identity requires that they have a separate voice, even if this defies the denomination paradigm based on which these forums were first established.

Theology: Denomination as One Model of Diversity

There still remains the question of what church unity will look like and, in particular, whether the model will be the conciliar one of a fellowship of churches or a more organic one more like that of the Catholic Church. While some Protestants have advocated organic unity, De Mey, speaking from a Catholic perspective, can see its weaknesses and some of the advantages of a conciliar model. He suggests that the Catholic Church needs to take greater cognizance of legitimate theological and regional diversity by recognizing intermediary bodies between the local congregation and the universal church, such as are represented outside Catholicism by denominations and the newer movements.

De Mey does not propose strengthening intermediate structures for theological reasons but for practical ones. However, Miroslav Volf argued in the 1990s that different church polities—he examined particular Catholic, Orthodox and Free Church ecclesiologies—are related to differences in theology, in this case different understandings of the Trinity.[4] Others have questioned this relationship, among them Pauw in this volume argues that church polity has more to do with local social patterns and exigencies, pointing out that Reformed churches in the United States have variously adopted congregational, presbyterian or episcopal structures. Nevertheless, such differences in polity are often justified biblically and theologically—for instance in the example Pauw cites: Presbyterians refer to the conciliar model of Acts 15 rather than to the promise of Matthew 16.18 that the church will be built on Peter as the rock which is favored by Catholics. It may be because they are linked to both theology and practice that differences in polity are so intractable. Diversity of theology and polity can only be expected to increase as new churches emerge in Africa and Asia, especially because theology and social organization are related to cultural and philosophical differences.

The stimulating contributions in this book have been responses to Ensign-George's thought-provoking opening paper, which raises the question of whether there is a theological foundation for "denomination". I do not think this volume has succeeded in advancing biblical and theological justification for universally adopting the concept of "denomination" as Protestants have conceived it. Instead "denomination" itself is revealed to be a construct of a particular part of the church, the result of historical circumstances in a particular part of the world, and a perception that is not shared by others. But this does not mean that there is no possible theological justification for denominations. Indeed, Ensign-George, Pauw, Richey, and Gesa Thiessen articulate theological arguments that have to do with divine delight in diversity, with Christian humility, and with biblical images of churches as branches of a vine (Rom. 11.17–24), members of the family of God (like the twelve tribes of Israel), particular gatherings of the people of God (like the church at Antioch, Acts 11.19–26), or particular parts of the body of Christ (1 Cor. 12–14). These theological priorities and biblical images are clearly not shared by some other churches referred to, which instead have a theology of guarding a truth which has been entrusted to them, which is also a biblical stance (e.g. 1 Tim. 6.20). While they may find ways of being open to others through a "receptive" form of ecumenism,[5] they would consider it disloyal to their ancestors and unfaithful to the revelation they have received to give up what they believe to be their particular heritage.

"Denomination" in the sense of the historic Protestant groupings is a shifting form, and likely to become less significant as other new forms of church and inter-church relations emerge. However, in so far as "denomination" is a theological attempt to justify legitimate Christian diversity, it makes a lasting contribution to ecclesiology. Christian diversity is here to stay because the spread of Christianity into so many cultures has increased its diversity in recent years. Furthermore, diversity has been an integral aspect of Christian history since biblical times. Contemporary biblical scholars such as James Dunn; scholars of liturgy such as Paul F. Bradshaw, and of the early church, including

Charles Freeman; and church and mission historians such as Dale T. Irvin and Scott W. Sunquist have emphasized that since the time of the Apostles Christianity has been diverse.[6] There were twelve apostles (not one) and traditionally they each went out in different directions to "all nations", following Jesus' command (Mt. 28.18–20; Mk 16.20; Acts 1.8). So throughout Christian history there have always been different churches with varied practices and theological perspectives. The early churches arose and existed in different locations and cultures.

Instead of seeing church history as a series of fragmentations of an original whole, contemporary interpreters recognize multiplicity in Christianity from the start. Periodically there were attempts to reconcile different traditions into one according to the needs of particular regions (for example, by Bishop Victor in late second-century Rome, at the Synod of Whitby in 664 AD, etc.). But globally, the diverse traditions of the churches of the different apostles were respected in the first centuries in the way that the world church met in the form of an ecumenical council and, as Ensign-George compellingly points out, in the decision to retain four distinct gospels in the Bible, rejecting the impulse to unify them. These were the gospels of different apostles and of churches in different parts of the world of that time. These churches were not "denominations" in the modern sense but they were prepared to accept that their gospel was complemented in some way by the other three.

Our early Christian ancestors found ways of dealing with the diversity of their age, and affirmed some distinct Christian identities when they compiled the canon of scripture. It is also important in our own age of world Christianity and global interconnectedness that we find ways of doing the same. One thing is certain: there will not emerge one single theological model of diversity. Christian diversity means that each part of the church or Christian movement is challenged to develop its own theology of accommodating other Christians. This discussion of "denomination" is one constructive attempt towards this end which I am sure will stimulate others.

Notes

1 Sebastian Kim, and Kirsteen Kim, *Christianity as a World Religion* (London: Continuum, 2008).

2 John Howard Yoder, *The Politics of Jesus: Vicit Agnus Noster*, 2nd edn (Grand Rapids, MI: Wm B. Eerdmans, 1994).

3 John S. Pobee, and Gabriel Ositelu II, *African Initiatives in Christianity* (Geneva: WCC Publications, 1998), pp. 29–30.

4 Miroslav Volf, *After Our Likeness: The Church as the Image of the Trinity* (Grand Rapids, MI: Wm B. Eerdmans, 1998).

5 Cf. Paul D. Murray (ed.), *Receptive Ecumenism and the Call to Catholic Learning* (Oxford: Oxford University Press, 2008).

6 James Dunn, *Unity and Diversity in the New Testament: An Inquiry into the Character of Earliest Christianity*, 2nd edn (London: SCM, 2006); Paul F. Bradshaw, *The Search for the Origins of Christian Worship* (London: SPCK, 2002); Charles Freeman, *A New History of Christianity* (New Haven, CT: Yale University Press, 2009); Irvin, D. T. and S. W. Sunquist (2001), *A History of the World Christian Movement*, Vol. I: *Earliest Christianity to 1453* (Maryknoll, NY: Orbis Books, 2001).

INDEX

CPSIA information can be obtained at www.ICGtesting.com
Printed in the USA
LVOW072151300513

336287LV00003B/91/P